PREPARATION FOR LIFE?

For Granny, and in memory of Nanna

Preparation for Life?

Vocationalism and the Equal Opportunities Challenge

SUE HEATH

LONDON AND NEW YORK

First published 1997 by Ashgate Publishing

Reissued 2018 by Routledge
2 Park Square, Milton Park, Abingdon, Oxon, OX14 4RN
711 Third Avenue, New York, NY 10017, USA

Routledge is an imprint of the Taylor & Francis Group, an informa business

Copyright © S. Heath 1997

All rights reserved. No part of this book may be reprinted or reproduced or utilised in any form or by any electronic, mechanical, or other means, now known or hereafter invented, including photocopying and recording, or in any information storage or retrieval system, without permission in writing from the publishers.

Notice:
Product or corporate names may be trademarks or registered trademarks, and are used only for identification and explanation without intent to infringe.

Publisher's Note
The publisher has gone to great lengths to ensure the quality of this reprint but points out that some imperfections in the original copies may be apparent.

Disclaimer
The publisher has made every effort to trace copyright holders and welcomes correspondence from those they have been unable to contact.

A Library of Congress record exists under LC control number: 97074445

ISBN 13: 978-1-138-32664-4 (hbk)
ISBN 13: 978-1-138-32666-8 (pbk)
ISBN 13: 978-0-429-44938-3 (ebk)

Contents

Tables	vi
Acknowledgements	vii
Abbreviations	ix
Introduction	1
1 Vocationalism and the 'problem' of gender	6
2 Education feminism and the school-work interface	22
3 TVEI and equal opportunities	45
4 Implementing TVEI at the local level	65
5 Managing equal opportunities	80
6 The curricular experiences of TVEI pupils	96
7 TVEI and the 'world of work'	114
8 Post-16 destinations: A 'touchstone' for measuring progress?	128
9 Into the labour market: Preparation for life?	144
10 The legacy of TVEI	161
Appendix 1: A note on method	185
Bibliography	196
Index	216

Tables

Table 6.1:	TVEI cohort membership in Masonfield by gender: cohort II (1987-89)	102
Table 6.2:	TVEI subjects available to cohort II and their prior gendered association	102
Table 6.3:	Uptake of TVEI subjects amongst cohort II pupils in 2 pilot schools	104
Table 7.1:	Occupational location of fifth year students' TVEI work experience	120
Table 7.2:	Fifth year students' activities in TVEI work experience	120
Table 7.3:	Work experience placements amongst a sample of cohort II pupils (numbers)	122
Table 8.1:	Destinations of 1989 pilot school leavers six months after leaving school (%)	136
Table 8.2:	Destinations of cohort II leavers by gender	136
Table 8.3:	Occupational Training Families of 1989 pilot school leavers by gender (%)	138
Table 8.4:	Non-traditional destinations of 1989 pilot school leavers	142

Acknowledgements

This book is based on research which I first embarked upon back in 1989, whilst working as a research officer for 'Masonfield' LEA's central TVEI team, at the same time as studying part-time at Lancaster University. Three jobs and eight years later I still remain fascinated by TVEI's equal opportunities policy, not least because of the light it has shed on my own experiences of schooling. I experienced secondary education during the second half of the 1970s, and attended a comprehensive school with a rather nice line in the mixed messages it gave out concerning gender and equal opportunities. A close friend, one of only three non-white pupils in the school, was the first girl to be allowed to take technical drawing 'O' level, whilst the rest of us were frightened out of the technology workshops by a loathsome teacher who unequivocally told us that workshops were dangerous and unsuitable places for young women, rather neatly underlining his argument by throwing a metal vice at a girl not paying attention. The dashingly handsome history teacher urged the besotted girls in his top class to aim high academically, whilst proudly wearing his 'male chauvinist pig' tie at all times and teasing us for being 'blue stockings'. The boys in my year took needlework, and were rather effectively turned off further study by being forced to make denim 'tabard tops' in true 1970s style. Having gained top science marks in my first year, by the end of my third year I was told emphatically that 'O' level physics and chemistry were not for me, although I might be able to manage biology (which I subsequently failed). Hindsight is a wonderful thing, and studying TVEI has provided me with plenty of it.

On a more serious note, I am of course indebted to a very large number of people for the crucial parts they played in allowing my research to get to this stage. The biggest thank you, of course, must go to all the teachers, careers officers, advisers, education officers, councillors and ex-TVEI students who were willing to give up their time to talk to me, give me access to data and documentation, and generally put up with all my questions.

I am particularly indebted to my ex-colleagues in Masonfield's TVEI Central Team - most notably the teacher advisers for Business Studies and for Home Economics, as well as the Central Team administrator - who taught me the ropes and made me feel so very welcome. It was a good time. Thanks too to colleagues at Masonfield Careers Service. A very special thank you must go to the central TVEI coordinator, the pseudonymous 'David James'. Without his constant support and encouragement, this research would have been impossible. His generosity in sponsoring the research in the first place will always be appreciated; that he was willing for me to publish the research more widely is positive proof of his commitment to educational research. It will no doubt amuse him to note that my original rather pessimistic conclusions have had to be modified somewhat in light of recent evaluations of TVEI's longer term impact! It is a shame I cannot give David James' real name, as he is a shining example of an educationalist fully committed to social democratic principles of education, and for whom I retain the utmost respect.

I am similarly very much indebted to Jennifer Mason and Penny Summerfield, my PhD supervisors. I have benefited greatly from their complementary insights, and am also very grateful for their friendship, help and support in many other respects. If I had to do it all over again (thankfully an unlikely occurrence!) I would choose Penny and Jennifer as supervisors without any hesitation. Thank you both very much.

I would also like to thank Rosemary Deem, Kevin Brehony and Angela Dale for support and inspiration during the final stages of writing up the thesis on which this book is based, and Teresa Rees and Murray Saunders for making the viva (on the whole!) an enjoyable experience. A special thank you must also go to Carol Vincent, who provided living proof of light at the end of the tunnel. Thanks, too, to friends at the University of Manchester, in particular Fiona Devine, Peter Halfpenny, Penny Tinkler, Stephanie Linkogle, Tracey Payne, Clare Holdsworth, Ruth Durrell and Jo Wathan. For frequent (and welcome) reminders that there is more to life than vocational education, thank you to lots of people, but especially Susie Smith, Helen Dodwell, Gwen Crawford, and James and Alison Place. I must also thank the editorial team at Avebury, Rachel Hedges in particular.

On a more personal note, a big thank you must go to Reg and Dorothy Heath for being such wonderful and supportive parents, and also to my many and various siblings, especially my sister Netty. Finally, a huge thank you to Steve New, for his unstinting faith in me, but mostly for all his love.

Abbreviations

BTEC	Business and Technician Education Council
CBI	Confederation of British Industry
CDT	Craft, Design and Technology
DES	Department of Education and Science
DFEE	Department for Education and Employment
EEC	European Economic Community
EOC	Equal Opportunities Commission
GATE	Girls And Technology Education
GCSE	General Certificate in Secondary Education
GIST	Girls Into Science and Technology
GNVQ	General National Vocational Qualification
HMI	Her Majesty's Inspectorate
ISS	Information Systems Strategy
IT	Information Technology
LEA	Local Education Authority
MSC	Manpower Services Commission
NEON	National Equal Opportunities Network
NFER	National Foundation for Educational Research
NUT	National Union of Teachers
OFSTED	Office for Standards in Education
ORT	Organisation for Rehabilitation and Training
OTF	Occupational Training Family
QCA	Qualifications and Curriculum Authority
SDA	Sex Discrimination Act
TVEI	Technical and Vocational Education Initiative
TRIST	TVEI-Related In-Service Training
UNESCO	United Nations Educational, Scientific and Cultural Organisation
WISE	Women Into Science and Engineering

WNC	Women's National Commission
YOPS	Youth Opportunities Programme
YT	Youth Training
YTS	Youth Training Scheme

Introduction

In November 1982, Prime Minister Margaret Thatcher announced to the House of Commons the launching of a pilot programme of technical and vocational education for 14-18 year olds within the British state education system. This was proclaimed as a response to 'a growing concern about existing arrangements for technical and vocational education for young people expressed over many years' (quoted in Dale, 1985, p.41). The proposed programme was thus designed to meet long-standing criticism from across the political spectrum that the education system was failing to meet the needs of employers by instead 'producing' young workers who were ill-prepared for life in a rapidly changing labour market. In autumn 1983, the first round of participating Local Education Authorities (LEAs) commenced on a five year pilot phase of the 'Technical and Vocational Education Initiative', with multi-million pound backing from the Manpower Services Commission and its various successors. Eventually, all education authorities in Britain were to become involved in TVEI, moving from an initial five year pilot period into a further five years of TVEI extension funding. Much has been written about TVEI's origins (Dale, 1985; Chitty, 1989), and about TVEI's impact on curriculum development and the management of educational change (for example, Dale et al, 1990; Gleeson, 1988; Saunders, 1990; Gleeson and McLean, 1994). Much less has been written about an aspect of TVEI which to many observers came to have much greater import: the unprecedented inclusion of a commitment to equal opportunities for boys and girls as a central and high profile funding criterion.

At the time of TVEI's introduction in the early 1980s, the promotion of gender equality was a relatively recent concern within British education and, as it remains, was a highly controversial issue. Nonetheless, as the first of TVEI's eight explicit funding criteria, progress in this area became a legitimate measure of the scheme's broader success or failure (Weiner, 1990a). This is particularly significant given that the inclusion of such an emphasis brought TVEI into direct confrontation with the difficulties which vocational education has traditionally generated for British policy makers attempting to frame an appropriate education for girls and boys. As Wolpe (1981), Hunt (1991) and Gomersall (1997) have all demonstrated, such attempts were usually strongly influenced by the entrenched belief that boys and girls had very different vocational concerns. In the decade preceding TVEI's launch in 1982, policy statements in the spheres of education and training had begun at last to emphasise the changing role of women, yet they had nonetheless led to broadly similar outcomes in terms of the domestic preparation of girls (Deem, 1981). Given this track record, it was arguable that a strongly vocational education initiative would overwhelmingly serve to emphasise and further reinforce sexual divisions in the labour market, rather than challenge them, by virtue of bringing discriminatory assumptions from the world of work directly into the classroom.

By exploring the seemingly paradoxical relationship between TVEI and its equal opportunities goals, this book is concerned with teasing out the nature of the challenge which vocational education poses for the promotion of greater gender equality in education and the labour market. Under TVEI, the issue of gender inequalities in education was transformed from a peripheral issue into a mainstream educational concern, and one of the major concerns of this book is to examine what actually happened to the conceptualisation of gender inequality at the moment of transformation. Attention is accordingly focused on the point when TVEI's commitment to the removal of gender inequalities was least diluted - during the pilot phase, when the greatest concentration of resources was targeted at the smallest number of pupils. By studying TVEI's impact on both policy makers and pupils in participating projects, including a detailed exploration of one specific project, important theoretical issues are raised concerning the complex relationship between schooling and a capitalist economy strongly shaped by gender differentiation. At first glance an equal opportunities perspective within the context of a vocational scheme could be seen to mark a potentially radical departure for British education policy. However, it could equally be interpreted as evidence of a theoretical naivety (with very real practical implications) concerning the centrality of the sexual division of labour to the successful operation of capitalism, and the key role played by schools in reproducing those divisions (Arnot and Whitty, 1982; Kelly and Nihlen, 1982; Wolpe, 1988). MacDonald's argument concerning the weakness of the simple correspondence theory developed by Bowles and Gintis (1976) could equally be applied to the philosophical underpinnings of vocational education schemes:

> Any theory of schooling which seeks to account for the form of schooling in terms of the mode of reproduction of the work force... must recognise the structure of male-female dominance relations as integral and not subsidiary organising principles of the work process (MacDonald, 1980, p.15).

It will already be clear to the reader that the focus of this book is on TVEI's attempts to tackle *gender* inequalities in education. This focus specifically on equal opportunities policies aimed at tackling gender inequalities, rather than equal opportunities policies in relation to other forms of oppression, takes its lead from the almost exclusive focus on gender within TVEI's own equal opportunities agenda. Under the extension phase of TVEI funding the equal opportunities statement was extended to cover issues of 'race', but at the level of practice most projects and individual schools still continued to focus on gender issues in isolation. Indeed, it was a strong feature of TVEI's approach to equal opportunities that gender and 'race' inequalities were largely regarded as separate issues, not as issues which were inextricably linked. As for more complex interconnections between gender and 'race' and *other* structures of inequality, based for example upon social class, disability and sexuality, these linkages were rarely made. This in itself highlights a major weakness of TVEI's approach to educational inequalities. As we shall see, from the outset TVEI was based on an assumption that 'boys' and 'girls', 'men' and 'women', formed homogeneous categories and shared a commonality of experience on the basis of their gender alone, due to their exposure to an undifferentiated process of socialisation and sex role stereotyping. Acker has pointed out that this perspective has been reflected more generally in 'official' British equal opportunity literature: 'Girls are simply girls: the differential impacts of class, ethnicity or other attributes upon their life chances appear a taboo topic' (Acker, 1994, p.47).

This narrow conceptualisation of male/female identity lies in stark contrast not only to the perspectives of radical and socialist feminism, which seek to develop a more complex treatment of gender difference, but also to the more recent insights of feminist post-structuralism (Weedon, 1987). Notwithstanding the many problems associated with this latter position, writers such as Kenway and Middleton (Kenway et al, 1994; Middleton, 1993 and 1995) have highlighted the 'multiple subjectivities' of boys and girls within the classroom: that is, boys' and girls' identities are not cast in stone, but are in constant flux, continually being constituted and reconstituted on the basis of their history and current experiences. Thus, in focusing on gender within this book, it is not my intention to reinforce TVEI's assumption of homogeneity: rather, my intention is to drive home the point that this assumption was *in itself* one of the 'problematics' of TVEI's equal opportunities approach and undoubtedly fed directly into the development of TVEI's deficit model of female achievement which is discussed in subsequent chapters.

An exploration of the lessons to be learned from TVEI's landmark equal opportunities commitment would seem to be a particularly salient task at the present time, given the current controversy surrounding the relative examination performances of boys and girls and the subsequent backlash in favour of schemes which focus on tackling the supposed underachievement of boys (Raphael Reed, 1997). This, too, is a debate which tends to be conducted around essentialist notions of 'girls' and 'boys'. Media rhetoric talks of young women 'fighting back', of young men 'losing out' to young women in the labour market (see, for example, Panorama, 1995). More significantly, official documents are also placing an increased emphasis on the educational needs of boys (OFSTED, 1996). However, it is crucial to note that despite higher levels of achievement at certain levels and amongst certain groups of girls (Elwood and Comber, 199; Elwood, 1996), this has *not* in fact resulted in the expected corollary of greater equality in the labour market - nor indeed in post-16 education. If young women now have a wider range of employment opportunities open to them, it is certainly *not* because they are moving into areas traditionally associated with young men, and may indeed be more to do with an unwillingness amongst young men to move into areas of the labour market which are increasingly characterised by low pay, poor working conditions and job insecurity. It is in these (as well as in other) areas that distinct gender inequalities remain, and it is hoped that this book will contribute to a broader understanding of the dynamics of educational initiatives which seek to bring about change in the sphere of gendered employment.

A detailed study of TVEI's equal opportunities policy is also timely given the significance accorded to TVEI in a series of recent reviews of gender equality in Scottish, English and Welsh education, sponsored by the Equal Opportunities Commission. Turner et al (1995), Arnot et al (1996) and Salisbury (1996) all point to the positive impact of TVEI on putting equal opportunities on the educational agenda. Arnot et al (1996) found, for example, that TVEI was cited as the impetus for the introduction of equal opportunities policies in 37 per cent of secondary schools in England and Wales, whilst Turner et al conclude that 'TVEI was generally seen to have been the most important development in drawing schools' attention to gender equality matters' (Turner et al, 1995, p.62). The change in culture around equality issues in schools is of course to be warmly welcomed. However, it is important to distinguish between the impact of TVEI's equal opportunities commitment on school organisation and management, and its impact on *pupils*. Whilst TVEI clearly resulted in significant organisational spin-offs, TVEI's chief concern was to create a generation of young people who were better prepared for the demands of the world of work. With respect to its equal opportunities element, TVEI hoped to promote a more flexible workforce, no longer hidebound by stereotypical notions of what constituted appropriate work for men and appropriate work for women. It is this central aspect of TVEI's equal opportunities commitment which forms the main focus of this book.

Chapter 1 is thus concerned with exploring the historical tension which has long existed between vocationalism and the notion of an 'appropriate' education for boys and girls. It demonstrates that misgivings concerning the assumption that boys and girls have very different vocational concerns are a relatively recent phenomenon. Chapter 2 places these concerns in a theoretical framework, focusing on mainstream and feminist critiques of the role of schooling in reproducing and reinforcing gendered divisions in broader society, both within and outside of the labour market. A range of feminist responses to vocationalism and the work-related curriculum are considered.

Chapter 3 starts by outlining the origins of TVEI, and then considers the origins of its specific equal opportunities element. It also briefly outlines the impetus which came from the National TVEI Unit once TVEI was operational, drawing on material taken from an interview with two of TVEI's former national equal opportunities consultants. Chapter 4 then introduces 'Masonfield' Local Education Authority, the LEA whose TVEI project forms the focus of the case study material used in chapters 5 to 9. A full description of the methods used in this part of the research can be found in Appendix 1. In summary, the case study explores the perspectives of TVEI policy makers and implementers of policy within Masonfield through analysis of a wide range of documentary evidence and through interviews with LEA officers, elected members and school-based TVEI personnel. The experiences and perspectives of the young people who were involved in TVEI as pilot pupils are considered by means of secondary analysis of Careers Service data, a postal survey a year after leaving school and follow-up interviews two years after leaving school.

Chapter 5 raises a series of concerns around the management of TVEI, including the representation of women within TVEI schemes and the development of the 'Information Systems Strategy' for equal opportunities work in the pilot schools. Chapter 6 then focuses on the curricular experiences of TVEI students in Masonfield, highlighting TVEI's major emphasis on the promotion of non-traditional option choices and the kind of intervention strategies that were accordingly developed. Chapter 7 explores the interface between TVEI and the 'world of work'. After a consideration of the careers education and guidance strategies experienced by TVEI pupils, the chapter then focuses on the role of work experience within TVEI's broader equal opportunities framework. Chapter 8 considers the actual post-school destinations of leavers from the pilot schools in the context of ethnographic studies of gendered transitions from school to work, whilst chapter 9 continues this theme by looking at the longer-term influence of TVEI on young school leavers by considering the experiences of ex-TVEI pupils in their first two years within the labour market. The extent to which TVEI's equal opportunities emphasis was regarded as having little relevance to their own concerns is highlighted, alongside evidence which demonstrates the extent to which their working lives were structured by gender differentiation in the workplace.

The final chapter in the book reassesses the significance of TVEI as a landmark policy in education. Recent evaluations of TVEI are referred to, alongside a consideration of the strategies for the management of change which were adopted by TVEI more generally, but which had particular implications for the success or otherwise of its equal opportunities work. The theoretical considerations raised in chapter 2 will be reassessed in the light of these considerations. Finally, the chapter will finish by outlining the framework for a feminist response to the ongoing vocational bias within education, based on a recognition of the experiences and needs of all young people, not just those who choose non-traditional pathways.

1 Vocationalism and the 'problem' of gender

Introduction

Vocationalism in its broadest sense is a standpoint which holds that education should be concerned with the preparation of young people for their post-school lives, although it is perhaps more widely associated in common usage with specific *occupational* preparation. In this narrower sense, the vocational bias of English education undoubtedly has a long history, with its roots lying in the education of monks and priests (Watts, 1985). During the Industrial Revolution, however, the more elite educational institutions attempted to distance themselves from the newly developing disciplines of scientific and technical education. Instead, they vigorously promoted the liberal ideal of education as a good in itself, leading to disdain for vocational application generally, and industrial manufacture in particular (Weiner, 1981; Watts, 1985). Hunt (1991) argues, however, that in practice there was often a tacit understanding by both liberal idealists and vocationalists that education should, at some level, be concerned with the preparation of young people for adult life. Conflicts arose from differing interpretations of what such a preparation should entail, liberals arguing that education should prepare young people for adult life in a general sense - spiritually and culturally, for example - and vocationalists arguing that education should prepare young people for specific occupational destinations. Antagonism between liberal idealists and vocationalists remains a strong theme within educational debate, a state of affairs which Quicke (1996) attributes to the 'conflicting imperatives' model of the relationship between democracy and capitalism:

> The contradictions that this gives rise to in schools are often experienced as a conflict between 'the world of education' and 'the world of work'... Although the defining attributes of the capitalist imperative are contested and its nature and

social impact can vary with context, the assumption is that both in terms of its current role in the global order and its central philosophical assumptions about human nature it will inevitably conflict with practices driven by the democratic imperative, of which the goals of liberal progressive education are an aspect (Quicke, ibid, pp.49-50).

Over the course of the twentieth century, these tensions have created dilemmas for educational policy makers seeking to develop an appropriate education for boys and girls. For much of the century it was deemed to be self-evident that a boy's adult life would be taken up in pursuit of a career or profession, but 'the powerful tendency was for girls' lives to be seen in terms of role, rather than career' (Hunt, 1991, p.118). Hunt argues further that vocationalism has consistently posed such a problem for those concerned with the education of girls in the twentieth century, and although in the latter years of the post-war period there was a grudging recognition of the changing role of women, girls' education was still chiefly concerned with preparation for domestic roles.

This chapter considers the poor track record which vocational education has had with respect to the promotion of gender equality. It starts with a consideration of official policy in the period running up to the Second World War, highlighting the tension between liberal and vocational ideals. It then looks at a series of key policy documents which were written in the two decades after the war, but which shared many of the pre-war assumptions concerning the assumed 'natural' interests of boys and girls respectively. The chapter then explores the impact of the Sex Discrimination Act on an educational world slow to take action to challenge gender inequalities, and highlights the eventual response of the Department of Education and Science. Despite a growing awareness during the late 1970s and early 1980s of the increased importance of economic activity to women, the final part of the chapter highlights the tendency of the education system to nonetheless prepare young women for 'women's work'. The chapter thus provides a historical backdrop to the introduction of TVEI in 1982 and demonstrates that given the prior track record on equal opportunities within the world of education, it is all the more extraordinary that TVEI emerged in the early 1980s with its colours so clearly nailed to the equal opportunities mast.

'Appropriate' education for boys and girls

Official policy 1900 to 1944

The development of mass education in this country can be traced back to growing concerns over the need for an educated workforce in the wake of rapid industrialisation. In 1870, elementary schools were established for children up to a maximum age of 10, whilst ten years later elementary schooling was made compulsory, with a small means-tested fee. In 1891, elementary fees were waived, and in 1900 free education was extended up to age eleven. Despite efforts to promote wider take-up of secondary education, attendance remained sporadic amongst the poorer sections of society, and if they did attend they were much more likely to be found within the rate-financed technical schools, rather than the voluntary or rate-financed grammar schools (Thane, 1982).

Gomersall (1997) provides an account of the gendered nature of education during the nineteenth century, based very much on differentiated curricular experiences for boys and girls, especially amongst children from the working classes. In the early years of the *twentieth* century, policy makers at the Board of Education were nonetheless keen to place a strong emphasis on the *liberal* basis of schooling. The 1904 Regulations for Secondary Schools argued for a general curriculum which did not overly emphasise either science, literature or languages, nor subjects which were primarily aimed at a vocational business education. Similarly, the 1905 Code for Higher Elementary Schools clearly stated that higher elementary schooling, which was designed to provide an advanced, practically-oriented education, 'must not be devoted exclusively to the cultivation of dexterity in the daily routine of a special employment... and must not displace the more general side of Elementary Education' (quoted in Hunt, 1991). However, in practice the Board's liberal idealism was undermined by what it regarded as its duty to cater for the 'special needs' of girls. The 1904 Regulations for Secondary Schools stated that 'it is left to school authorities to consider how far the same kind of school curriculum is desirable for girls as to boys... due regard (should be) had to the differences inherent in the nature of the two sexes...', whilst the 1905 Code noted that 'a common curriculum for both boys and girls will not as a rule be approved' and the girls' curriculum 'will, as a rule, be expected to include a practical training for home duties' (ibid). The resulting emphasis on domestic subjects for girls therefore belied any claims to a liberal basis for educational provision:

> Girls' abilities were underrated, they were assumed to have a common vocation, dictated by their gender, even where their scholastic ability (or social status or both) was high, and it was assumed that this vocation demanded training at school. Such training, because of its practical and vocational nature, was less esteemed than, even antithetical to, the highly valued principle of a liberal education (Hunt, 1991, p.69).

Thus there was a tension between the Board of Education's liberal ideals and the notion of role-directed education. The only way to have overcome this tension would have been to grant domestic subjects equal educational status to other subjects. Liberal educationalists found this impossible to admit, however: to have done so would have publicly undermined the Board's cherished liberal principles. Moreover, the failure to do so contributed to the view that girls' domestic subjects were necessarily educationally inferior, a view that is still widely held (Attar, 1990).

In the Welsh context, it has been argued that whilst secondary schools for girls were modelled on the academically-orientated curriculum of the English grammar schools, by 1914 there were strong demands that domestic studies should be seen as valid alternatives to foreign languages, mathematics or science (Evans, 1990).

In 1920, the Consultative Committee to the Board of Education of England and Wales was asked to consider whether such differentiation in the secondary curriculum was justified. The Committee received a mass of contradictory evidence concerning supposed physical and mental differences between the two sexes. Ultimately, however, the Committee concluded that the existence or otherwise of such differences was in a sense irrelevant: what *was* relevant was the extent to which boys and girls had different functions to perform, both at secondary age and on leaving school. On the grounds that they *did* appear to have different functions, it was felt that there was some justification for the continuation of a differentiated curriculum. Consequently, in its 1923 Report, *Differentiation of the Curriculum for Boys and Girls Respectively in Secondary Schools*, the Committee concluded that whilst the main aims of education were to prepare children to earn their own livings and to be useful citizens, for girls there was a third aim: to prepare them to be 'makers of homes' (Hunt, 1987, p.18).

Educational policy and discussion in the pre-war era continued to reflect these assumptions, with many of the major Education Acts being framed principally with the vocational concerns of young men in mind. The curricular experiences of males were overwhelmingly constructed as the educational 'norm', and the curricular experiences of females, to use Hunt's phrase, tended to be constructed as either 'the norm minus' or 'the norm plus'. The raising of the school leaving age to fourteen in 1918, for example, was in part a response to the need for a better skilled workforce (Thane, 1982). That this workforce was envisaged as being predominantly male is evident from the parallel disquiet regarding 'maternal ignorance', which resulted in an increased emphasis within girls' education on practical domestic subjects such as needlework, cookery and 'housewifery' (Turnbull, 1987).

The tripartite system, first recommended by the 1926 Hadow Committee and subsequently built into the implementation of the 1944 Education Act, was similarly explicitly organised on the basis of young people's likely occupational destinations. The influential Norwood Report (Secondary Schools Examination Council, 1943), which in the run up to the 1944 legislation re-emphasised the supposed benefits of a tripartite structure, did not appear to view women as an integral part of the world of work (Wolpe, 1981). The grammar schools were designed to prepare pupils for white collar and professional occupations, technical schools for technician-level occupations, and secondary modern schools for blue collar occupations. Girls in general, however, were considered to be best suited to the secondary modern school, which would cater for their specific needs as future wives and mothers, rather than future workers, whether at professional or technician level.

Against the backdrop of these assumptions, the years of the Second World War witnessed a mass mobilisation of women into the labour market. The number of women in the engineering sector, for example, rose from 97,000 in 1939 to 602,000 at the height of the war effort in 1943 (Summerfield, 1989). By 1943 women represented a third of all employees working in the previously male-dominated 'essential' industries such as engineering, ship building and public utilities, compared with only 14 per cent in 1939. At the same time, the overall numbers of women in 'female' occupational areas, such as textiles and clothing, and food and retail services declined quite substantially. In addition, by 1943 there were almost half a million women in the armed forces.

Summerfield (1989) refutes the popular view that women were systematically excluded from paid labour in the immediate post-war years (Friedan, 1965; Mitchell, 1974). On the contrary, most occupational areas saw a return to pre-war patterns of expanding employment opportunities, with women's participation in 'male' industries continuing to increase not just absolutely but proportionately in comparison with their pre-war involvement. However, it is important to note the extent to which women were affected by horizontal segregation: despite working within 'male' industries, women were predominantly employed within *female sectors* of these industries (Hakim, 1978). Thus, if the war years resulted in a shift in the assumptions and ideologies surrounding women's paid labour, it was, 'in the direction of the idea that women could combine paid and domestic work without damage to industrial productivity and without undermining the concept that their first responsibility was to their homes' (Summerfield, 1989, p.188).

These arguments are important in understanding the subsequent vacuum in post-war policies with regard to women's education and training, which continued to be based on pre-war assumptions about different vocational concerns. Thus, women's increasing participation in the labour market was largely ignored - as were their specific educational and training needs. In particular, there was an expansion of clerical and caring work in the post-war period, principally affecting women, yet the training needs of women in these areas were largely neglected. Four official reports from this period stand out as significant in this regard - the Norwood Report (1943), the Crowther Report (1959) and the Newsom Report (1963) in the sphere of education, and the Carr Report (1958) in the sphere of training. All four reports made assumptions about the 'natural interests' of boys and girls, the former being dominated by their future occupational roles, the latter dominated by - if not confined to - their future roles as wives and mothers (CCCS, 1981; Wolpe, 1981; Wickham, 1985; Arnot, 1986). Given that the goal of education was viewed by Norwood, Crowther and Newsom as the preparation of children to fit into the adult world as citizens and workers, the assumed divergent interests of boys and girls dictated the necessity of a differentiated curriculum in order to cater for these particular concerns. Moreover, the 'natural interests' of girls precluded their involvement in training programmes on leaving school.

Wolpe (1981) argues that *The Norwood Report on Curriculum and Examinations in Secondary Schools* (Secondary Schools Examinations Council, 1943) clearly regarded women's war work only as a temporary 'intrusion' into the formal economy. Accordingly, the report rejected the view that girls and boys should have access to non-traditional subjects within single-sex schools - 'such opportunity must be offered to those who desire it through 'scouting' or 'guiding' or similar interests' (SSEC, 1943, p.20). It did note, however, that some co-educational schools had a small number of pupils taking non-traditional subjects, 'which we would bring to the notice of co-educational schools in general' (ibid). Girls were largely rendered invisible by the bulk of the report, only being explicitly mentioned in a discussion of secondary modern schools. Such schools, as opposed to grammar and technical schools, were seen as providing the most suitable type of education for girls, catering for their specific needs and interests as future wives and mothers.

The Crowther Report, *15 to 18* (Central Advisory Council for Education [England], 1959), was concerned with a review of educational provision for 15-18 year olds, 'in relation to the changing social and industrial needs of our society and the needs of the individual citizen' (CACE, 1959, p.xxvii). This was a reference to the increase in the levels of skills demanded by industry and the corresponding decrease in the numbers of unskilled jobs during this period. The report noted that young women were less likely to take up part-time training and other educational opportunities for early leavers (those who left school at 15), and that this was a good reason in itself for raising the minimum leaving age. However, they attributed these differences to the 'fact' that 'the bulk of women's employment is not in fields where considerable technical knowledge is required' (ibid, p.124), a function of the 'special interests of women' in early marriage and parenthood. Indeed, at one point it was argued that 'the prospect of courtship and marriage should rightly influence the education of the adolescent girl... her direct interest in dress, personal experience and in problems of human relations should be given a central place in her education' (ibid, p.34). Whilst the Crowther Report undoubtedly shared many of the assumptions of the Norwood Report, it at least accepted that women were involved in paid labour. However, the report relegated them to jobs not requiring 'considerable technical knowledge', thereby ignoring the thousands of women who had developed a high level of technical skill in the context of in-service training rather than in part-time courses (Wolpe, 1981, p.151).

The Newsom Report, *Half Our Future* (Central Advisory Council for Education, 1963), was concerned with the education of 13-16 years olds of average or less than average ability, again with regard to the need for a better qualified and more highly skilled workforce. The report did acknowledge the changing role of women and the challenge that this posed to young women:

> This is a century which has seen, and is still seeing, marked changes in the status and economic role of women. Girls themselves need to be made aware

of the new opportunities which may be open to them, and boys and girls will be faced with a new concept of partnership in personal relations at work and in marriage (CACE, 1963, p.28).

However, the report later outlined what it considered to be the primary concern of young women: 'For all girls, too, there is a group of interests relating to what many, perhaps most of them, would regard as their most important vocational concern, marriage' (ibid, p.37). The role of the school in preparing girls for this particular 'vocation' was clearly spelt out within the report, particularly the need for older girls to realise 'that there is more to marriage than feeding the family and bathing the baby, and that they will themselves have a key role in establishing the standards of the home and in educating their children' (ibid, p.137). Thus, once again, girls were assumed to have a 'natural interest' in domestic roles, and even when possible occupations for women were mentioned - despite the earlier comment about the new opportunities opening up for women - it was in terms of traditional female areas - clerical work, catering, retail and the clothing industry.

Common to all three reports is the way in which they consistently ignored the mounting evidence of the increased importance of women workers within the economy, albeit largely in part-time rather than full-time posts (Elliott, 1991) and, conversely, the increasing importance to women of assuming wider roles within society (Wickham, 1985). By 1961, for example, 30 per cent of women aged 20 to 64 were working full-time, whilst amongst women aged 15 to 59, 47 per cent were working either full-time or part-time (Hakim, 1993). Such participation rates are hardly marginal, yet,

> where (the report writers) have considered educational problems for girls as distinct from those of boys they have revealed that they have presupposed what will and should be the lives of girls as adults. In other words, they have shown that they accept implicitly the dominant cultural values of society and have disregarded in the main the stark substantive data of the situation - they have been guided by their ideological assumptions rather than by a disciplined analysis (Wolpe, 1981, p.143).

This same ideological blinkering was also evident in the Carr Report, *Training for Skills: The Recruitment and Training of Young Workers in Industry*, (Ministry of Labour, 1958). This report contained one short section on training opportunities for women. Again, marriage was assumed to be their primary interest and, accordingly, training was not considered to be a priority. Some concern was expressed, though, about grammar school educated girls of above average ability who might be expected to make a sustained contribution to the labour market in occupational areas such as teaching and nursing (Wickham, 1985). However, the consequences of overemphasising a narrow range of professional careers suitable for girls were highlighted in Rauta and Hunt's study of schoolgirls' aspirations in the 1970s, where it was argued that 'since girls who are not attracted to school teaching, nursing or welfare work see few other prospects if they require high qualifications, it is scarcely surprising that many of them forgo further study and take jobs requiring lower qualifications' (Rauta and Hunt, 1975).

The election of a Labour government in 1964 led to the widespread introduction of comprehensive schooling, although some LEAs had experimented with 'multilateralism' prior to the Labour victory. The dismantling of the tripartite system should have been to the general advantage of girls, given that they were overrepresented in secondary and technical schools. However, the rhetoric of comprehensivisation was principally concerned with equality of opportunity along lines of class, rather than gender. Thus, there was actually a further polarisation of male and female curricular areas (Arnot, 1986), whilst one of the most damaging consequences of the shift towards comprehensive schooling was the closure of many single sex schools (Deem, 1981). Further, the move away from single sex schools was actually justified in part in terms of the supposed greater academic benefits to boys of being educated in a mixed environment, where they could use girls as 'a negative reference point', despite the social and academic benefits to girls of single sex education (Dale, 1969). One of the main motivating forces behind the move towards comprehensive schooling was the need to exploit the talents of all young people in the interests of the economy (CCCS, 1981). However, Deem argues that 'in so far as working class girls could have contributed to this, it would have been only in those unskilled jobs for which greater or better education was not required' (Deem, 1981, p.233). She concludes that comprehensive schooling made little practical difference to the lives of working class girls, whilst Arnot (1984) has argued that although working class and middle class girls were offered slightly different versions of femininity through their educational experiences, both versions nonetheless placed greater emphasis on training for family life than for paid employment.

For most of this century, therefore, there was a tendency within education policy for boys and girls to be regarded as two distinct groups. Each group was assumed to have different 'special interests' which were deemed to be unproblematically shared by all boys or all girls (Wolpe, 1981). In terms of educational organisation, the assumed *group* interests of boys or of girls were given priority over the *individual* interests and aptitudes of all children. Policy makers have often been in the unenviable position of being 'damned if they do, damned if they don't' with regard to the education of girls (Hunt, 1991), and it is of course all too easy from the perspective of the late twentieth century to be critical of the 'political incorrectness' of earlier times. In the first half of this century, to have abandoned the notion of role-directed schooling would have left the Board of Education open to severe criticism for ignoring what was after all an important aspect of women's lives. However, its response - to deny girls a broad-based education and to subordinate the education of girls to that of boys - did nothing to question the extent to which, by so doing, schooling actually served to reinforce the notion of separate spheres for men and women.

Education, employment and equal opportunities legislation

Although for most of the 1960s vocational education and training policies still remained largely dominated by explicit appeals to the assumed separate spheres of men and women, by the end of the decade demands for equal treatment were beginning to be heard. Prejudice and discrimination were increasingly being recognised as barriers to women's education, employment and equality more generally (Rendel, 1985; Arnot, 1986). Momentum had been building up both inside and outside Parliament in favour of the introduction of anti-discrimination legislation and in 1972 an anti-discrimination Bill, introduced by Labour backbenchers but with cross-Party support, was finally referred to a Select Committee to receive evidence on the need or otherwise for a legal framework. A mass of evidence was received from a diverse range of sources, including evidence from the National Union of Students who argued that sex-stereotyping in schools was a form of discrimination against girls, and from the Confederation of British Industry, who were actually opposed to legislation, but who claimed that women's restricted employment opportunities and low pay resulted directly from their educational experiences (Rendel, 1985). The Conservative Party Women's National Advisory Committee (also opposed to legislation) argued that the solution lay with the provision of better education concerning the opportunities now available to women (ibid).

The Department of Education and Science, however, emphatically denied that discrimination was a problem in schools. The following statement was given as evidence in 1973 by the Secretary of State for Education - Margaret Thatcher:

> It is alleged that rather fewer girls take scientific subjects than boys. I think that is so. It may be so because rather fewer girls want to take scientific subjects... or because... they do not find that they have sufficient employment opportunities at the other end... In view of the great debate for relevance as far as education is concerned, there would seem to be some sense in most girls doing some of the domestic science subjects, and there is not the time for everything in the curriculum (Quoted in Rendel, 1985, pp.87-88).

This stance (promoted, ironically, by a female chemistry graduate) was strongly criticised in the Select Committee's final report. It concluded that,

> There remains a widespread feeling that discrimination between boys and girls exists in the educational field however difficult it may be to identify... We believe that the DES have been complacent in its (sic) reactions to these criticisms. We recommend that the Secretary of State should establish

machinery to keep these areas of concern under regular review (ibid, p.88).

On the 29th December 1975 the Sex Discrimination Act (SDA) finally came into effect. Under the new Act, anti-discriminatory legislation was extended to wider employment and training issues, and to a number of other related areas including, significantly, education. Alongside the granting to individuals of direct access to courts and industrial tribunals in pursuit of their claims of discrimination and the groundbreaking recognition of indirect discrimination (Gregory, 1987; Lupton and Russell, 1990), the Act also made provision for the setting up of the Equal Opportunities Commission (EOC), invested with powers to police the Act. This was to be done by means of formal investigations into discriminatory practices, by the issuing of 'non-discrimination' notices enforceable through the courts and by encouraging equal opportunities 'good practice', as well as by conducting and commissioning informal inquiries and research. In practice, however, the EOC deliberately adopted a non-confrontational approach to law enforcement, earning itself a reputation for timidity and indecisiveness (Meehan, 1985). The EOC's political influence was further weakened by two early decisions. The decision to base the EOC in Manchester was interpreted as a marginalisation of its role away from the seat of government in London (Rendel, 1985), whilst the EOC's Commissioners were not originally selected on the basis of any commitment to sexual equality but in order to achieve political balance and the representation of a wide range of interests. Indeed, the Commissioners have at times included avowed anti-egalitarians (Gregory, 1987).

The inclusion of education under the Sex Discrimination Act was viewed by the DES as a highly controversial decision and the eventual price for the inclusion of education within the successful Bill was that the EOC was proscribed from issuing non-discrimination notices in relation to education (Rendel, 1985). Further, all complaints about education were initially to go through the Secretary of State for Education (ibid). Thus, the place of education within the EOC's brief was always likely to be somewhat sensitive. Wickham (1986) notes, for example, that the DES did very little to publicise the SDA's few requirements on schools (that schools must not discriminate in admissions to coeducational schools and in the nature of courses offered to pupils), whilst David (1980) argues that there were frequent quarrels between the DES and the EOC over their legal powers.

In practice, the EOC erred on the side of caution in its dealings with the DES. In 1976, it took up complaints about sex discrimination in admissions to secondary schools in Tameside, where more boys than girls had been provided with grammar school places as a result of the High Court's earlier decision to allow Tameside to retain selective schooling. The EOC took over a year to publish the findings from this investigation and eventually upheld the actions of the LEA, justifying its decision on the grounds that one of the schools was a single sex school and therefore not subject to the requirements of the SDA (David, 1980). In 1979, the EOC decided for the first time to support an education test case in the County

Courts. In *Whitfield vs London Borough of Croydon and Woodcote High School*, Helen Whitfield appealed against her school's ruling that she make a special application if she wished to study a craft subject in the upper school. Before the case could be heard, however, the EOC withdrew its support without explanation, whereupon the girl's mother applied for a judicial review. The EOC's Annual Report subsequently gave as its reason the belief that the case had no reasonable prospect of success and that there was 'a serious risk that the case would result in a narrowly restrictive interpretation... of the Act' (Fourth Annual Report, EOC, quoted in Gregory [1987]). Indeed, the case against the school was lost; the judge ruled that as boys in Helen Whitfield's school also had to make special applications to study Home Economics subjects, the school was not in breach of the SDA. In the judge's view, cooking and needlework were anyway more advantageous to girls than 'technical' subjects, whilst he held that Helen Whitfield had been 'used as a weapon... in her mother's campaign for equal rights.'

As an immediate spin-off from this case, however, the EOC issued advice to LEAs on how to comply with the SDA, in recognition of the fact that, despite the judge's ruling and the EOC's reluctance to support the case, such practices were in fact illegal (EOC, 1979). Simultaneously, the EOC also instigated a formal investigation into the training of craft, design and technology teachers. Rendel (1985) concludes from this that litigation alone cannot be used as a measure of the Act's effectiveness; in a sense she is right, but one could similarly argue that this is evidence of the EOC's general unwillingness to exercise its powers of litigation, unlike the Commission for Racial Equality, which has been prepared to adopt a more confrontational stance (Lupton and Russell, 1990). David (1980) and Arnot (1986) both conclude that the SDA and the EOC have had little impact on the curriculum or on the reform of educational practice more generally. The EOC did, however, draw attention to issues such as the lack of scientific education for girls and the limited pattern of girls' option choices and has produced a considerable amount of resource materials for teachers to draw on in equal opportunities work (Rendel, 1985).

The discovery of gender inequality by the Department of Education and Science

Only two years after Margaret Thatcher's denial of the existence of discrimination within schooling, and whilst Parliament was debating the final shape of the SDA, Her Majesty's Inspectorate (HMI) conducted a major investigation into the nature and extent of sex discrimination within the curriculum. Its report, *Curricular Differences for Boys and Girls* (DES, 1975), was published in the summer before the Bill became law, possibly in order to forestall the unwelcome interventions of the EOC: if the DES appeared to be facing up to the issue, then there would be a weaker case for the inclusion of education under the SDA. Whatever the rationale, the report recognised for the first time the problem of differential uptake of subjects and the implications this had for wider society in terms of the 'wastage of talent' brought about by restricted economic opportunities for girls. The report did not, however, attempt to argue the case for a curriculum common to both girls and boys:

> Equal opportunities are not necessarily synonymous with identical opportunities. Discriminatory treatment as between the sexes may indeed be to the advantage of both boys and girls... equal opportunities does not necessarily imply identical programmes or the use of identical materials (DES, 1975, p.20).

Instead, it argued that curriculum differences should be based on 'genuine choice', rather than stereotyped assumptions. However, the report failed to tackle the effects of the 'hidden curriculum', which largely determined those 'choices'. Rather, it noted that,

> educational establishments do not exist in isolation from the community and will continue to take some account of tradition and custom (which are themselves changing) both in the family and the labour market (ibid, p.20).

Thus, the report fell back onto the 'natural interests' argument in justifying the way in which schools tended to perpetuate curriculum differences (David, 1980). The causal factors for those differences were located largely outside of the school's sphere of influence, effectively letting schools 'off the hook' (Orr, 1985).

Education in Schools (DES, 1977), written in response to Labour Prime Minister Jim Callaghan's landmark Ruskin College speech, pointed to what it saw as a blurring of the distinctions between 'male' and 'female' subject areas, and claimed that in many schools both boys and girls were being educated for domestic responsibilities, including parenthood, in line with wider societal change. This was a remarkable assertion, coming only two years after *'Curricular Differences'* had identified the scale of the problem, and it is difficult to understand on what evidence these claims were made. School ethnographies written at the time certainly provide little or no evidence in support of this claim (Willis, 1977; Sharpe, 1976). Nonetheless, the report called for a curriculum which responded to individual need and which was not based on stereotyped assumptions of what those needs might be. However, it still ascribed to the 'equal opportunities are not synonymous with identical provision' school of thought developed in *Curricular Differences*. Moreover, its emphasis was very much on the needs of *girls*:

> Schools should not by their assumptions, decisions or choice of teaching materials, limit the education opportunities offered to girls... Care should be taken to see that girls do not, by subject choice, limit their career options (DES, 1977, pp.6, 41).

The following year, HMI published *Girls and Science* (DES, 1978), and once again explored the economic impact of girls' unwillingness to opt for the physical sciences in their final years of compulsory education. Although the report was in many ways based on a deficit model of young women and the rationality or otherwise behind their subject choices, a section on the teaching of science noted the lack of positive images of women in relation to science as a possible factor in explaining young women's 'negative' attitudes. It also noted that classroom comments made by male pupils which undermined girls' confidence were not always rebuked by teachers and that this, too, tended to have a negative effect. This certainly marked a break with the tradition of blaming every other factor but the school, in particular the individual girl herself.

Aspects of Secondary Education in England (DES, 1979a) repeated many of the concerns expressed in *Education in Schools* (DES, 1977). This report once again acknowledged the loss of opportunities occasioned by stereotypical curricular choices, but noted with some optimism that, 'traditional attitudes were observed to be changing during the survey, and more pupils were taking advantage of a free choice of craft subjects' (DES, 1979b, p.15). It concluded that,

> close to the heart of any formulation of the aims of education must lie concern to develop the potential of all pupils... including their part in the economic life of the country. Curricular provision, therefore, ought not to be such as to shut off any pupils from important areas of knowledge and experience, or to suggest quite different views of their future role in society (ibid, p.265).

So why the conversion to the cause of equal opportunities? The passing into law of the SDA must be partially responsible for the way in which gender slipped onto the educational agenda of the mid- to late 1970s, whilst given the mutual suspicion and hostility between the DES and the EOC, it would not be surprising to learn that the DES was keen to outwit the EOC by pre-empting likely causes of complaint. However, the prime factor must be the economic imperative arguments that were emerging during the 1970s and which, as we shall see in chapter 3, led to the eventual emergence of TVEI itself. Indeed, the reports highlighted above were unashamedly blatant about this: there were few appeals either to the requirements of legislation or the cause of social justice. In short, Britain needed to harness the talents of *all* young people, regardless of their gender, if it was to compete successfully in a recession-hit world economy and, although reference was occasionally made to the need for young men to learn to adapt to greater domestic responsibilities, the overwhelming need was for young women to learn to adapt to the world of work.

Education for women's work?

It is undoubtedly the case that in the wake of the SDA educational policies increasingly gave greater recognition to the role of women within the labour market. Nonetheless, despite its rhetorical commitment to the promotion of equal opportunities, the DES - in common with the EOC - lacked the political muscle necessary to bring about any great change at the level of official policy. By the early 1980s, few LEAs or schools were seriously concerned with the issue of equal opportunities (Dale et al, 1990). A survey conducted in 1981 by Pratt et al (1984), for instance, found that thirteen per cent of schools still continued (illegally) to offer subjects where allocation was wholly determined by sex. Half of the schools in the sample had been nominated by their LEAs as sites of equal opportunities good practice, yet single-sex options were offered in similar proportions in both nominated and control schools. Further, only eighteen per cent of nominated schools, and nine per cent of control schools, had a member of staff or a group of teachers with a special interest or responsibility for promoting equal opportunities. At the level of practice, therefore, equal opportunities still appeared to be a long way down the educational agenda.

Moreover, upper school option choices continued overwhelmingly to reinforce gender divisions, with the exercise of free choice at this stage of a pupil's education largely resulting in a well-documented polarisation between curriculum areas dominated by boys - technical subjects and the physical sciences - and those dominated by girls - biological sciences, social studies, home economics options and languages (Reid et al, 1974; DES, 1975; Woods, 1976; Hurman, 1978; Ryrie et al, 1979; Ryrie, 1981; Gaskell, 1984; Pratt et al, 1984; Riddell, 1992a). It was therefore commonplace by the early 1980s for all secondary-age pupils to receive a programme of careers education and guidance in which they were encouraged to consider their future working lives, and in which the importance of further education and training was stressed. Nonetheless, it was clear that most pupils continued to make very stereotyped choices in line with their stereotypical career aspirations (Riddell, 1992a). More significantly, studies such as Pratt et al's highlighted the extent to which stereotypical aspirations went largely unchallenged - and were often reinforced - by teachers and careers officers alike. This was despite the fact that the process of choosing options for the final two years of compulsory schooling undoubtedly marked a pivotal point in a young person's education, with serious and far-reaching consequences for their future direction. By rejecting certain curriculum areas, young people were in effect narrowing the range of their future career options, such that if they subsequently wanted to change their plans, they would find it difficult, if not impossible, to pursue a radically different career. This was particularly likely to be the case with regard to 'non-traditional' careers, where their job chances were likely to have been affected not so much by the lack of a particular knowledge base (although this may have been the case with regard to jobs in the technical and scientific sector), but by the implicit lack of a prior interest

(Banks et al, 1992).

In general, therefore, by the early 1980s schooling may no longer have been *overtly* preparing young women for primarily domestic roles, but the bias inherent in the curricular experiences of most young women arguably served a similar function in terms of preparing them for careers which would cast them in the role of service-provider. Indeed, many of the more popular career choices of young women, such as child care, nursing and catering, which tended to be predicated on the choice of related subjects at school, directly replicated domestic roles, thereby serving the purpose of providing 'apprenticeships' for young women's future roles as unpaid domestic workers (Deem, 1978). These trends were graphically illustrated by a number of important studies conducted during the 1970s, which highlighted the extent to which young men and women had both very different aspirations and very different post-16 experiences of paid employment (Sharp, 1976; West and Newton, 1983; Griffin, 1985). Brelsford et al (1982) also found in their study of a Youth Opportunities Programme that young men and women were almost completely segregated within post-16 work experience schemes: young men were clustered in commercial and industrial placements, whilst young women were concentrated in care work and office work in statutory or voluntary organisations. Further, gender segregation tends to be most marked within semi-skilled and unskilled manual occupations (Ashton et al, 1987); this had particular implications for young female school leavers of the late 1970s and early 1980s, given that the concept of 'skill' is itself inherently biased against women's labour market experiences. As Blackmore (1992) has noted, the more widely shared is the competence at a particular occupational task, the more it tends to be devalued and labelled 'unskilled'. This of course has serious implications for women's labour: given its concentration in fewer occupational areas than men's, there is a lessened likelihood of workers in these areas receiving accredited training, particularly amongst un(der)qualified school leavers.

Conclusion

This chapter has considered the 'problem' which gender has presented for policy makers concerned with developing an 'appropriate' education for boys and girls. Educational policy over the course of the century has largely been characterised by differentiated curricular experiences on the basis of assumed vocational differences. For much of the century, official policy has been explicit in its objective of preparing young women for primarily domestic careers. Policy statements in the post-SDA era increasingly stressed the changing role of women, yet they nonetheless led to broadly similar outcomes in terms of the domestic preparation of girls. Given this track record, it is arguable that any vocational emphasis within schooling, far from challenging the sexual division of labour, would inevitably serve to *emphasise* segregation within the labour market, by bringing discriminatory assumptions from the world of work directly into the classroom (Blackman, 1987). However, a central question begs to be asked: to what extent is it fair to cast schools as central agents in the reproduction of a sexually divided labour market? Indeed, to what extent is it fair to cast schools as agents in the reproduction of gender divisions within *schooling itself*, let alone more widely? These questions are addressed in chapter 2, which considers mainstream and feminist attempts to theorise the relationship between schooling and the labour market.

2 Education feminism and the school-work interface

Introduction

Chapter 1 highlighted the extent to which education policy over the course of the century has been based on the assumption that boys and girls have very different vocational concerns. Indeed, it could be argued that the outcomes of schooling for boys and girls in terms of their occupational location and their domestic orientation served to add normative weight to those assumptions. This is to assume, however, that schools are not themselves implicated in the reproduction of gender divisions within wider society - or indeed within schooling itself; rather, that they act as neutral arbiters of the choices made by young people as they move through the education system (Arnot, 1982). These are matters over which feminist educational sociologists have argued long and hard over the last two decades, and the conclusions that have variously been reached on the relationship between schooling and post-16 experience of the labour market can be seen to mark quite substantial differences between alternative strands of what Stone (1994) has referred to as 'education feminism'.

Education feminism in its various guises has a long and distinguished history, and its campaigning has invariably been focused - directly or indirectly - around vocationalist issues. In the second half of the last century, for instance, women worked together towards gaining equitable access to secondary and higher education, whilst in the 1920s and 1930s women teachers fought for equal pay and an end to the marriage bar (Oram, 1987; Weiner, 1989; Purvis, 1991; Miller, 1996). More recently, the passing of the Sex Discrimination Act in 1975 signalled for many feminist teachers the start of a new campaign for gender equality in education. Such campaigning has highlighted the widely held view that education is an important tool in the emancipation of women, in particular with respect to its contribution to raising women's aspirations beyond traditional, stereotypical expectations of 'women's roles', whether that be within the private or public sphere. Feminist campaigners throughout the last century have, therefore, sought to demonstrate the effects of a lack of access to 'male' curriculum areas: the effective cutting off of young women from job opportunities in a wide range of occupational areas, which has had considerable implications for women's wider economic position.

This chapter explores various feminist responses to the tendency of schooling to reproduce existing sexual divisions of labour, both within the school and without. Over the last twenty years, second wave education feminists have had a great deal to say about gender inequalities in schooling (Weiner, 1986 and 1994); this chapter will confine the discussion more specifically to a consideration of the main feminist critiques of vocational education and the work-related curriculum. In so doing, it will make broad distinctions between liberal, socialist, radical and post-structuralist feminisms. Whilst this categorisation is a useful device for highlighting key points of difference, it should be noted that in practice such divisions are often blurred; as Deem has argued, 'what counts is what happens afterwards and where and to whom, rather than the ideological purity of those involved (in gender reform) and the rationale with which it is cloaked' (Deem, 1987, p.160). The chapter starts, however, with an overview of mainstream - or 'malestream' - accounts of the relationship between schooling and the economy, before going on to consider a variety of feminist alternatives.

'Malestream' voices on schooling and the economy

Sociologists of education in the 1970s witnessed the emergence of a critique of the role of schooling in reproducing class relations within society. The key voices in these debates were social reproduction theorists such as Althusser and Bowles and Gintis, who sought to explain the role of schooling in reproducing a class divided labour force, and cultural reproduction theorists such as Bourdieu and Bernstein, who were concerned with the role of schooling in legitimating the dominant cultural forms of the ruling classes (Ashton, 1988). Both perspectives shared an underlying view that 'students are shaped by their experiences in schools to internalise or accept a subjectivity and a class position that leads to the reproduction of existing power relationships and social and economic structures' (Weiler, 1988, p.6). The work of these theorists was groundbreaking and continues to represent a significant and important force within educational sociology, but it has also been heavily criticised for failing to provide an adequate explanation for the role of education in the reproduction of the *sexual* division of labour. This section will briefly outline the main features of these 'malestream' explanations and the central criticisms which have been levelled at them with respect to the gender question.

Social reproduction theory

The central premise of both Althusser's *Ideology and State Apparatus* (1971) and Bowles and Gintis' *Schooling in Capitalist America* (1976) is that the education system plays a critical role in the reproduction of the capitalist mode of production, both in terms of the reproduction of productive forces and the reproduction of the social relations of production (that is, the class relations operating within the structuring of the labour process). The education system is thus seen to perform two main functions: the production of the necessary skills and techniques required for adequate job performance, and - more critically - the assumption of responsibility for 'submission to the ruling ideology' (Althusser) or the 'reproduction of consciousness' (Bowles and Gintis). Thus, even when schooling is not explicitly vocationalist in content, social reproduction theory argues that schooling nonetheless does an effective job in preparing young people for specific class-based occupational locations. Social reproduction theorists have, however, been criticised for either ignoring gender differences altogether or failing to face up to the complexities of the interaction between class and gender. As we shall see, neither Althusser nor Bowles and Gintis acknowledge - let alone seek to explain - the centrality of the sexual division of labour within the broader process of the reproduction of class divisions within the economy.

For Althusser, the school is the dominant 'Ideological State Apparatus' within capitalist society, and is the chief means by which young people acquire a distinct disposition which prepares them for their role within the class structure: as the exploited, the agent of exploitation or the professional ideologist. These mechanisms are concealed by an ideology of the school which represents the educational system as an ideologically neutral environment, in which teachers act to expand the horizons of young people (Althusser, 1971). Althusser is totally silent, however, on the importance of gender within this process, leading one to conclude that he either assumed that the education system did not differentiate between the experiences of boys and girls or, if it did, that such differentiation was irrelevant to the broader project of reproducing class divisions. Further, whilst he writes of the importance of the 'education-family couple' in reinforcing appropriate ideology, he does not attempt to address the extent to which this process may be highly gendered, given the assumed role of mothers in home-school links (David, 1980 and 1984; Vincent, 1996).

Bowles and Gintis (1976) have rather more to say about gender inequalities in education and the labour market, but still fail to develop an adequate explanation of the relationship between the education system and the position of women within the occupational hierarchy. Their model of social reproduction is based on the 'correspondence principle', whereby the structure of hierarchical social relations in the school serves to reproduce the hierarchical class division of labour by once again preparing young people for different levels within the occupational structure. This process is made legitimate by the semblance of equality of opportunity within a liberal educational regime which claims to be a meritocracy; any inequalities that remain are therefore supposedly innate within the individual, rather than structural in origin (Bowles and Gintis, 1976).

However, Bowles and Gintis consistently fail to acknowledge the centrality of the sexual division of labour as an organising principle of the labour process, and instead assign it to a position of secondary importance. They also fail to acknowledge its centrality as an organising principle *within the school*. In *Schooling in Capitalist America*, for example, they claimed that sexual inequality persisted in wider society 'despite the fact that women achieve a level of schooling (measured in years) equivalent to men' (ibid, p.35). More recently, they have argued that 'the formally equal status of women as citizens, gained early in the twentieth century, virtually ensures that the state political mechanism will come to supply relatively equal education to men and women' (Gintis and Bowles, 1988, p.23). By making such claims, Bowles and Gintis' arguments ignore the findings of a mass of research which suggests that *within* the educational system young women continue to have a qualitatively different experience of schooling from that of young men, even if in one respect - formal examinations - *some* girls (predominantly middle class) are now doing much better than *some* boys (predominantly working class). They assume, therefore, that boys and girls receive equal educational opportunities, with the determining factor of a differentiated educational experience being not gender (nor ethnicity), but *class alone*. By accepting at face value the claims of sexual equality in the classroom, however, Bowles and Gintis miss the opportunity to develop a powerful argument for the legitimation of differential outcomes for boys and girls. Unfortunately, they appear to have accepted a version of their own meritocracy argument to account for the educational experiences of girls: that is, because *some* girls manage to do well and achieve mobility, *all* girls have the potential to do likewise. Their 'failure' to do so is therefore related to issues such as individual ability and motivation, rather than any failings of the 'system' through which they pass.

Bowles and Gintis argue further that the roots of sexual (and racial) inequality lie *outside* of the educational system. More specifically, they argue that the prime agent for the reproduction of the sexual division of labour is not the education system, but the family:

> Like the educational system, the family plays a major role in preparing the young for economic and social roles. Thus, the family's impact on the reproduction of the sexual division of labour, for example, is distinctly greater than that of the educational system (Bowles and Gintis, 1976, p.143).

Family life, with its 'teaching by example' of sex roles, is therefore assumed to be far more important than schooling in determining a young woman's future direction, yet the relative impact of family life on young men is apparently negligible. As Wolpe (1988) argues, it is difficult to sustain a claim that implicitly suggests that education has very little importance in shaping girls' lives. Undoubtedly the family does have a major impact - on both boys *and* girls - in shaping young people's perceptions of appropriate gender roles (Furlong, 1986), but Bowles and Gintis appear to ignore the fact that gender-based hierarchical relationships within the home, which are deemed to have such a strong influence on young women, exist just as strongly within the educational system. Moreover, within education these relationships are reinforced by a hierarchy of knowledge that puts greater value on 'male' areas of knowledge than on 'female' areas of knowledge.

Cultural reproduction theory

The two main figures within the cultural reproduction tradition are Bourdieu and Bernstein. Bourdieu's work on education (Bourdieu, 1973, 1976a and 1976b; Bourdieu and Passeron, 1977) regards the principal function of schooling as the reproduction and legitimisation of hierarchical relations between different groups or classes in society. This is achieved via the system of teaching and the language used as the basis of communication in the schools: the 'cultural arbitrary', which is the dominant system of values, norms and languages. He also argues that the formal examination system acts as a selection filter, which selects children from the dominant groups for promotion and selects out children from the subordinate classes. The working classes are selected out by means of the different 'cultural capital' they bring to their schooling by virtue of their family background. Cultural capital is important in determining not only a young person's educational success, but the kind of work they will do on leaving education and the kind of life they will lead, including the determination of their attitudes and values. Social class, however, 'is important only because it is reproduced in the structures of the school system: it is the basis of divisions in the schools, but is not in itself the source of adult values and attitudes' (Carnoy, 1982, p.104).

Bourdieu has very little to say about sexual divisions within schooling and how they might interact with class-based divisions. In *Reproduction* (Bourdieu and Passeron, 1977), he comments on the apparently weaker performance of women students in university arts faculties and notes that it is 'understandable' that their performances should be weaker in comparison with their male counterparts,

> since we know that female students are twice as likely as male students to enrol in Arts course and that, compared with men, for whom the other faculties open their doors more widely, women Arts students... are less strongly selected than the male students in the same faculty (Bourdieu and Passeron, 1977, p.76).

He therefore rejects any attempts at 'fictitious explanations' based on 'natural inequalities between the sexes', yet he does not explain why it is that these differences in uptake, choice and selection exist in the first place. Neither does he comment on sexual divisions within the wider society that schooling serves to reproduce. David (1980) argues that this is because Bourdieu *assumes* the importance of sexual divisions, in particular the role of women, as mothers, in the cultural reproduction of the educated classes. Further, although he regards the examination system as a filter for selecting children from the dominant groups for promotion, and for selecting out children from the subordinate classes, Bourdieu ignores the fact that girls with similar - or even better - qualifications to boys do not receive the same economic rewards in line with those qualifications (Arnot, 1986). His arguments are ultimately unsatisfactory in explaining gender divisions in educational experience and post-school experience. Whilst he argues that a young person's cultural capital will determine her or his future, he fails to address the question of the gendered nature of young people's futures. He offers no analysis of the differences in cultural capital between young men and women, of the differential 'status' of subjects traditionally pursued by young men as opposed to those pursued by young women, nor of the specific roles of different family members in the inculcation of cultural capital.

Bernstein's work (1971, 1977, 1990 and 1996), which is concerned with the importance of a school's culture in terms of the curriculum and its moral and social order and how these serve to legitimate dominant cultural forms, is rather more helpful in this respect. His work also provides tools which have allowed feminists to reflect on the role of gender as an organising principle in schools. For instance, he makes explicit the way in which gender can be used as an organisational category within schools. He argues that schools order, integrate and control their heterogenous populations by means of a number of differentiating 'rituals' based on age, 'house', loyalty and sex, and he argues that in co-educational settings, 'sex rituals' will act to reinforce sex stereotyping. Further, he argues that in advanced industrial societies the social purpose of the school is increasingly concerned with education for *diversity* and, as such, sex (and age) tend to become less relevant as general social categories for distinguishing and separating groups within the school, whilst ability becomes the most important category by which pupils are organised. As the organising categories in school change, so the significance of the family as the principle determinant of occupational status is reduced, whilst at the same time sex stereotyping is also reduced, the net effect of which is 'to increase the possibility of innovation within a society and to widen the area of individual choice' (Bernstein, 1977, p.59). Thus, Bernstein's model allows for change and progression, unlike Bourdieu's, which tends to see the status quo continually reinforced.

Bernstein also discusses the role played by women, as mothers, in the process of the reproduction of the educated classes and, by extension, the reproduction of sexual divisions within the labour market. He notes that historically women, as mothers, were not important as transmitters of symbolic property (language, cultural tastes and manners) or of physical property. However, under capitalism, 'the (middle class) mother is transformed into a crucial preparing agent of cultural reproduction who provides access to symbolic forms and shapes the dispositions of her children so that they are better able to exploit the possibilities of public education'

(Bernstein, 1977, p.131). Thus the role of the *middle class* mother is complementary to the role of the school. This is in stark contrast to the role of the working class mother, whose informal teaching and pedagogic values are 'irrelevant, if not downright harmful' (ibid), as the concepts with which the working class mother will instil her children are at odds with those which are valued within the (middle class) education system: 'If the mother is to be helpful, she must be resocialised or kept out of the way... the teacher has the power and the mother is as much a pupil as the pupil' (ibid, p.139). (Recent work by Vincent [1996] tends to confirm the marginalised role of the working class mother.) Bernstein therefore regards the family, and not the school, as exerting the strongest influence on young people's dispositions towards particular locations in production. He does not see this as the primary role of education, and is critical of Bowles and Gintis on this point, arguing that only a small fraction of the output of education bears a direct relation to the requirements of production. This suggests that the family will also be the chief influence on a young person's *gendered* location within production, not least because Bernstein's comments about the effect of the progress of industrialisation on sex typing suggest that he sees the school as generally *less* sex typed and more progressive with regard to the bounds of appropriate gender behaviour than wider society. As such, the school is likely to be at odds with the family's role as the transmitter of traditional gender roles in production. Presumably, then, a school may attempt to promote equal opportunities in option choice and career possibilities, only to be undermined by the stronger influence of the family.

Bernstein's work has also provided tools which can be used for considering the gendered organisation of schooling. Central to Bernstein's work on classroom codes - regulative systems which underlie various message systems, especially curriculum and pedagogy - are the concepts of *classification* and *framing*. The former refers to the construction and maintenance of boundaries between different categories of knowledge and the latter to the form and degree of control within pedagogic relations. Bernstein uses the term 'visible pedagogy' (VP) to refer to strong classification and framing, and 'invisible pedagogy' (IP) to refer to weak classification and framing. MacDonald has used these concepts in order to investigate 'the ways in which schooling transmits a specific gender code whereby individuals' gender identity and gender roles are constructed under the school's classification system' (MacDonald, 1980, p.22). In traditional schools, she argues, classification between definitions of masculinity and femininity will be strong. These categories will be used as organising principles, which will be implemented and reinforced by means of a pedagogy characterised by strong framing along gender lines, with a child's behaviour being evaluated against a yardstick of gender-appropriate criteria and expectations. MacDonald argues that this model is particularly strong in schools serving communities where there is a strongly demarcated sexual division of labour both at home and in the labour market. In schools serving suburban middle class or semi-skilled and skilled groups, classification may be weakened within the school as a whole, with less stress on the necessity of boys pursuing 'boys' subjects' and girls pursuing 'girls' subjects', yet framing is still likely to be strong within the classroom.

MacDonald was of course writing before the rise of New Vocationalism in education and training, and she concluded that, given the strong sexual division of labour within capitalism, it was not surprising that the dominant gender code of British schooling is that of strong classification and framing. However, Bernstein's more recent writings have discussed the forms of classification and framing which have characterised vocational education initiatives. In a modification of his earlier work on visible and invisible pedagogies, Bernstein draws a distinction between *autonomous visible pedagogy* (AVP) and *market-dependent visible pedagogy* (MVP). AVP is based on the acquisition of knowledge for its own sake, whilst MVP is based on a rejection of this assumption and stresses the economic necessity of relevant skills (Sadovnik, 1991). Nonetheless, although earlier vocational initiatives may well have been based on visible pedagogic practices, TVEI prided itself on its encouragement of student-centred teaching and learning styles, and contrary to Bernstein's view could best be characterised by a reliance on invisible pedagogic practices (relatively weak classification, very weak framing with implicit hierarchy and weak sequencing and pacing).

The reason this is of relevance to an understanding of gendered transitions is because Bernstein argues that the roots of the IP lie within the family structure and processes of the new middle class, 'that is, those who work in the agencies of symbolic control, not directly in production' (ibid, p.55). He asserts that whilst visible pedagogy is based on the processes of the old middle class family, the 'masked and often diffuse hierarchical rules (of IP) are a reflection of the socialisation practices of the new middle class family, with its emphasis on the internalisation of authority relations, rather than on the response to external control or force' (ibid, p.55). Key to these relations are an integrated, not a segregated, division of labour within the middle class home, implying that pupils whose family life is based on equitable gender relations will reap greater benefits from the vocationalist classroom than pupils from families where a stricter division of labour is in evidence. These pupils will be disadvantaged by IP, because they are likely to misread the significance of classroom practices. Although Bernstein does not state this himself, this seems to imply that daughters of the new middle classes will perhaps reap the greatest benefits of all, with both working class girls and boys remaining disadvantaged within the school. If this is the case, this would actually go a long way towards explaining current trends in exam performance, as it tends to be *middle class* girls who are doing well, leaving behind both working class boys *and* girls. This would seem to be a fruitful avenue for further research to explore.

Education feminisms and the school-work interface

The previous section outlined the key mainstream perspectives on the school-work interface. Each of the approaches which have been highlighted have generated a vast amount of controversy and debate over the years and, although later developments have taken on board many of the criticisms levelled at the early work in this area, Moore (1988) has noted that the basic, deterministic models have remained pretty much intact. As we shall see, the various strands of education feminism have reacted to these models in different ways: liberal feminists have eschewed the structuralist approach entirely; socialist feminists have largely attempted to build on the basic model; radical feminists have placed far greater emphasis on sexual politics alongside 'economic' politics; and post-structuralist feminists have emphasised the importance of 'individual subjectivities' and have accordingly been highly critical of the over-determinism implicit not just within 'malestream' accounts but within some feminist accounts too.

In the sections which follow, each of these four positions will be examined in turn, firstly to highlight their distinguishing features and then to consider their specific perspectives on the school-economy interface and their implications for vocationalism and the work-related curriculum.

Liberal feminism: challenging stereotypes

The liberal feminist perspective on education is a perspective which informed many of the early campaigns for women's rights within the education system. In its 'second wave' manifestation, it has been strongly influenced by the social democratic tradition in education, an egalitarian movement which reaches back to, and is enshrined within, the 1944 Education Act, which held out the promise of secondary education for all (CCCS, 1981; Jones, 1989). For most of the post-war period, the social democratic tradition was concerned primarily with the promotion of class-based equality. It was not until the end of the 1960s that concerns with regard to women's access to education and training began to reappear on the egalitarian agenda, but even then within a framework which, ironically, tended to focus on middle class girls and women (Millman and Weiner, 1987).

The liberal feminist approach, also sometimes referred to as the egalitarian or equal opportunities approach, is essentially a reformist perspective, seeking to bring about progressive change within the education system on behalf of girls and women, as well as on behalf of boys and men where inequalities are seen to affect them. The implicit assumption of the liberal approach is that changes in organisation and practice within the education system - which is considered to be essentially benevolent - will automatically lead to changes in social relationships (Weiler, 1988). Associated with this assumption is a strong belief in the individual nature of social aspiration, mobility and achievement such that, given access to opportunities, girls will compete on an equal footing with boys (Arnot, 1983). Accordingly, liberal feminists have concentrated their efforts on the elimination of sex-role stereotyping within education, and with respect to the work-related curriculum there has been much to do. Indeed, in the wake of the SDA, a steady stream of feminist research began to emerge which pointed to the forms and extent of sexual discrimination within education, invariably with a focus on the implications of such discrimination on the post-school experiences of pupils. Much of this early research - clustered, according to Weiner (1989), around the three broad themes of teacher attitudes, school organisation and resources, and the activity of women in the labour market was informed by a liberal feminist concern over the effects of stereotyping and the need for awareness raising measures in schools. Having established the nature of the problem, feminist teachers and researchers were keen to translate research into action, and the measures which tended to develop were often characteristic of a liberal approach to inequality.

Early liberal initiatives, for example, sought to promote the wider take-up of science and technology amongst girls, in part through the provision of greater information and awareness-raising measures, including initiatives to challenge the sexist imagery so often contained within school text books. Liberal feminists also called for - and, subsequent to the introduction of the National Curriculum, have welcomed - the introduction of a common curriculum, whereby 'boys' subjects' and 'girls' subjects' have been made compulsory for all pupils (Byrne, 1975, 1978 and 1985). In similar vein, they have stressed the need for equal opportunities to be seen as a professional issue, as a question of good educational practice, whilst equal representation of women in each tier of the education system has been seen as an important goal in itself.

Perhaps the most well known action research project of this period was the 'Girls into Science and Technology Project' (GIST) (Kelly, 1985a; Whyte, 1986), which sought to investigate the causes of female underachievement in science and technology, and to change the situation by encouraging more girls to opt for physical science and technology subjects in the upper school years. A similar project, which has continued into the 1990s, is the Women Into Science and Engineering campaign (WISE). WISE was established in 1984 with joint sponsorship from the EOC and the Engineering Council, and aims to encourage more women into careers in science, engineering and technology. WISE-coordinated initiatives include visits of the WISE campaign bus to selected schools, taster courses for GCSE and 'A' level students, an annual award for the best team of girls in the Young Engineers for Britain competition, and the provision of posters and leaflets with information on career openings in science and engineering. Both Rees (1992) and Henwood (1996) have pointed out, however, that WISE places greater emphasis on the need for girls and women to change their attitudes to careers in science and engineering than it does on the need for industry to change its approach to female employees. This is exemplified by the language used in various WISE publicity leaflets: 'BE WISE. Girls can *no longer afford to ignore* the challenging opportunities which careers in engineering open up for them' (Engineering Council, 1988); 'Women are as likely as men to have the personal qualities that make a good engineer: all that remains is for more of them to *give themselves the chance* of entering this challenging world by acquiring the necessary qualifications' (DES, 1984).

WISE remains a classic example of a vocationalist strategy informed by liberal feminist notions of the individualistic nature of aspiration and the assumed efficacy of awareness raising. Kelly has described such initiatives as 'publicity stunts', which 'run the risk of trivialising the whole issue by making it appear that all that is needed is a conference and goodwill' (Kelly, 1985, p.145). This view is shared by Riddell (1992b), who argues that WISE is based on a simplistic notion that equality will be achieved simply by enlisting females into male occupational areas, without necessarily altering the occupational structure and ethos. Kelly, who was GIST's co-director, has subsequently argued that this was a weakness of GIST: it was limited in its effect in part because it deliberately did not pose a threat to existing gender relations in education (Kelly, 1985a). In the short term this benefited the project by avoiding the alienation of male teachers upon whose goodwill the project relied. However, it backfired in the longer term, as most teachers failed to 'make the links between their own assumptions and girls' underachievement' (ibid, p.141) and therefore sought to change girls' attitudes rather than their own practices, a point confirmed by an independent evaluation of GIST (Payne et al, 1984).

GIST and WISE are both illustrative of one of the inherent weaknesses of liberal feminism: a failure to contextualise gender inequalities within schooling and wider society (Kessler et al, 1985; Weiler, 1988; Gewirtz, 1991). Thus, radical and socialist feminist critics of the liberal perspective argue that gender inequalities in education are directly related to the general subordination of women by men within patriarchal society, which in turn is interlinked with class-based and racial oppression within capitalism. The liberal approach, in contrast, is happy to work within existing structures and does not seek to challenge the basis of those structures or their part in the creation and reinforcement of social inequalities. It is an approach that underpins the work of the EOC, based on the notion of *formal equality*: the prior disadvantages of gender, race and class are thereby ignored, leading to the reinforcement of the substantive inequalities which prevent people from competing on equal terms (Gregory, 1987). As a result, liberal feminists hold to the view that boys and girls should be treated in identical fashion; many liberals, for example, are uncomfortable with the provision of 'special' treatment for girls (such as single sex classes), and regard such action as a compromise of the commitment to equal treatment. Indeed, they may well view it as a form of discrimination in itself (ibid; Connell, 1985).

The liberal feminist approach is also strongly underpinned by a rather deterministic model of sex role theory and socialisation, which assumes that young people are socialised into particular gendered behaviours in a fairly uncritical fashion. There is also an assumption, though, that the socialisation process can be 'undone' by awareness raising measures, which compounds the error of assuming that young people effectively 'soak up' messages which are directed towards them. In this respect, therefore, the liberal approach can be regarded as a social engineering model of gender reform. Pupils tend to be viewed as homogenous groupings - *boys* and *girls* - with distinct interests and having gone through distinct processes of socialisation, with little account taken of diversity and the capacity to resist socialisation processes (Connell, 1987).

The liberal feminist perspective also has a rather naive faith in the impact of school-based gender reforms on the wider labour market. Whilst schools may succeed in encouraging girls to take non-traditional subjects at GCSE or even at 'A' level, there is no guarantee that young women will subsequently be able to pursue careers in those areas. Ethnographies by Griffin (1985), Cockburn (1987) and Stafford (1991), for example, have highlighted both the obstacles which invariably stand between young women and access to non-traditional career pathways, and the high social costs of surviving within male-dominated working environments. Moreover, the economic restructuring of the late 1980s onwards has radically altered the potential demand for recruits to traditionally male occupational areas (Haywood and Mac an Ghaill, 1996). Manufacturing industry has continued its long decline, with the growth areas now being within the female-dominated service sector, an area characterised by casualised labour, low pay and poor working conditions - the typical features of 'feminised' occupational areas (Reskin and Roos, 1990). These are processes which tend to be underplayed within liberal feminist accounts of gender reform.

It is important to end this section by highlighting the achievements of liberal feminism within education. Whilst its theoretical base is rightly regarded as weak, it is a perspective which nonetheless wrought considerable organisational change throughout the 1980s. Both Arnot (1991) and Acker (1994) have noted the appeal of the liberal approach to policy makers; indeed, Acker argues that the liberal equal opportunities approach 'is virtually the only one acceptable to the general public' (Acker, 1994, p.45). Its appeal lies in its consensual approach to change, marked by the setting of achievable targets and workable strategies within existing resources. At the same time it holds out the promise of teacher autonomy, treating teachers as potential agents of change, with the actions of policy makers largely limited to the provision of support services and in-service training. This has a downside, of course, in that this approach also allows teachers the space to decide *not* to take action.

Socialist feminism: challenging oppression

In contrast to liberal feminism, the socialist feminist approach is concerned with exploring the structural roots of educational inequality in the context of a capitalist society. Accordingly, socialist feminists are concerned with the role of the school in reproducing existing sexual and class divisions of labour and the mechanisms by which this is achieved. Weiler (1988) has provided a useful commentary on the work of these writers and has written that,

Basic to their approach is the view that women's oppression in the paid workforce and in domestic work is reproduced through what happens in schools... The major focus of this approach is on the connection between sexist practices in the schools and women's oppression in society as a whole... Work, both paid and unpaid, becomes the central focus of analysis... (and) they focus on the way schools work ideologically to prepare girls to accept their role as low paid or unpaid workers in capitalism (Weiler, 1988, pp.31, 32).

The relationship between schooling and the economy therefore provides a central focal point within this perspective and, not surprisingly, the starting point for socialist feminist perspectives on education is a critique of existing social and cultural reproduction theories. Indeed, most of the criticisms of mainstream theory noted in the first section of this chapter have been made by writers who would locate themselves within the socialist feminist tradition. In response to the failure of mainstream theorists to provide adequate accounts of the impact of gender on the processes they describe, socialist feminists have developed versions of reproduction theory in which the relationship between gender as an ideology and women's role in production is central. Anne-Marie Wolpe's work (1978, 1981 and 1988), for example, has pointed to the ideological assumptions underpinning official educational policy statements in the post-war era. She argues that the assumption that women function only (or, at best, chiefly) as wives and mothers, along with the failure to acknowledge women's participation in paid labour, encouraged girls to see their own work (paid and unpaid) as insignificant, thus serving to reproduce women's oppression and subordination within the economy. Weiler (1988) has criticised Wolpe, however, for inadequately addressing how these assumptions are put into practice in schools, or how students and teachers accept and incorporate them. She argues that,

This is not to discredit or discount Wolpe's analysis, but to point to the limitations inherent in a view of ideology as the uncontested imposition of a view of reality or set of values... It is Wolpe's reliance on reproduction and her failure to address the question of human agency that ultimately limits her work (Weiler, 1988, p.33).

Rosemary Deem's early work (1978, 1980 and 1981) also emphasises the role of schooling in preparing women for certain kinds of paid and unpaid work, pointing to the domestic nature of the curriculum followed by girls, particularly working class or non-academic girls. Deem does not argue that sexual and class divisions are *created* by schooling, but she does stress that schools rarely do anything to challenge those divisions; rather, in their authority structures and expectations they transmit different cultures to boys and to girls, which also differ according to a pupil's social class location, and which in turn influence the stereotypical 'choices' made by pupils. Deem's work has also emphasised the continuity between women's work as mothers in the home and as teachers in the primary school, and the effect this has on children's understanding of women's roles within society. More recently, Deem has focused her attention on the impact of the Conservative educational reforms of the late 1980s. Her work on school governing bodies (Deem, 1989; Deem, Brehony and Heath, 1995) has highlighted the gendered assumptions concerning appropriate roles for women governors, particularly those who serve as parent governors, and how these too tend to reinforce stereotypical notions of the appropriateness of certain spheres of influence.

The assumed role of mothers within the education system is a key theme in the writings of Miriam David (1980 and 1993; David, West and Ribbens, 1994). Her work has also highlighted debates over the role of education for parenthood within schools, which overwhelmingly has been translated into education for *motherhood*, and accordingly been directed almost exclusively at girls, particularly working class girls for whom it is assumed that (early) motherhood will be their chief vocation. Recent research by Mac an Ghaill (1994) has, however, highlighted the extent to which courses based around 'parentcraft' - dressed up as 'care work' under a New Vocationalist guise - have become contested territory within schools, with many female pupils resenting the attempts to be taught skills in areas where many of them already have considerable experience and expertise.

This last point relates to a general criticism, made by feminists and non-feminists alike, that mainstream social and cultural reproduction theories take little account of the possibilities for resistance and contradiction within schooling. Social feminist writers such as Arnot (MacDonald, 1980; Arnot, 1983, 1984, 1991 and 1993), Weiler (1988 and 1993) and Yates (1993) have put a further spin on this by pointing to the neglect of possibilities for a (re)negotiation of dominant gender codes, whether on the part of pupils or of teachers. They argue that the processes of social reproduction are represented as 'a relatively smooth process of structures and apparatuses, unconcerned with the erratic or impassioned actions of flesh-and-blood human beings' (Weiler, 1988, p.8). In contrast, whilst recognising that schools *can* be the terrain of social control, it is argued that they can also be sites of ideological and political struggle (Apple, 1982; Arnot and Whitty, 1988; Moore, 1988; Weiler, 1988). Thus, although schools will tend to reinforce the 'norms of the enterprise', this is not necessarily so: individual schools, or individual classrooms within schools, may actually succeed in being 'relatively autonomous' to the wider enterprise. Moreover, the social reproduction model is based on the premise that young people accept without question the messages they receive within the classroom, and feminist reproduction theorists have therefore sought to question the extent to which pupils and teachers do remain passive within the process of reproduction. Kelly and Nihlen (1982), for example, have argued that there may be a world of difference between what children are *taught* and what they actually choose to *learn* about the 'norms' of society, and they conclude that women, as both teachers and as pupils, do *not* accept the ideological messages of the education system uncritically.

Arnot (1982) has argued further that writers who fail to engage with notions of resistance and contradiction are in danger of falling into the trap of social determinism, leading to a sense of overwhelming pessimism and helplessness, especially amongst women teachers. Moreover, an overly-deterministic model tends to overlook historical gender campaigns within education, most notably the fight for the right to education for women - 'the most public of gender struggles' (Arnot, 1982). This of course highlights a central paradox in women's relationship to education: access to formal education, whilst being implicated in women's wider oppression, can also be a liberating experience for women (Arnot, 1984; Weiner and Arnot, 1987). Indeed, Yates has criticised feminist theorists who overlook this latter point, and notes that their own existence undermines their arguments:

> Feminist theorists, themselves usually the products of high levels of formal education, generally fail to acknowledge that this education may have contributed to their ability to criticise or 'see through' the sexist forms of contemporary society (Yates, 1993, p.184).

Radical feminism: challenging patriarchy

Acker (1994) argues that socialist feminism is often viewed as a largely academic force amongst education feminisms, that although it provides theoretical insights it does not necessarily provide much in the way of practical strategies for change in schools. This charge is of course contestable, but is certainly not one that could be levelled at radical feminism as a force within education. Radical feminism - sometimes referred to as the anti-sexist approach - is very much an action-orientated feminism but one which, unlike liberal feminism, sets the issue of male power and control at the very centre of its thinking:

> (Radicals) have expressed doubts about the value of policies of equal opportunity which deny or ignore competing educational (and economic) interests, and have criticised policies of educational change which fail to acknowledge the constant competition for power and control between men and women, black people and white, and between class interests (Weiner, 1986, p.269).

As this quotation suggests, radical feminism is often used to describe a variety of approaches, including black radical feminism and lesbian radical feminism. There may be subtle differences between the different radical approaches, but they are all concerned with prioritising the experiences of young women within the education system, a system which is regarded as fundamentally flawed and androcentric. Thus, to see real change, radical feminists argue that groups within education that are currently privileged by patriarchy need to relinquish their hold on that system and that girls need to be placed at the centre of the educational process. To prioritise the needs of young women in this way is not to discriminate unfairly in their favour, as many liberal feminists would see it, but to treat girls in the same manner that boys have *always* been treated.

Radical feminists have concentrated their efforts on two main areas of school life and, although Acker (1994) argues that radical feminists have made few attempts to relate school life to the economy, both areas of concern do have implications for a critique of a work-related curriculum. The first area relates to the male monopolisation of culture and knowledge within the education system, and the second area relates to the sexual politics of everyday life in school. With regard to the first area, radical feminists have highlighted the extent to which 'male' forms of knowledge are granted higher status than 'female' forms of knowledge within schools, with a consequent downgrading of 'female' knowledge areas and of the occupational spheres which are linked to those knowledge areas. The resultant polarisation of option and career choices both pre- and post-16 is of course an issue of concern to liberal feminists too, but the proposed solutions tend to be rather different in emphasis. For liberal feminists, the solution to unequal take-up of gendered subject areas has been the provision of equal access or the imposition of a common curriculum. Both solutions tend to assume that young people's negative attitudes towards particular subject areas are the main obstacle to take-up. However, radical feminists have argued that the 'problem' should not be located with pupils; rather, that their supposedly 'negative attitudes' should be taken seriously and their criticisms taken on board in revising curriculum content. A good example of this alternative approach is the 'Girls into Technology Education' project (GATE) which in looking at the low take-up of technology options (and subsequent careers) amongst girls sought - in contrast to WISE - to redefine the nature of the 'problem': rather than implicitly blaming girls for having negative attitudes towards technology, GATE sought to bring about change in the teaching of technology towards a more 'girl-friendly' approach (Grant and Harding, 1987; GATE, undated). Thus, it sought to reclaim an area of knowledge largely appropriated by boys and men.

This distinction between 'male' knowledge and 'female' knowledge - in turn linked to assumptions about gendered interests and learning styles - is a recurring theme within radical feminist debates, yet it is not unproblematic and has indeed attracted considerable criticism. Kenway (1993) has argued that the radical position paradoxically serves to perpetuate the gendered dualisms of which it is so critical by giving credence to these polarised positions. Thus, the solution to the 'masculinisation' (and hence, assumed superiority) of the physical sciences, for example, is seen to lie with the development of a feminised version of science, within which 'female' cognitive styles and 'psychic preferences' are given priority:

> This underwrites rather than challenges the masculine, monopolistic claim on certain forms of intellectuality, such as the 'rational', 'objective', 'impersonal' and

so on. Further, gendered dualisms are confirmed, not transcended, and ironically, women and girls remain locked into traditional rather than expansive versions of femaleness - hence female difference is both naturalised and (re)produced (Kenway, 1993, p.88).

The second main area of concern - the sexual politics of everyday life in school - is very much a hallmark of the radical approach, and highlights a willingness to tackle areas of school life which tend to be neglected within a more liberal framework. Thus, radicals are not afraid to tackle issues such as sexual harassment and sexuality as sites of struggle within schools, and have sought to provide spaces both within and without schools for these and related issues to be confronted - notwithstanding the severe limitations placed on some aspects of this work by Section 28 of the 1988 Local Government Act, which made it illegal for a local authority to 'intentionally promote homosexuality' or to 'promote the teaching in any maintained school of the acceptability of homosexuality as a pretended family relationship' (Sanders and Sprigg, 1989). Studies by radical feminists such as Carol Jones and Pat Mahoney (Jones, 1985; Mahoney, 1985; Jones and Mahoney, 1989) have highlighted issues of sexual violence in school, whilst Debbie Epstein's work has drawn attention to the difficulties experienced in school by lesbian and gay pupils and teachers (Epstein, 1994 and 1997; see also Cooper, 1989).

These and similar studies have contributed to a broader understanding of the likely impact within schools of an equal opportunities orientated work-related curriculum, whether explicitly or implicitly. By focusing on sexuality as a key site of struggle within education, they have emphasised the centrality of sexual identity to issues seemingly as uncontentious as the promotion of non-traditional careers and options for boys and girls. Girls who choose 'boys' subjects' and 'boys' jobs', for example, are often accused of having ulterior motives: they either want to be *with* the boys or be *like* the boys. Cockburn's ethnographic study of young women working within a male-dominated Youth Training workshop demonstrates this point: if the young women showed any interest in their fellow male workers they were accused of being sexually promiscuous, yet if they ignored them they were accused of being lesbians, both labels being viewed as slurs on their reputations (Cockburn, 1987; see also Stafford, 1991). Similarly, boys who choose to study 'girls' subjects' or to follow 'girls' careers' are faced with accusations of being 'sissies' by their peers (see Walker, 1988; Mac an Ghaill, 1994; Abraham, 1995). In contrast, 'traditional' subjects offer protection from such onslaughts, providing safe environments within which one's sexuality is not constantly subjected to 'policing'. Thus, the radical feminist focus has highlighted the extent to which the convention of 'compulsory heterosexuality' (Rich, 1980) may play a crucial part in reinforcing traditional choices within a vocationalist framework.

Moreover, environments dominated by one sex to the virtual exclusion of another can be uncomfortable places to be, above and beyond the questioning of one's sexuality, resulting in the calls for greater use of single sex teaching and training opportunities. Strategies in schools have included the provision of women's studies courses and girls' support groups, for example, whilst outside of school radical feminists have exploited the opportunities for using youth workers to encourage young women to join together in challenging oppressive structures. Arnot (1991) and Spence (1996) note in particular the development in some LEAs of youth work aimed specifically at black and lesbian young women. This highlights the refusal of radical feminists to shy away from making explicit the interconnections between 'race', class, sexuality and gender in the perpetuation of educational inequalities, instead arguing that strategies for combatting racism, sexism, homophobia and class bias are less effective if these issues are treated as completely unrelated to each other (Weiner, 1989; Gewirtz, 1991; Haw, 1991). The emphasis is very much on the *empowerment* of students, so they in turn can challenge the hierarchies of oppression which they experience in their schooling and, in contrast to the liberal stance, the radical approach tries to take into account the *real*, and not stereotyped, experiences of girls and young women. Implicit in the approach is the importance of struggle, the politics of change, and the development of subversive strategies (Weiner, 1986).

Finally, it is important to note the strong link between education-based radical feminism and the rise of New Left 'municipal socialism' in the 1980s (Arnot, 1992), most notably in authorities such as Manchester, Birmingham and the (then) Greater London Council. This period witnessed an expansion of local government equal opportunities programmes, in relation to both gender and race, which inevitably spilled over into work in schools (Jones, 1989; Lupton and Russell, 1990). However, Arnot has noted that, 'the development of local authority policies on race and sex equality did not facilitate a coherent political ideology, and instead brought to the fore competing interests between different groups of women and different ethnic communities' (Arnot, 1991, p.456).

Paradoxically, this highlights a further weakness of the radical approach, namely its tendency to present a rather undifferentiated view of the behaviour of boys and men in school, and of the responses of girls and women to that behaviour. The implication of the work of Jones (1985) and Mahoney (1985), for example, appears to be that all males within a school are potential harassers of women, or that all males are motivated by misogyny in their behaviour towards women. To make such a claim is to repeat the essentialist error made by liberal feminists in assuming that girls and boys form homogenous groupings and accordingly share a commonality of experience on the basis of their gender alone. Although radical feminists may be more likely than liberal feminists to take account of differences between, for example, black working class young women and white middle class young women, they may still be guilty of assuming that *within* each of these categories young women share essentially the same experiences and outlooks. It is a concern with this final point which is one of the defining characteristics of feminist post-structuralism, which forms the focus of the final section of this chapter.

Feminist post-structuralism: challenging discourse

Feminist post-structuralism is in many senses the 'young pretender' in debates over gender and education. It is an approach which not only stands in contrast to the three broad approaches described so far, but one which also includes at its heart a specific critique of these other perspectives.

Post-structuralism at its most general is concerned with the importance of *meaning*: 'the way in which meaning is struggled over and produced, the way it circulates amongst us, the impact it has on human subjects, and finally, the connections between meaning and power' (Kenway et al, 1994, p.189). Drawing heavily on the work of theorists such as Foucault, post-structuralism focuses on the shifting significance of different 'discourses' and 'texts', discourse being defined by Dant as 'the material content of utterances exchanged in social contexts that are imbued with meaning by the intention of utterers and treated as meaningful by other participants' (Dant, 1991, p.7). Particular 'utterances' obtain dominance through being inscribed within apparatuses of power and social practices, and 'from within a post-structuralist perspective, the various feminist theoretical typologies themselves are seen as inscribed in multiple power relations' (Middleton, 1993, p.128). Feminist post-structuralism therefore offers tools for understanding the ascendency of dominant gendered discourses, including for example the greater acceptability within schools of liberal feminism in comparison with socialist and radical feminism.

Feminist post-structuralists focus their attention on schools as sites made up of a wide range of different - and competing - discourses, including discourses around issues of gender and sexuality. They seek not only to place these discourses at the centre of analysis, but to present a challenge to inequitable power relations based on gender and/or sexuality (Kenway et al, 1994). Key issues for post-structuralist feminism include, therefore, the processes by which discourses on gender and sexuality which are inimical to women's interests gain ascendancy within schools, and the ways in which counter discourses can be mobilised. However, the broader theoretical context within which these issues are explored is very different to that of liberal, socialist or radical education feminisms, of particular relevance here being the post-structuralist rejection of the logic of binary oppositions and the notion of the 'unified subject'.

With respect to the first of these issues, Kenway (1993) argues that liberal and radical feminism in particular have always had problems with coping with male-female dualism, a dualism which almost invariably constitutes women as the negative other. Liberal feminists have tended to encourage girls to move across to the male side of the binary, by choosing non-traditional subjects and careers for example, whilst radical feminists have tended to elevate and celebrate the feminine side, by means of a 'reclaiming' of 'girls' subjects', for example, or an emphasis on an essentialist view of female nature. Such strategies have had variable success in challenging gender inequalities in schools, yet they have rarely attempted to transcend and transform the very basis of the binary divide. Such a transformation is, however, a project for post-structuralist feminism, which is concerned with deconstructing dualisms and revealing their hierarchical nature. A post-structuralist response to the need to dismantle the binary divide with respect to vocationalism might therefore include a redefinition of notions of skill, or an attempt to move beyond the labelling of certain occupational spheres as being 'essentially male' or 'essentially female' in nature.

This relates to the second key distinction: the rejection of the notion of the 'unified subject'. Post-structuralists argue that, rather than possessing stable identities, individuals are made up of ever-fluctuating 'subjectivities', the on-going result of the discourses that have shaped their specific histories and worlds, and which are thus constituted and reconstituted on a daily basis. Even the concept of gender itself is subject to scrutiny and the meaning of fundamental terms are called into question: for example, 'what it means to be a 'woman' and/or to be acceptably 'feminine' shifts and changes as a consequence of discursive shifts and changes in culture and history' (Weiner, 1994, p.64). Accordingly, post-structuralist feminism is critical of approaches which ignore difference and the importance of the individual, as girls' identities are in constant flux:

> Rather than insisting that girls are one thing or the other, (post-structuralism) recognises that they are all the above at different moments and in different circumstances. It recognises girls as subjects who are variously 'rational' and 'irrational' and acknowledges their commonalities and their many differences (Kenway et al, 1994, p.201).

This approach highlights the need for gender reform programmes to take into account the gap which will inevitably exist between the intentions of policy makers and the interpretations - and subsequent responses - of pupils. There has, for example, been a tendency within many programmes to assume that pupils will automatically recognise the benefits of changing their behaviours and attitudes, with surprise consequently expressed when they invariably fail to do so. However, post-structuralist feminists argue that young people 'read', and often 'rewrite', the messages they receive around gender and their own gendered identities in highly complex and subjective ways. Thus, an equal opportunities initiative may be variously viewed as threatening, irrelevant, coercive, patronising or confusing, despite the view of its architects that the initiative is definitely in the best interests of those at whom it is aimed.

Post-structuralist feminist theorising has recently been used to great effect in a series of studies around schooling and masculinities (Connell, 1987 and 1995; Mac an Ghaill, 1994; Haywood and Mac an Ghaill, 1996; Pye et al, 1996). These studies place great emphasis on the existence of *multiple* masculinities, in contrast to earlier, rather uncritical, studies of masculinity by writers such as Willis (1977) and Walker (1988), as well as the writings of radical feminists which have presented a rather undifferentiated view of the behaviour of boys and men in school (Mahoney, 1985, for example). Thus, rather than viewing boys and men as a homogenous grouping of misogynists and potential (if not actual) harassers of women, it is argued that certain groups of young men are *also* marginalised by the power relations of the school. Connell (1995) describes this differentiation in terms of 'hegemonic' and 'subordinated' masculinities; the former are given tacit approval and hold sway within an institution, the latter are seen as inferior and are consequently marginalised and held up to ridicule. Whilst gay masculinities are perhaps the most conspicuous forms of subordinate masculinity, the term also refers to the marginalised masculinities of groups such as Willis' 'ear'oles', Abraham's 'Gothic punks' or Walker's 'three friends' (Willis, 1977; Abraham, 1995; Walker, 1988).

This approach builds upon the arguments advanced in the previous section concerning the importance of the sexual politics of the school to an understanding of gendered option and career choice. It takes these arguments forward, though, by highlighting the complexity of both boys' and girls' responses to their schooling, as well as the fluidity of their responses. Thus, masculinities and femininities do not remain static, but are subject to constant change and redefinition. This sheds light not only on young people's decision making processes whilst still at school, but also on the decisions they make on entering the labour market. Certain forms of work are seen to be integral to particular versions of masculinity and femininity, with the labels of 'men's work' or 'women's work' not only serving to reinforce hegemonic and subordinate masculinities and femininities, but also serving, crucially, to mark out men from women. Indeed, many studies of young women in transition from school to work (described in greater detail in chapter 8) have found that 'women's work' is valued precisely for the clear-cut versions of masculinity and femininity that are thus presented (Sharp, 1976; Griffin, 1985; Wallace, 1986). For example,

> the archetype of the secretary has many of the qualities of the 'ideal woman'... and for young women, struggling in their mid-teens to achieve a workable gender identity, a job that is unambiguously feminine, safe from competition from men, and bestows a little extra femininity on you, is a secure place to be (Cockburn, 1987, p.118).

The insights of post-structuralist feminism have undoubtedly brought a welcome freshness to debates around gender and educational inequalities, not least perhaps because they also contribute to an understanding of the power struggle which exists between competing discourses such as liberal, socialist and radical feminism (Middleton, 1993). There are, however, a number of problems with the position which need to be borne in mind. Firstly, and crucially, post-structuralism is underpinned by the relativist notion that all world views and ideologies are equally valid, that grand theories meet as competing interests. However, at the heart of a feminist perspective lies a belief that 'women are oppressed in relation to men'. This may be a minimalist definition of feminism, but it is one which nonetheless assumes a 'privileged reading': it is certainly privileged over a reading which says 'men are oppressed by women'. If it is the case that grand theories are no more than competing interests, then feminism loses its validity within such a relativist framework: feminist interpretations of schooling become no more or less valid than any others, including those which may be inimical to women's interests, such as anti-feminist masculinist frameworks (Tett, 1997).

A second problem with post-structuralist feminism is that although an insistence on 'the death of the universal human subject' inevitably leads to the welcome deconstruction of the 'unitary white male rational subject', it also deconstructs the categories 'woman' and 'girl', which have been of such overriding importance to feminism and on which earlier feminist critiques of schooling have been based. Thus, on occasions an individual girl may have less in common with the girl sat next to her in the classroom than with the boy sat across the table from her. Admittedly, on occasions gender is undoubtedly less important than other aspects of a person's 'subjectivity' - as earlier sections have emphasised, socialist feminists have particularly emphasised the importance of class, whilst radical feminists have variously flagged up the importance of factors such as 'race' and sexuality - but a dangerous relativism beckons if the category is seen to lose all validity.

Post-structural feminists' treatments of these two dilemmas has been less than satisfactory: how are we to continue to focus on gender differences if gender is a meaningless, or constantly shifting, category, and feminism just one more truth claim amongst others? This criticism goes to the heart of a complex debate which cannot adequately be dealt with here, but which is also inadequately treated in most accounts of post-structuralist feminism. As Martin asks, 'How do feminists participate in struggles over the meaning(s) of woman in ways that do not repress pluralities without losing sight of the political necessity for fiction and unity?' (Martin, 1988, quoted in Kenway et al, 1994, p.207). If at the present time this tension seems to be largely unresolved, this should not prevent us from appreciating many of the insights that post-structuralism has undoubtedly provided. As Weiner argues, post-structuralism's emphasis on plurality and diversity rather than unity and consensus have undoubtedly 'enabl(ed) an articulation of alternative, more effective ways of thinking about or acting on issues of gender' (Weiner, 1994, p.63).

Conclusion

This chapter has covered a great deal of ground. It started by exploring mainstream theories concerning the relationship between schooling and the economy, highlighting its treatment of the role of schooling in reproducing gendered divisions of labour. The bulk of the chapter has been concerned with exploring the implications of the four main education feminisms - liberal feminism, socialist feminism, radical feminism and post-structuralist feminism - for an understanding of this relationship. Each approach undoubtedly has its strengths as well as its weaknesses. Together, though, they provide us with a broad range of tools, some admittedly more useful than others, for understanding the complexity of pupils' responses to the work-related curriculum and a hidden curriculum which tends to reinforce existing sexual divisions within wider society. Indeed, Kenway et al (1994) argue that these different strands should be viewed as 'strategies rather than truths for pedagogy' and that they should be 'selectively and judiciously employed' in accordance with the particular circumstances of a school: 'feminism itself is a discursive field of struggle, not only with different 'horses for different courses' but also with different dividends for different punters' (ibid, p.207).

3 TVEI and equal opportunities

Introduction

The previous two chapters have set the scene - historically and theoretically - for a detailed consideration of the development and impact of the equal opportunities policy which was included as a funding criterion of the Technical and Vocational Education Initiative. This chapter starts by briefly outlining the origins of TVEI, which emerged from the convergence of three strands of influence during the mid-1970s and early 1980s: the legacy of the 'Great Debate' on the aims of education, the impact of rising youth unemployment and increasing employer dissatisfaction with school leavers, and the ascendancy of the Manpower Services Commission. Turning specifically to TVEI's equal opportunities commitment, this chapter will then problematise its inclusion and question the intentions of TVEI's architects by considering a range of official justifications for its equal opportunities policy, alongside a range of alternative explanations for its inclusion. The chapter ends with a brief overview of the mode of equal opportunities work which developed at the national level.

The origins of TVEI

At the time of its launch, the Technical and Vocational Education Initiative was but the most recent manifestation of the vocational bias of the English education system. Indeed, TVEI and the various forms of youth training which appeared from the late 1970s onwards, collectively became known as the 'New Vocationalism' of the 1980s. New Vocationalism emerged from the convergence of three strands of influence during the mid-1970s and early 1980s: the legacy of the 'Great Debate' on the aims of education, the impact of rising youth unemployment and increasing employer dissatisfaction with school leavers, and the ascendancy of the Manpower Services Commission. Dale (1985) provides a fascinating and detailed account of TVEI's specific origins; the following is a brief summary of these three main strands of influence.

The 'Great Debate'

It was noted in the introduction that TVEI was announced in response to 'a growing concern' regarding the apparent failings of the education system. This was undoubtedly a reference to the anxieties highlighted by the 'Great Debate' on the aims of education, which was set in motion in October 1976 by the Labour Prime Minister Jim Callaghan. Callaghan's watershed speech at Ruskin College marked the end of the period of educational expansion which had been largely promoted by his own party. His speech called into question the very basis of liberal educational philosophy, based on comprehensive reorganisation and educational expansion as the keys to tapping the talents and abilities of working class youth. However, as Britain moved deeper into economic crisis in the 1970s, political commentators argued that these policies had clearly failed to forestall the nation's economic decline (CCCS, 1981; Bailey, 1988; Brown, 1988). Far from creating a new generation of highly skilled and highly employable young people, schooling had inadequately prepared them for the world of work, not least because a predominantly academic curriculum in the nation's schools had led to an in-built prejudice against employment in productive industry. As a result, it was argued that pupils were leaving school with little or no understanding of the economy (DES, 1977; Chitty, 1989).

The Ruskin College speech, which picked up on earlier discontents expressed by *right* wing critics in the 'Black Papers' on education (Cox and Dyson, 1969, 1970a and 1970b; Cox and Boyson, 1975), acted as the catalyst for a sequence of regional conferences, consultative documents and White Papers which addressed the vexed question of the relationship between education and industry. Much of the emerging material was strongly based on a deficit model: economic decline was not a structural problem, but a problem situated within the work force itself, amongst younger workers in particular, and by extension situated within the educational system through which they had passed. In *Education in Schools: A Consultative Document*, it was noted that whilst some of the criticism directed towards the education system was unfounded, not all of it had been misplaced:

> There is a wide gap between the world of work and the world of education. Boys and girls are not sufficiently aware of the importance of industry in our society and they are not taught much about it (DES, 1977, p.2).

The White Paper accordingly argued for much closer links between education and industry, that it was the duty of each school to 'help children appreciate how the nation earns and maintains its standard of living and properly to esteem the essential role of industry and commerce in this process' (ibid, p.6). Two years later the message was repeated: 'It remains a matter of concern that... many pupils are not being taught how industry creates national wealth and the ways in which we depend on industry for our standards of living' (DES, 1979b).

The impact of youth unemployment

In the years prior to Callaghan's Ruskin College speech, youth unemployment had begun to rise dramatically as the country sank into economic recession. Youth unemployment increased steadily over the 1970s, but the biggest increases in absolute terms occurred in the early 1980s: indeed, the net increase in 1980 alone was greater than that over the whole of the 1970s (Raffe, 1987). Thus, whilst adult unemployment took a temporary downturn at the end of the decade, youth unemployment continued to increase, and by 1982 affected over a quarter of all 16-19 year olds (Roberts, 1984). Neither was youth unemployment uniformly distributed: in the early 1980s, unemployment amongst young men grew faster than that amongst young women, with males accounting for the greater proportion of the young unemployed (Raffe, 1987; Brown, 1997). Young people from ethnic minority groups were particularly badly affected, with rates for West Indian young men being twice as high as the rate amongst white young men, and rates for Asian young women being twice those of white young women (Rees and Atkinson, 1982).

Youth unemployment rates were exacerbated by a corresponding rise in labour supply. Increasing numbers of school leavers were joining the labour market as a result of the mid-1960s 'baby boom'; fewer adults were reaching retirement age due to the 1914-18 trough in births; and women were returning to the labour market in increasing numbers (Marsh, 1988). Moreover, there were changes in the economic structure itself, with the decline of certain industries that had traditionally been major recruiters of young people, manufacturing and assembly being prime areas (Rees and Atkinson, 1982). In these areas, the number of apprenticeships available had declined rapidly, from 40 per cent of male school leavers in the 1960s to less than 20 per cent by the end of the 1980s.

Once again, the Labour government shied away from the suggestion that youth unemployment was a structural problem and opted instead for the deficit model, sympathising with employers who complained that the overall quality of school leavers had dropped. Thus, school leavers of the 1970s were uniformly characterised as disinterested, unmotivated and undisciplined (Finn, 1982). In 1977, the Manpower Services Commission published the findings of a major survey of 16-19 year olds and employers (MSC, 1977), which included an examination of factors which were reputedly contributing to the problem of youth unemployment. The Holland Report argued that the assertion that young people were inadequately equipped to compete favourably in the job market had some substance. It suggested, for example, that young people were 'over-aspirated', on the evidence that 53 per cent of those who were still in full-time education felt that job satisfaction was the most important factor in their choice of career. The report argued that,

> It may be that the concern and expectation of some school and college leavers that work should be interesting and varied causes conflicts when they are faced with what may be dull and routine tasks in a job. This could be a factor in what employers describe as a poor attitude towards work (MSC, 1977, p.35).

Such attitudes were clearly regarded as a failing, even though they could equally be interpreted as a measure of the success of liberal educational philosophies in giving young people a sense of self-worth. The question thus became one of whether schools had a responsibility to produce critical and independent thinkers or 'ideal workers' (Finn, 1982; Bates et al, 1984). As youth unemployment continued to rise, it was widely regarded as all the more essential that a work-related curriculum be developed in schools. With previous generations, the early years in work were seen as the means of instilling the 'right' attitude into young workers; with rising unemployment, the responsibility for this process of socialisation came to be seen increasingly as that of the school, in conjunction with the Manpower Services Commission. Thus, as a contemporary commentary put it,

> schooling for unemployment involves, paradoxically, more efficient education for *employment*: it is as if teachers now have to instill the work ethic deeply enough for it to survive lengthy periods out of work (Finn, 1982, p.49).

The ascendancy of the Manpower Services Commission

The third factor in TVEI's genesis relates to the rise in influence of the Manpower Services Commission (MSC) under the Conservative government. After coming to power in 1979, the Conservatives had initially reduced the MSC's budget, seeing it as an unwelcome arm of Labour 'statism'. However, the 1981 inner-city riots were widely regarded as a direct consequence of high youth unemployment, particularly amongst black youth. In the wake of the 'moral panic' that gripped the nation and the sense of urgency that the riots generated, the Government was obliged to reconsider the MSC's role. Youth unemployment was evidently too explosive to be left to market forces, and the Government was forced to provide increased youth training provision under the remit of the MSC, paving the way for the MSC to increase its interventionist role within the economy more widely (Benn and Fairley, 1986; Ainley and Corney, 1990).

As its role expanded, the MSC became sufficiently confident to intervene within the education system itself. Thus TVEI was not, as one might reasonably expect, a creation of the (then) Department of Education and Science, but of the MSC. Indeed, its announcement apparently caught the DES, Local Education Authority associations and the teaching unions by surprise, particularly as the teaching unions had at the time been working with several agencies - including the MSC and the DES - in drawing up plans for a jointly sponsored initiative to tackle the skills gap amongst school leavers (see MSC, 1981a). The significance of TVEI's MSC 'pedigree' is that it reflects the view that the DES was considered to be too cumbersome and resistant to change to be trusted with the responsibility for a major educational initiative. The MSC, in contrast, was a relatively new body, without precedents or an established bureaucracy; not only was it created to respond to specific situations and given power to respond as changes occurred in those situations, it also had the power to initiate policy (Chitty, 1989). Moreover, it enjoyed unquestioned political backing: indeed, the MSC's Chair, David (later Lord) Young, was adamant that the MSC would set up its own schools if existing state schools refused to cooperate. In the event, initial resistance to TVEI (particularly from Labour-controlled LEAs) soon crumbled as it became evident that very large sums of money would be made available to participating projects (Ainley and Corney, 1990).

TVEI in practice

One of the main objectives of TVEI was to develop a stronger relationship between schools and the labour market. This was done by means of both curriculum development and the introduction of new approaches to learning as part of a four year integrated course for students of all abilities in the 14-18 age range, although many TVEI pupils left at 16. TVEI introduced a series of new and enhanced courses leading to nationally recognised qualifications, and emphasised a number of other core elements: most notably, work experience, records of achievement and student-centred teaching and learning styles. In a letter to Chief Education Officers, David Young stated that:

> Our general objective is to widen and enrich the curriculum in a way that will help young people to prepare for the world of work, and to develop skills and interests, including creative abilities, that will help them to lead a fuller life and to be able to contribute more to the life of the community... Secondly, we are in the business of helping students to *learn to learn* (quoted in Hitchcock, 1988, p.2, emphasis in original).

The first round of 14 pilot projects commenced in 1983, followed by a further 47 in 1984, and by the end of the 1980s all LEAs in England and Wales had embarked on a five year period of pilot funding. The first 14 LEAs shared 51.5 million pounds over a five year period, whilst projects in subsequent rounds each received funding of 2 million pounds, representing a huge injection of capital into state schooling. Most projects spent around 60 per cent of their funding on extra staff, 25 per cent on equipment and the remainder on administration, including at least 1 per cent on TVEI evaluation (Dale et al, 1990). In 1986, it was announced that

TVEI funding would be extended for a further five year period to all schools and all pupils in projects which had completed at least three years of pilot. Eventually, all education authorities in Britain became involved in TVEI, with funding finally ceasing in 1997 (McKinnon et al, 1995).

Debates surrounding TVEI's origins and its impact on curriculum development and the management of educational change are well rehearsed (Dale, 1985; Chitty, 1989; Dale et al, 1990; Gleeson, 1988; Saunders, 1990). More recently, Gleeson and McLean (1994) have argued that TVEI represented an important 'transitional moment' in educational policy, a moment in their view characterised by the transition from local to central determination of the curriculum. This, they argue, was crucial for smoothing the path for the subsequent introduction of the National Curriculum under the Conservative government's 1988 Education Reform Act. The significance of TVEI's inclusion of an equal opportunities policy, however, tends to be glossed over in most of these accounts of TVEI's impact on schools, even though for many observers this could be seen as a far more important development. Indeed, TVEI's equal opportunities commitment should *also* be viewed as a moment of transition. Under TVEI, the issue of gender inequalities in education was transformed from a peripheral issue - for the most part championed on the margins of school life by individual feminist teachers (notwithstanding the radical policies of certain 'New left' local authorities) - into a mainstream educational concern.

But why was the equal opportunities commitment given such a high priority? We have already seen that gender issues had been taken up by the DES with a marked lack of enthusiasm, and within rather narrow parameters. Neither did the MSC have a particularly impressive record in this regard. Nonetheless, the inclusion of an equal opportunities policy within an overtly vocational framework implicitly assumed that it was possible for schools, via TVEI, to act as agents of change with respect to ongoing gender inequalities both within schools and within the labour market. This appears to fly in the face of some of the arguments explored in the previous chapter which suggest that, even taking into account the relative autonomy of schooling and the potential for individual and group acts of resistance, schools will overwhelmingly serve as key agents in the reproduction of 'male-female dominance relations'. Thus, from a socialist and radical feminist perspective, TVEI's apparent optimism could be construed as a 'misrecognition of the actions of the state' (Arnot, 1993), an attempt to transform gendered relations within society which schooling - as an agent of the state - had historically helped to construct, most notably through the overt gender essentialism of successive vocational initiatives (Hunt, 1991).

All of these factors suggest that the inclusion of an equal opportunities commitment as a funding criterion was unrealistic in its aspirations given the broader context from which the policy emerged. The question of motive is accordingly explored in the next section of this chapter. The MSC's record on equal opportunities with respect to the training needs of young people in the run up to the introduction of TVEI is explored firstly. There then follows a consideration of some of the official justifications which were advanced in defence of the inclusion of an equal opportunities policy, before a consideration of a number of possible alternative explanations. It is argued that the official justifications were based on a misreading of the gendered working of the labour market, and that the alternative explanations shed some light on this misreading.

The MSC's record on the promotion of gender equality

Although the Equal Pay Act was passed in 1970, it was not until 1973 that women's unequal access to training finally appeared on the government's policy agenda, in the form of the Employment and Training Act. It was this Act which made provision for the establishment of the Manpower Services Commission (known variously as the Training Agency and the Training, Employment and Education Department, before finally being phased out and its duties largely devolved to Training and Enterprise Councils in the early 1990s). In a move predating the Sex Discrimination Act, the Act also incorporated measures to encourage increased training opportunities for women, including the provision of experimental part-time training courses in commercial and clerical training, areas already female-dominated. The provision of childcare facilities, the lack of which was likely to hinder access for some women, and similar measures which would facilitate ease of access, were not included in these proposals (Wickham, 1985). Just before the SDA became law, the Training Services Division of the MSC published a report on *Training Opportunities for Women* (MSC, 1976), which asserted that women's training needs ought to be made a national priority. The report recognised the inadequacy of existing arrangements and admitted that there was an unsatisfied demand for women's training. It argued that there were legislative, economic and social justifications for providing such training, although Evans (1992) contends that the overriding justification was economic rather than social. However, whilst the report should be recognised as the first major initiative by the state in the post-war period to consider the training needs of women, the MSC appeared to lack the political commitment necessary to translate the report's recommendations into concrete practice (Wickham, 1985). During this period, for example, the overall numbers of women involved in the Training Opportunities Scheme (TOPS) gradually increased, yet the opportunities that were available to women were limited both in terms of their range and their level.

The 1977 Holland Report, *Young People and Work* (MSC, 1977), paved the way for the MSC to intervene in youth training and provision. The report, as noted above, was concerned with the training needs of young people who would be entering the labour market at a time of peak youth unemployment. The solution to the needs of both young men and young women was seen to lie in the provision of work experience programmes and 'skills training' - which meant social skills as much as specific vocational skills. Two years later *Opportunities for Girls and*

Women in the MSC Special Programmes for the Unemployed (MSC, 1979) was published. Starting from the assumption that 'there are practically no jobs which cannot be done by girls, given the opportunities and appropriate training', it also recognised the specific forms of disadvantage suffered by the female work force, including lack of confidence to enter new areas and problems arising from having had different educational experiences to men. The report stressed the potential of using Section 48 of the SDA to encourage women into non-traditional areas of employment, yet once again practice failed to match up to the policy commitment (Wickham, 1985). For instance, when the Youth Opportunities Programme (YOPs) emerged at the end of the seventies, young women constituted 50 per cent of all young people involved, yet the range of opportunities available to women was extremely limited, based on stereotyped notions of appropriate female employment. Moreover, YOPs actually resulted in a *greater* narrowing of opportunities for female trainees: pre-YOPs, 68 per cent of young women were found in clerical, retail, catering and personal service work, compared with 74 per cent after its introduction.

In 1981, the MSC published a major consultative document, *A New Training Initiative* (MSC, 1981b). As a consequence of the report's recommendations, YOPs was replaced in September 1983 by the Youth Training Scheme (YTS), at the same time that the first TVEI pilot schemes were launched. The MSC recognised the equal opportunities inadequacies of YOPs and hoped that YTS would be able to go some way towards redressing the balance, yet the same patterns appear to have been repeated (Marsh, 1986; Cockburn, 1987; Hollands, 1990; Bates and Riseborough, 1993). Once again, therefore, the MSC failed to recognise the structural impediments to women's take-up of training opportunities and, in the absence of a more radical approach, their efforts consistently failed to meet their objectives. Seen in this context, the MSC's eventual intervention within education begins to make some sense. If, as *Opportunities for Girls and Women* argued, women were often hampered by their prior experience of education, then the MSC could only hope to make an impact post-16 by means of an early equal opportunities intervention within the school curriculum.

The origins of TVEI's equal opportunities commitment

> Equal opportunities should be available to young people of both sexes and they should normally be educated together on courses within each project. Care should be taken to avoid sex stereotyping (TVEI Unit, 1985).

The MSC had clearly not managed to acquire an exemplary record in the realm of equal opportunities by the early 1980s. Whilst its policy documents gave priority (to a lesser or greater extent) to issues of gender inequality in education and training, it had not translated these policy statements into positive outcomes for women. Indeed, many critics accused the MSC of lacking the political muscle, if not the political will, to do so (Wickham, 1985). This did not augur well for the likely success of TVEI's equal opportunities commitment. It is of course important to note that TVEI emerged within a climate where the odds were heavily stacked against success. This can be illustrated by the coexistence of a number of contradictory forces prevalent in the wider economic and political spheres. Firstly, TVEI was heralded as the much needed panacea to the severe effects of high rates of youth unemployment which had rapidly developed as a consequence of the economic crisis of the 1970s, as well as the panacea for the education system's supposed failure to produce 'good workers' and thereby forestall the economic crisis (MSC, 1977). However, as jobs became increasingly scarce towards the end of the 1970s, female school leavers found themselves competing unfavourably with their male counterparts (Rees and Atkinson, 1982). Thus, even if they managed to acquire the 'non-traditional' skills which TVEI was encouraging them to pursue, it was extremely unlikely that employers would give preference to young women over young men, particularly given the sharp decline over the 1970s and 1980s of employment opportunities in manufacturing industries (Millman, 1985).

Moreover, TVEI's equal opportunities policy assumed the existence of a ready pool of girls willing to pursue male-dominated career paths, yet such a policy operated against a strong tide of resistance. Blackman (1987) has argued, for example, that the threat of unemployment will invariably result in the lowering of job expectations, and that pupils will tend even more towards traditional occupational areas in order to maximise their employment chances. McKinnon and Aloha-Sidaway (1995) have made similar points in relation to attempts to promote non-traditional career routes for young women in the context of Canada's economic recession. Cockburn also highlights the 'embarrassing fact' that few young women aspire to traditionally male occupational areas at any time, regardless of the economic climate, and that it is perhaps more surprising that some young women *do* decide to do so, given 'the high social costs that we all pay if we disobey gender rules' (Cockburn, 1988, p40). (The exception to this may be wartime, when traditional gender boundaries become eroded by the concept of patriotism [Summerfield, 1989].) It could also be argued that training girls only to have their hopes dashed was not a particularly 'girl-friendly' strategy to adopt (Yates, 1985; Eden and Aubrey, 1988), given their far greater chances of gaining employment in traditionally female-dominated occupational areas, where they also have a better chance of promotion than within male-dominated spheres. Indeed, Cockburn (1987) has taken this argument further by arguing for the 'ring fencing' of traditional areas of female employment, in order to ensure that it is women rather than men who acquire the better paid jobs in these areas.

Further, TVEI's commitment was at odds with the anti-egalitarian direction of Thatcherite government policy in other areas, particularly family-related policy, which was exhorting a return to the much-trumpeted 'Victorian values' (Weiner, 1989 and 1993; David, 1993). Above and beyond any misgivings at the level of theory, therefore, there would seem to have been strong grounds for doubting the likely success of TVEI's equal opportunities criterion, given the MSC's earlier track record and the broader context within which TVEI emerged. Given these contradictions, the question arises as to why the equal opportunities element was given such a high priority, and the following sections address this question by considering some of the 'official' and alternative explanations for its inclusion.

Official justifications

Official justifications for the inclusion of TVEI's equal opportunities commitment, published once TVEI was well-established, tended to put forward a strongly economic argument. The most coherent versions of these arguments are contained in two papers published towards the end of the 1980s: *Promoting Equal Opportunities for Boys and Girls within TVEI: A Strategy Guide* (Skinner and Jones, 1987) and an introductory paper within *TVEI Developments 2: Equal Opportunities* (Cross, 1988). The former was one of a series of TVEI Unit papers on various aspects of TVEI, circulated to Central project teams, whilst the latter was the second issue of the regular 'TVEI Developments' series, widely circulated within TVEI schools. Both documents contain prefaces which 'set out supporting reasons to underpin the criterion' (Skinner and Jones, 1987), and both share a number of common themes.

'A matter of human rights'

Both accounts begin with a rights-based argument for the promotion of equal opportunities. Cross argues that,

> It is first and fundamentally, a matter of human rights. No system can be called fair, just or democratic, if it is organised on the assumption that people of one sex are basically inferior and not entitled to the same educational and career opportunities as those of the other (Cross, 1988, p.vii).

The wider context of Cross' article makes it clear that it is women's position in society with which he is principally concerned, although this statement does not rule out the possibility that in some settings it could be boys and men who are regarded as the 'inferior sex' and their rights also therefore in need of protection. As we have seen, this is a sentiment which is strongly associated with liberal perspectives on gender equality and which also underpins the SDA (Smart, 1989). Skinner and Jones' initial argument is similarly ambiguous concerning the gender of those most likely to be currently affected by discrimination:

> People need equality of opportunity in order to develop and maximise their intellectual and social potentials and achieve self-fulfilment in ways which may

be, currently, denied to them because of traditional expectations of the social group with which they identify, or are identified' (Skinner and Jones, 1987, p.1).

This statement is vague concerning the basis of discriminatory action against individuals; the possibility of discrimination based on a whole range of factors, including race, class, sexuality, intellectual and physical ability as well as gender is not therefore ruled out by this statement, unlike most TVEI statements on equal opportunities which tended to concentrate solely on gender. In practice, however, as subsequent chapters will demonstrate, TVEI's equal opportunities work remained narrowly focused on gender in isolation, tending to play down differences which existed *between* boys and *between* girls.

Preparation for changing roles

Skinner and Jones argue further that equal opportunities are essential for equipping young people with the necessary competencies to make the most of changing work, social and family roles, and that equal opportunities should encourage both 'greater diversity of role expectations' and the acquisitions of skills to respond to change. However, one of the central tensions within TVEI's position on equal opportunities is encapsulated in a development of this argument:

> In particular, with regard to the role and status of working women, new and extra demands may be imposed upon their existing social and domestic roles, whilst not necessarily affording them the status enjoyed by their male counterparts, and this calls for the development of new and greater capacities including organisational, negotiating and decision-making skills to which schools and colleges have a major contribution to make (Skinner and Jones, 1988, p.2).

Although implying initially that both sexes will increasingly need to adapt their lifestyles, this statement makes it clear that in practice young women will need to show greater flexibility, in order to cope with the double burden of being active in both the public and domestic spheres, young men being less willing to respond to the additional responsibilities of a world in 'permanent, constant flux.' Thus, in their broader discussion of the importance of equal opportunities in contributing to the creation of a flexible and gender neutral workforce, there is a clear expectation, to paraphrase crudely, that 'all young people are gender neutral, but some young people are more gender neutral than others.' Again, that expectation was clearly translated into practice, with young men rarely being urged to pursue female-dominated subjects and occupations with quite the same urgency as young women were being encouraged to consider male-dominated areas.

'Fighting the economic war with both hands'

A further argument relates specifically to the needs of the economy:

> In order to halt the decline in international competitiveness, the country needs to be able to harness the talents of all its people to their fullest extent. To do anything else is to fight an economic war with one hand tied behind our backs (Cross, 1988, p.vii).

Behind this particular concern lay the anticipated impact of the 'demographic timebomb', the projected 23 per cent drop in the number of pupils leaving school by the late 1980s (Beavis, 1988). It was supposed that employers would be crying out for skilled workers, regardless of gender, and also regardless of age (Maguire, 1992). Despite a great deal of rhetoric concerning the 'economic necessity' for women of all ages to enter non-traditional labour markets, most women stayed firmly within 'traditional' sectors, either because few desired such careers or because the obstacles to gaining access to non-traditional areas proved insurmountable. Thus, the idea of women moving towards non-traditional work in large numbers proved to be more a myth than reality (Lupton and Russell, 1990). Rather, women 'returners' were increasingly found in low paid, part-time employment in traditionally female-dominated service-orientated occupations.

Cross' argument is also weakened by the examples he draws on in illustration. Firstly, he holds up the example of the United States, a country which he argues has 'begun to show the way' in harnessing the talents of all its citizens by means of positive action programmes. His second example relates to the (then) USSR, a country where, he notes, over half of all doctors and four out of ten engineers are women - 'as, of course, are almost all the street cleaners'. However, he omits to mention the inferior status, pay and conditions associated with the 'feminisation' of these jobs in the USSR, in comparison with their American and British counterparts (Scott, 1976; Buckley, 1992). Neither is this process confined to former communist bloc countries: pay and conditions in previously male dominated areas of employment in Britain, such as clerical work, also deteriorated as women moved into them in large numbers over the course of the century (Lane, 1988; Blackmore, 1992; Rubery and Fagan, 1995). Further, Cross fails to acknowledge that measures designed to promote the horizontal integration of young women within the labour market do not necessarily lead to the erosion of vertical segregation.

The development of new technologies

A fourth argument relates to the development of new technologies on a mass scale during the 1970s and 1980s:

> The world of work is changing fast; there are many teachers who have not yet

perceived the implications of technological change. It is no good talking about 'a man's job' and directing boys and, if possible, some girls, towards that particular market, when it no longer exists... Strength is not much in demand; it is skills which are desperately needed and most of them can be acquired equally well by girls (Cross, 1988, p.vii).

The future is too uncertain to make more than educated guesses as to the specific skills/knowledge/experiences that will be needed; thus, as groups, both sexes will need similar broad ranges (sic) of achievements to equip them at the start of their adult, working lives (Skinner and Jones, 1988, p.3).

Many new technologies had already been developed in sectors where women traditionally formed the bulk of the unskilled or semi-skilled workforce, so it might have been considered sensible to train young women to fill the emerging skills gaps. Moreover, it was argued that most major changes in the labour market in future years would be related to the further development of new technologies. If the workforce was to adapt sufficiently to ensuing changes, it was argued, it was clearly critical that new technology be seen as a 'gender neutral' area of employment, as a non-segregated workforce would be a far more flexible workforce (Weis, 1990).

However, this argument overlooked evidence which questioned the emergence of 'gender neutral' new technologies, and which had suggested that new distinctions between tasks tended to emerge, such that gender continued to form the basis of a differentiation between certain jobs, as well as grades within jobs (Reskin and Roos, 1990). Thus, Game and Pringle (1983), Cockburn (1985), Roberts et al (1988) and Dex (1988) all concluded that continuing distinctions are shaped by the 'ideological context' of the new jobs: 'It would appear, therefore, that new jobs and new technologies only modify the gendered distribution of jobs and that when new jobs are created, old symbolism is drawn on to decide whose jobs they are' (Dex, 1988, p.299).

In sum, these arguments for the inclusion of an equal opportunities policy appear to represent a pragmatic response to the anticipated impact of the demographic shift away from a large pool of school leavers. However, it was a response which ignored the effect that high rates of youth unemployment would have on the availability of employment opportunities for school leavers. These arguments also demonstrated a naivety concerning the extent to which young people were prepared to innovate with regard to sex-stereotyped occupations, the willingness of employers to allow them to innovate, and the extent to which new technologies would remain gender neutral. Moreover, policies promoted primarily to meet temporary labour shortages can, of course, be easily dispensed with once those shortages disappear (Acker, 1984; Purcell, 1988). Nonetheless, these arguments imply that the inclusion of an equal opportunities policy was a deliberate policy move on the part of the MSC, and had been intended from the start. However, a number of other factors should also be considered, all of which suggest that the policy may have been developed with little real commitment from those responsible for developing TVEI policy more generally. If so, TVEI's apparent challenge to the traditional gendered assumptions of vocational education should be viewed as more of an accident than design.

Alternative explanations

Equal opportunities as a sweetener

At the time of its introduction, concerns were expressed that TVEI would be the means of reintroducing selectivity and elitism within secondary education (Dale, 1985). Pilot funding was typically extended to no more than five schools in each participating LEA, and to only a selected cohort of around fifty pupils per year group in each of those schools. Moreover, TVEI was often accused of being aimed at 'middle ability' pupils, offering little to less academically-inclined pupils, a group so often neglected by educational reforms. Accordingly, many LEAs, particularly Labour-controlled administrations, were initially very resistant to an initiative which benefited only a small number of pupils. TVEI's equal opportunities commitment may well have been included, therefore, as a 'sweetener' to convince reluctant LEAs that TVEI was in fact deeply concerned with at least one facet of equal opportunities - conveniently overlooking the central contradiction of an equal opportunities scheme aimed at a *selected* group. Its inclusion could thus be construed as a rather inept good will gesture designed to render the scheme politically (more) acceptable to its critics. This strategy has overseas precedents: Yates (1993), for example, points to the shrewdness of the Australian national government in choosing a policy on equal opportunities as its first national (as opposed to state) education policy, thus wrong-footing critics of the government's extension of powers.

Equal opportunities as a containment policy

Given the timing of TVEI's launch, there is a rather more cynical, but nonetheless plausible, argument to be made that its equal opportunities commitment was deliberately included in an attempt to stem and contain more radical policies such as those which had emerged in many 'New Left' authorities during the late 1970s and early 1980s (Jones, 1989; Jones and Mahoney, 1989; Lupton and Russell, 1990). Arnot (1992) has argued that whilst these policies did not have a *major* impact on the state education system, it would be naive to assume that they had *no* impact. Alongside similar developments in anti-racist education, anti-sexist approaches were regarded as subversive of a government which was becoming increasingly influenced by New Right thinking. The pillorying of the so called 'Loony Left' by the Right, both in the media and in Parliament, pays testimony to this. Thus, the development of a high profile equal opportunities policy would have allowed the government, via the MSC, to redefine the nature of the issue. In place of policies which emphasised radical sexual politics, therefore, TVEI redefined the issue in purely vocational terms and as an educational problem demanding an educational solution. More recently, a similar process has been played out with respect to the National Curriculum. Much has been made of the uniform access which pupils now 'enjoy' to a core curriculum, even though the core itself enshrines 'male' forms of knowledge at its heart. Arnot (1991), for example, has highlighted the priority given to subjects such as science, mathematics and technology, all of which were predominantly associated with boys in pre-National Curriculum days and which attracted criticism from feminist educationists for marginalising female experience in their content.

Pressure from women's lobby groups

Thirdly, the inclusion of an equal opportunities policy might be seen as a victory for lobbying groups such as the EOC and the Women's National Commission, who for some time had been exerting pressure on the government to increase educational and training opportunities for girls and women. As a complement to the role of the EOC, the Women's National Commission had been set up as part of the Cabinet Office with the express purpose of providing advice to the government on issues relating to women (Rees, 1992). Both groups had been involved with the MSC in an advisory capacity in connection with the promotion of equal opportunities within the Youth Opportunities Programme (Millman, 1985), so would have been well aware of the potential dangers of stereotyping within a vocational initiative. The WNC was certainly concerned with TVEI *after* it had been announced: Millman (1985) points out that it had sought to influence the MSC's selection of first round TVEI projects by spelling out its own interpretation of equal opportunities 'good practice'. A commitment on paper to equal opportunities at a time when such intervention was likely to have minimal impact on the labour market would cost the MSC very little, of course, whilst enabling them to satisfy their critics and win them new allies (Wickham, 1986).

The European and international dimension

Similarly, the MSC might have been complying with pressures from outside Great Britain. Both UNESCO and the EEC had passed equal opportunity resolutions in the mid-70s in relation to vocational education and training (Byrne, 1989). In a set of recommendations which were finally ratified in 1980, UNESCO sought to ensure that girls should have the same educational opportunities as boys, that special provision should be made for women returners, and that vocational guidance for girls should cover the same range of training and employment opportunities as those for boys. Within the European context, an EEC resolution in February 1976 stated that the achievement of equal opportunities in all forms of education was an essential aim for all member states. The following December the EEC adopted an action programme which included action to ensure educational opportunities for girls (Byrne, 1989). From 1978 to 1982 the EEC funded a community action programme entitled 'Transition from Education to Working Life', with most schemes concentrating on vocational preparation and guidance. Varlaam (1984) has noted, however, that whilst the specific needs of girls within this context were often mentioned as a secondary aim, few schemes were actually successful in keeping equal opportunities on the agenda.

The extent to which the MSC would have been influenced by these external developments remains uncertain, however, particularly given the reluctance of Conservative governments since 1979 to comply with social policy aspects of European legislation (Savage and Robins, 1990). The MSC must have been aware of European policy and of UNESCO's policy stance (although it is worth noting that the UK opted out of UNESCO not long afterwards), but it is difficult to find evidence for TVEI being directly influenced by them, although one of the few questions ever asked in the House of Commons concerning TVEI centred on whether the government had taken measures to encourage boys and girls within TVEI schemes to consider non-traditional areas of study, subsequent to the government's response to a United Nations questionnaire arising from the Decade for Women (Hansard, 1985).

Policy making 'on the hoof'

Finally, material taken from an interview with the two pilot TVEI national equal opportunities advisers - 'Len Jones' and 'Joan Gray' - provides some evidence to support a further argument, that an equal opportunities component was included more by chance than by design. Prior to TVEI, Len Jones had been closely involved in a number of working parties of the National Union of Teachers concerned with education, training and equal opportunities. When TVEI was announced, he was asked to act as a consultant and in this capacity he had seen the TVEI funding criteria in draft form:

> But he (the drafter) had no mention of the equal opportunities on it. So we phoned him up and said, where's the equal opportunities aspect of this? You can't have this, it's going to be all about boys, it's David Young's baby' (Len Jones, August 1991).

This is a reference to the imputed influence on TVEI's origins of the Organisation for Rehabilitation and Training (ORT), an organisation principally concerned with developing the skills of potentially deviant young men, which was supposedly the MSC Chairman's 'favourite charity' (Dale et al, 1990).

Right, he said, if you draft something, we'll see it gets through, so we drafted something - and that's how it came to be. And it was added on because they couldn't figure out - if you look at the rest of the criteria, where the hell would equal opportunities fit? They didn't want it to go at the end, so that's why it's number one! And it's as simple as that.'

This account suggests that equal opportunities was included as an afterthought, and certainly was not uppermost in Lord Young's thoughts. As such, the economic justifications which later emerged could be seen as *post hoc* rationalisations. Comments taken from a further interview with officials from the Equal Opportunities Commission tend to add weight to this version of events. The view of the two officials interviewed was that little thought could have gone into this element of TVEI given the lack of consultation with the expert body in the field, the EOC itself:

I think the haste of the initiative surprised many people, including educationalists, and it wasn't until the initiative had been formally announced... that the Commission became fully aware of the nature and implications of the initiative. The Commission most certainly wasn't alerted or tipped off or formally involved in the planning stages. In fact, I think with hindsight there were no planning stages whatsoever (Interview held with two EOC education specialists, August 1992).

If this account is accurate, then many of the puzzles and contradictions surrounding the introduction of the equal opportunities dimension are rendered largely irrelevant, as it becomes clear that the implications of its inclusion had not been seriously considered:

I don't think that anybody in those days had actually thought through the implications of an issue about equal opportunities... It hadn't been thought through at all, because there had been no real thinking (Len Jones, August 1991).

Ball (1990 and 1994) has highlighted the extent to which educational policy making is invariably a far from rational process. In this light the above account does possess a certain authenticity, particularly given that the existing 'official' justifications appeared long after the introduction of TVEI. This suggests at the very least that little coherent thought had gone into its inclusion. The other factors considered here may have contributed to some extent, whilst the *post hoc* economic arguments may well, with hindsight, have been sincerely ascribed to by TVEI's policy makers. However, in the absence of a more coherent account of its inclusion, this account probably stands as the most likely explanation for a somewhat muddled decision which was subsequently justified largely in terms of economic arguments.

Equal opportunities work at the national level

This final section is concerned with the dominant mode of equal opportunities work which developed at the national level (a more detailed account can be found in Heath, 1994). Regardless of the rationale for its inclusion, the appointment of Len Jones as a TVEI consultant undoubtedly marked a significant starting point, not least because Jones already had a strong track record on equal opportunities: he had been the Chair of the Schools Council Sex Differentiation in Schools Working Party (see Weiner, 1985a, for a full account of this project) and had been instrumental in establishing the NUT's equal opportunities group. He was not specifically appointed as an equal opportunities adviser but, in the absence of a formal lead on equal opportunities coming from anywhere else within TVEI, he decided to focus his attentions in this area. This apparent lack of direction in the early stages of TVEI is confirmed by Dale et al (1990), who note that the MSC were slow to provide any guidance on how the elimination of gender inequalities might be achieved (see also Millman and Weiner, 1987; Arnot, 1992). The EOC and the WNC, however, wasted little time in jointly organising a one-day seminar in Clwyd LEA on equal opportunities (gender) in February 1984, aimed at coordinators of pilot projects. In June of that year, the DES ran a similar event in Birmingham, attracting many TVEI staff (see Dale et al, 1990).

On appointment, Len Jones followed suit and arranged a series of national workshops for pilot project personnel. He was particularly keen to see attendance by personnel in key positions, most notably LEA project coordinators. To this end, he stressed the contract compliance obligation of equal opportunities in the hope that these people would feel obliged to attend. However, in the event few who attended these first workshops were people in influential roles: 'Most people would say, equal opportunities, that's something for young Jane to go to, or young Janet or whoever it was' (Joan Gray).

At these early meetings, which were run by two private sector equal opportunities consultants, discussions centred on a four stage model of equal opportunities developed by one of the consultants, which was subsequently used widely as a model for developments within TVEI (see for instance Chambers and Raffe, undated; McIntyre, 1987; Bridgwood and Betteridge, 1989). Each stage described a particular stance on equal opportunities which a school might adopt: the unlocked door, the open door, the special escalator and equal outcomes. The *unlocked door approach* was based on the premise that TVEI options were 'open' to both sexes in the sense that a school considered there to be no barriers in the way of free choice, but the onus was very much on individual pupils to push open the door to gain access to non-traditional subjects. The *open door approach* recognised that pupils did not make 'free' choices in the sense implied by the first approach. Differences in prior experience were acknowledged and attempts were made to broaden the appeal of subjects to both genders. The *special escalator approach* was based on a positive action model, with conscious and deliberate efforts made to 'enable, persuade (and) encourage' pupils into non-traditional areas (see Chambers and Raffe, undated, p.10). Within this model schooling is seen as a means of combatting gender inequality. Finally, the *equal outcomes approach* sought to secure equitable take-up, qualifications and subsequent achievement amongst young men and women in both their schooling and their adult lives. This model involved the clear identification and monitoring of target outcomes and again reflected a strong belief that schooling provided a means of combatting discrimination in wider society.

By the academic year 1985/86, Joan Gray, a former NUT Executive Member, had been appointed to work alongside Len Jones as a second equal opportunities consultant. The second round of workshops, which succeeded in getting more senior people to attend, were in two parts: an initial workshop in which coordinators were asked to devise an equal opportunities strategy for their own schools, and a follow-up workshop for reporting back on progress. A number of TVEI coordinators even elected to work alongside the external consultants, with varying degrees of success. The following year, workshops were held for the coordinators of fourth round TVEI projects (which included the case study project). Joan Gray described the fourth round coordinators as 'quite a different breed of people':

> A lot of them had been project coordinators somewhere else or deputies and had got promoted, and this was the group to become quite key and quite influential... And they didn't want to mess about, they actually wanted to get somewhere, and as a result we came up with a whole number of recommendations, of ways in which equal opportunities should be taken forward (Joan Gray).

One of these recommendations was the establishment of a national network for the monitoring of equal opportunities, coordinated by regional project advisers. In October 1987 the first issue of 'NEON' was produced, the termly newsletter of the National Equal Opportunities Network, which was described in its editorial as 'something of a milestone in helping to promote Equal Opportunities consciousness within TVEI projects throughout the country' (NEON, 1987, p.2). It also noted that the Steering Group were planning to establish a database on equal opportunities initiatives and were responsible for acting on suggested strategies put forward by a larger, advisory group:

> The emphasis is on practical strategies, since we feel that issues of equal opportunities in TVEI (and elsewhere) have been explored so exhaustively that the talk has almost become an end in itself... There is a great deal still to be done, but a great deal *is* being done, as this newsletter shows... Many of you will be doing quite small seemingly unimportant things but these are the backbone of equal opportunities development (ibid, p.2).

The success of the network was heavily dependent on the commitment of individual regional advisers. The region in which the case study project is located had a particularly committed adviser, who set up a regional steering group with clearly stated objectives, and ensured that they met regularly to review progress. The group also produced a directory of good practice across the region's projects, which proved to be an extremely useful means of networking committed individuals across the region. By the early 1990s, the group began to focus more on equal opportunities developments with regard to race, although often *as opposed to*, rather than intersecting with, gender.

The other significant development to have arisen from the fourth round workshops was an emphasis on tools for the management of change, which led to a reappraisal of the way in which Jones and Gray had been working:

> We'd learnt the hard way of what couldn't be done, that you can't give people a workshop, send them away and expect them to do something without the skills - the management, strategic coordination and delivery skills to be able to do it (Len Jones).

As a result, the 'Information Systems Strategy' (ISS) was born, designed 'to bring about whole-school, equal opportunities objectives-setting and attainment by making progress towards these outcomes through agreed and recognisable target achievements' (Chambers and Raffe, undated, p.9). The region in which the case study project is located became very involved in the ISS, and chapter 5 provides a full account of the ISS strategy and its success in promoting equal opportunities.

Conclusion

This chapter has outlined the origins of TVEI and has explored the development of its equal opportunities commitment at the national level. It would appear that there were a number of basic economic - not to mention theoretical - contradictions inherent in promoting equal opportunities within a vocational context at a time of high youth unemployment. Moreover, there would seem to be little evidence of much prior thought behind the development of its equal opportunities dimension. Nonetheless, many TVEI officials, such as Len Jones and Joan Gray at the national level, and committed coordinators at local project level, were able to take full advantage of the policy's inclusion, regardless of its rationale or its lack of coherent thought. Subsequent chapters are concerned to explore the impact of TVEI's equal opportunities policy 'on the ground'. This is achieved mainly through a detailed examination of the development and impact of TVEI within one case study project, 'Masonfield' TVEI but, wherever relevant, material relating to national trends is referred to alongside that relating specifically to Masonfield.

4 Implementing TVEI at the local level

Introduction

This chapter introduces 'Masonfield', the city in which the case study research was conducted. Following a description of the city, it outlines the origins and early development of TVEI in Masonfield Education Authority, provides a short description of the five high schools which participated in TVEI pilot, and then considers the state of play with respect to equal opportunities prior to the introduction of TVEI in the city. The final section considers both the appropriateness of Masonfield as the case study site and the strengths of methodological triangulation in carrying out the case study research.

The city of Masonfield

The city of Masonfield, in the county of Sandfordshire, is often perceived as a grimy industrial city with row upon row of dense terraced housing. A third of the city's housing stock does in fact fit that description, but it coexists with pockets of considerable affluence, as well as areas of prime agricultural land. These contrasts are located within a geographically small area with a relatively high population density, albeit one which has been in decline over the last fifteen years. At the last Census, non-white ethnic minorities accounted for only 2.2 per cent of Masonfield's population, alongside an Irish (and predominantly Catholic) immigrant community of similar proportions (OPCS, 1993). Across the county, Masonfield has the highest proportion of households containing at least one person with a limiting long-term illness (32 per cent), the highest proportion of lone pensioners (18 per cent), but the lowest proportion of pensioners living in households without central heating. Rates of car ownership are low, with almost fifty per cent of households lacking access to a car, whilst council housing accounts for 35 per cent of all housing in the city (ibid).

Masonfield's traditional industrial base has experienced serious decline over the last twenty years, leaving the city with a major unemployment problem. The general decline in the total number of jobs available in the city from the mid-sixties to the mid-seventies was accelerated during the period 1977-81, with losses during that period accounting for nearly a third of the total stock of jobs which had been available in 1965 and a sixth of those existing in 1977 (City of Masonfield Education Department, 1985). By the early 1980s, major job losses had been experienced in clothing, footwear, electrical engineering, chemical and allied industries, vehicles and textiles. More recently, further heavy losses have been sustained in mechanical engineering and the manufacturing of metal goods, whilst the anticipated increase in jobs in the construction industry during the eighties failed to materialise (Masonfield TEC, 1990). However, many new jobs have been created in Masonfield's burgeoning service sector, most notably in banking and public administration, as well as in the hotel, catering and tourism industries. In recognition of this, many secondary schools in Masonfield began to offer a 'Travel and Tourism' GCSE in the early 1990s. Reflecting national trends, many full-time jobs in the male-dominated manufacturing and construction industries have been replaced by part-time jobs in female-dominated service industries and, by 1991, 39 per cent of female employees were working part-time (ibid).

Masonfield's inner city areas have been worst hit by declining job opportunities. In April 1990, the year after the group of young people who form the main focus of this research had left school, five inner city wards had male unemployment rates of over 20 per cent (including one with a rate of 24 per cent). Masonfield's overall employment rate at that time stood at 9.3 per cent, compared with 5.5 per cent nationally. Youth unemployment stood at 8.6 per cent. Long-term employment is a particular problem: in April 1990, two out of five unemployed people had been out of work for over a year (as high as one in two in four wards), whilst just over a quarter of the total had been out of work for more than two years (MRIPU, 1991).

Masonfield has a relatively low (but increasing) staying-on rate amongst 16 year old school leavers. In 1989, 37 per cent of leavers chose to continue in full-time education, whilst 17 per cent and 30 per cent respectively found jobs or YTS places. By the December of 1989, the unemployment rate amongst school leavers was believed to be at least three per cent, although a further eight per cent remained untraceable, some of whom undoubtedly would have boosted the unemployment rate if they had been traced (City of Masonfield Careers Service, 1990).

Traditionally, Masonfield has been a Labour-controlled council, but has always been keen to avoid the 'loony left' tag of some of its neighbours. Indeed, some observers have spoken of the council as being 'Labour with a small c'! Consequently, the elected members of the council have proceeded cautiously and pragmatically in dealing with central government. Whilst not afraid to voice their opposition to Conservative government measures (as indeed they did initially with regard to TVEI), at the same time they were not prepared to sacrifice the interests of Masonfield's citizens for the sake of political principle. This attitude was captured by a comment of the Principal Education Adviser:

> They are still very much middle-of-the-road socialist folks whose main criteria is, 'is it right for the people of Masonfield?' Now you may disagree with the conclusion they came to, but I don't think you can in any sense question their motive, whereas some authorities are there not to do what is right for people in wherever, they're there to oppose the government, regardless. And fortunately, we've not really got involved in that (Principal Education Adviser).

Masonfield's Education Department operates under a motto which reflects its broad commitment to social democratic ideals of education: 'High quality education for all'. These opportunities start at an early age in Masonfield, the city having a national reputation for the quality of its nursery provision. At the time of this research (1989-92), the secondary sector comprised of 18 mainstream secondary schools and three schools catering for special needs students, whilst the post-16 sector included three sixth form colleges and an FE college. Comprehensivation in the mid-70s and falling rolls over the 1980s resulted in a series of closures to produce this picture. At the time of the research, the local education authority still maintained a strong and well-respected advisory service, but this has now contracted considerably as a result of a series of deep cuts to the education budget imposed on Masonfield by the Conservative central government of the early 1990s.

The origins of TVEI in Masonfield

When TVEI was first announced in November 1982, one might have supposed that the possibility of obtaining funding for a scheme which promised to enhance the opportunities of young people in a restrictive economic climate would be welcomed with open arms by the officers and elected members of Masonfield. In fact, Masonfield had a rocky relationship with the MSC, and did not bid successfully for TVEI funding until the fourth round of applications. An initial bid in round one was actually withdrawn following submission, due largely to what were to be ongoing concerns about the 'difficulty in reconciling the requirements of the scheme with the principles and practice of neighbourhood comprehensive schools', and 'it being not practical to apply the scheme to part of the city only' (Minutes of Education Committee, 23/2/83).

Additionally, the Chief Education Officer at the time was personally very hostile to TVEI, and shared the opinion that was forming amongst Labour politicians up and down the country that TVEI was merely a Trojan horse for the reintroduction of elitism and selectivity in secondary education (Dale, 1985). Labour politicians were opposed not only to TVEI's content, but to the mechanics of its introduction, as the then Chair of the Education Committee explained:

This was the first shot across the bows of LEAs, in that they were required to bid for monies rather than develop their own initiatives, and the first reaction to that sort of, as we saw it, dilution of what we thought was right, was resisted. So it was resisted more on principle than anything else... it was a political reaction against the government's interference into LEA planning for education. It was as simple as that - a resistance to what the government was doing (Chair of the Education Committee).

In the autumn of 1983, the MSC invited a second round of applicants. By this time, it was becoming clear that considerable financial benefits were accruing to participating LEAs. However, as Saunders (1990) has argued, and perhaps more important than the financial benefits for the purposes of swaying the political arguments surrounding TVEI, the potential for LEAs to subvert the MSC's agenda was beginning to emerge:

It became evident that once the education world had got hold of the idea and begun to modify it a bit, that we were talking about something that was more about education than training and therefore was more attractive to us and the authority - and certainly more attractive to members (Principal Education Adviser).

It now seemed appropriate for the authority to bid seriously for TVEI funding - but only on its own terms. The major hurdle was the MSC's insistence that LEAs adopt a 'cohort' approach to TVEI pilot. In Masonfield this would mean the involvement of only 250 pupils a year across only five schools, which was felt to be against the spirit of Masonfield's commitment to high quality educational opportunities for *all* pupils. Attempts were therefore made to circumvent these restrictions, and the final bid proposed the introduction of TVEI into *all* schools with the cohort spread thinly across them all. Unsurprisingly, the bid met with a resounding 'no' from the MSC. The elected members were outraged by the rejection, and as a direct result no bid was made in the third round.

Following the appointment of a new Chief Education Officer in 1984, a fresh bid was made in round four. His view was that TVEI provided a golden opportunity to bring much-needed finance into Masonfield. Youth unemployment was continuing to have a devastating effect on the city and the need to take drastic action was evident. As many councillors remained to be convinced of TVEI's educational benefits, the officers arranged a series of visits to established TVEI projects in other Labour-controlled authorities, and a consensus emerged that if these LEAs could overcome their ideological qualms, then Masonfield should consider doing likewise. The government's decision to extend TVEI to *all* schools in participating authorities at the end of the five year pilot phase also played a key part in Masonfield's change of heart.

The final distribution of the cohort remained a highly contentious political issue and it was eventually decided to involve five schools representing five broad geographical areas in the city. The final selection attracted a great deal of criticism. For instance, none of the four Catholic schools were represented, even though the only Church of England school in the city was later included when one of the original five schools decided to opt out of pilot. Ostensibly this was because the Catholic schools had only just reorganised following comprehensivisation and needed time to adjust, yet two of the chosen schools were themselves facing amalgamation at the time.

A further bone of contention was the MSC's insistence that pilot schemes should be developed and administered centrally, with each school following essentially the same scheme within any given LEA. From long years of curriculum experience and from observation of other TVEI schemes, the officers in Masonfield were convinced that such a path would be disastrous in Masonfield. For the scheme to succeed, they argued, account would need to be taken of the individuality of each school, in preference to attempting to impose an LEA-wide model. It seemed evident to the officers that valuable time and resources would otherwise be wasted by the schools in modifying the scheme in order to exercise some form of personal 'ownership' over it. This proved to be a perennial battle with TVEI officialdom, but one which Masonfield won, and the notion of a 'school led' initiative, with common elements across the LEA, was allowed to stand.

The Masonfield bid was finally approved by the MSC in January 1986, with pilot scheduled to begin in the autumn term. Intermediate funding was acquired from the MSC to work on the bid with headteachers and the newly appointed school coordinators, and in September 1986 the Central Team Coordinator, David James, took up post, having come to Masonfield from the central TVEI unit of an LEA which had been one of the fourteen first round TVEI projects. Over the five year period of pilot, approximately one thousand pupils were officially involved in successive cohorts, although in reality it affected the education of thousands more, as many aspects of TVEI were soon extended to other pupils in the pilot schools. In September 1989, TVEI extension was introduced in Masonfield, eventually involving all schools and all pupils in the secondary sector, albeit with considerably reduced funding. The last cohort of pilot pupils left school in 1991, at the same time as the first group of leavers from the extension schools. Extension funding finally came to an end in July 1995.

Despite their earlier misgivings, the elected members proved to be extremely supportive of TVEI and took a great interest in its development:

> The thing in Masonfield is that once they take something on board, they really do tend to be very enthusiastic about it... They always expected TVEI to be able to deliver something really good for Masonfield's schools and although they really didn't have much of a financial commitment to that, they were very interested and very committed to what was coming out of it and wanted to promote that (Principal Education Adviser).

A number of structures were put into place with the introduction of TVEI pilot. Each of the five pilot schools appointed a coordinator who had responsibility for planning, implementing and monitoring TVEI in his or her respective school. Allowances were also made available to other members of staff who assumed responsibility for aspects of the pilot scheme such as Records of Achievement, work experience and - as discussed later - equal opportunities. Each school also appointed a clerk and/or a technician from TVEI funding.

At the central LEA level, a project coordinator was appointed who was directly accountable to the Senior Adviser for Secondary Education. At the beginning of pilot the Central Team also included a careers officer and three curriculum assistants, with responsibility for technology, Business Studies and Records of Achievement. From these modest beginnings, the central team began to expand, reaching its peak in the academic year 1989/90 when the Central Team incorporated the central coordinator and a deputy coordinator (who was also the teacher adviser for technology); an administrator, a finance officer and three part-time clerks; teacher advisers for teaching and learning strategies, business studies, travel and tourism, post-16 issues, information technology, citizenship and law-related education; an education-industry liaison officer, a senior careers officer and an assistant principle careers officer; and lastly, a full-time researcher. In addition, over the life of the pilot project a number of teachers were seconded to the central team for periods ranging from one term to a full year, to coordinate projects in the performing arts, art and design, home economics, National Curriculum technology, and modern foreign languages. Three secondments were also made to the careers service.

Finally, the Education Sub-Committee formed a consultative committee at the behest of the MSC, made up of councillors, MSC officials, officers and representatives from industry, parent groups, unions and other interested parties. The group had ceased to meet by the end of 1988, although individual members of the central team continued to present reports to the Schools Sub-Committee on a regular basis.

The five pilot schools

Although all five pilot schools were chosen to represent different geographical areas of the city, there were also pedagogic reasons for their selection. All five schools had 'proven experience in aspects of school management and curriculum development considered essential for potential success' (City of Masonfield Education Department, 1985). This was elaborated further: 'Each school is experienced in curriculum review, has initiated at least one cross-curricular project, contains staff committed to alternative approaches, is supportive and cooperates with Authority initiatives, and encourages school-based self-evaluation and staff development' (ibid). There follows a brief description of each of the pilot schools;

unemployment rates and other statistical information relates to the situation in the early 1990s, when the young people who form the major focus of the case study were first in the labour market.

Greenwood High School is located in the heart of inner-city Masonfield, an area which was extensively developed in the 1960s and 1970s and which contains a mixture of high rise council housing and back-to-back terraced housing. The school's catchment area covers the district which has been hardest hit by the erosion of the city's manufacturing base over the last two decades. It has a predominantly white, working class population. Adult employment in the area stood at 16 per cent in April 1990, and at 21 per cent amongst adult males, whilst youth unemployment stood at 14.5 per cent (MRIPU, 1991). The school has always had considerable difficulties with truancy, particularly amongst girls. In the autumn term of 1988, for example, 20 per cent of girls were in school for less than 15 per cent of the time, compared with six per cent of boys. Discipline is a related problem and female teachers in particular - although not exclusively - are treated with little or no respect by many pupils. For the first three years of Pilot, the school had a male TVEI coordinator, then a female coordinator for two years, and finally a male coordinator for the duration of Extension.

Seddon Park High School, a medium sized high school with a predominantly white intake, is located on the outskirts of the city and serves an area which acted as an overspill estate from inner-city Masonfield following slum clearance in the late 1960s and early 1970s. More than ten per cent of the local population are registered disabled. Three quarters of the school's pupils come from economically disadvantaged backgrounds, whilst the school's intake contains few high academic achievers (HMI, 1991). Both pupils and their parents reportedly have low expectations of their futures, bolstered by the above average unemployment rates, particularly amongst adult males. In 1986, the illegitimacy rate in the area stood at 46 per cent of all births in the area (Boseley, 1988). It is not uncommon for the school to have four or five 'schoolgirl pregnancies' each year, whilst many more young women become pregnant within a year of leaving school. The second of the school's two male TVEI coordinators argued that these patterns were symptomatic of the strong 'macho' culture predominant in the area, which he felt was strongly influenced by parental views.

Mosslands High School is situated in the 'agricultural hinterland' of the city. It is a very large, purpose-built community school serving a mixed residential area. It is geographically isolated from the rest of the city and as a result serves an extensive catchment area. At the time of TVEI Pilot it had a small but growing intake of non-white pupils, mainly Chinese and East Asian. Unemployment, although slightly higher than the national average, is not as high in this part of the city as it is in other areas. There are considerable employment opportunities in agriculture and horticulture, as well as in light and heavy industries situated in the area. The young people in the area have a reputation for being extremely parochial in outlook: it is often said that many have never ventured into the centre of Masonfield, some ten miles away, let alone over the city borders into the large neighbouring city centre. Mosslands had a male coordinator for the first four years of Pilot. He then left for a job in industry and was replaced by a woman for the final year. The Extension coordinator was a male teacher, the female coordinator having left the area for a promotion.

The Croft High School serves an old industrial area - which once included a coal mine within its boundaries - which has experienced decline in recent years, although unemployment is relatively low in the immediate vicinity of the school. Like Greenwood High School, the Croft was created out of an amalgamation of two schools onto the site of the school which had been involved in TVEI. At the time of the merger, the non-TVEI school had had a female deputy head whilst the TVEI school had no women in senior management. On amalgamation, an entirely male senior management team was created (headteacher and three deputies) and this situation held true for the entire period of Pilot. In line with this male dominance, the school had two male coordinators, with the latter continuing as the Extension coordinator.

The fifth school, *St Catherine's Church of England High School*, was not actually one of the original schools selected for Pilot (although it had made a bid to be involved), but was asked to step in when the school originally chosen faced closure. Although a church school, it had similar characteristics to the original school, serving as a medium-sized neighbourhood comprehensive school within a large council estate. Formerly a 1960s-built secondary modern school, it serves an area which has traditionally been dominated by heavy engineering, but in the last fifteen years many firms have closed down or reduced the scale of their operations, with massive redundancy programmes. Adult unemployment, although lower than the city average, was at the time of the research still higher than the regional average, whilst youth unemployment was particularly high, outstripping adult unemployment - one of only two wards in the city where this occurred (MRIPU, 1991). The school originally appointed two joint coordinators, a man and a woman. The male coordinator left the school in September 1988 to take up the reins of TVEI in the city's FE college. The female coordinator remained in post throughout Pilot and on into Extension, the only coordinator to have seen the project through from start to finish in the same school.

Equal opportunities in Masonfield pre-TVEI

It was noted in chapter 2 that the early 1980s witnessed an expansion of gender and race-related local government equal opportunities initiatives, yet Masonfield City Council could not have been further removed from the radical stance of these pioneering authorities. In line with the Council's noted conservatism, there was little evidence of any genuine political commitment to the promotion of equal opportunities when TVEI Pilot was launched in autumn 1986. Indeed, the Council did not establish any form of equal opportunities sub-committee until 1990, concentrating then on strategic issues of relevance to women returners across the city rather than on issues concerning its own employees.

David James took up post as the central TVEI coordinator in autumn 1986. He had arrived from a relatively progressive local authority and felt that,

> It was a bit of a culture shock, quite frankly... it was, and still is to a degree, fairly conservative; they cling to what they know. It was certainly very, very hostile to equal opportunities issues - throughout the authority, I think. I mean, there was nominal agreement, but in reality people were not prepared to do anything and stick their heads above the barricades (Central TVEI Coordinator).

There are at least two explanations for Masonfield's conservatism regarding equal opportunities. Firstly, Masonfield was still reeling from the blows dealt to its industrial base in the late 1970s. Given the dramatic collapse in employment and training opportunities for the city's school leavers, the need to cope with the associated difficulties was seen as the overriding priority of those concerned with policy issues in the educational arena. In particular, many collapsed industries were located within occupational areas which had been major recruiters of young men - engineering and allied industries, for example - and it would have been regarded as insensitive and inappropriate to have actively encouraged young women to pursue these careers.

Secondly, it was noted above that Masonfield councillors had reacted strongly against the perceived extremism of many 'new left' authorities, and were anxious not to become associated with the radical policy initiatives of such administrations:

> Not only was equal opportunities not an issue, it was considered dangerous extremism to raise it, because there was a caricature of what had been going on in some authorities, with an emphasis on gay rights and lesbian rights, and what that had meant in some schools, and what had been going on in ILEA - or what the media said had been going on in ILEA: the very high profile feminist activities and so on, and that was very much the stereotype, and so whenever you raised the equal opportunity issue there was this parrot cry, 'we're not ILEA', and it was always juxtaposed with 'we're not going to deal with lesbian issues, gay issues in the classroom here (Central TVEI coordinator).

In spite of the general indifference towards gender issues, there was at least one strategically placed councillor who was concerned about equal opportunities. In the early stages of the TVEI bid, Councillor Mrs Lewis was the deputy Chair of the Education Committee and, by the time TVEI was launched in 1986, she had become its Chair. The Principle Education Adviser described Councillor Lewis as 'quite an equal opportunities gender champion', and both he and David James believed that she had played a key role in ensuring that the issue of equal opportunities was not ignored by councillors following TVEI's introduction:

> It was an advantage having Mrs Lewis as Chair of Committee; clearly she had a personal commitment to equal ops. When I came in... the deputy chair was Councillor Mrs York, so we had two women in senior positions, and there's no doubt that Mrs Lewis must take a lot of the personal credit for certainly pushing the senior officers, to make sure that there were at least no obstacles to what we were doing (Central TVEI Coordinator).

At the political level, therefore, few Councillors were interested in equal opportunities prior to TVEI's launch. There were few women Councillors at that time, with even fewer in positions of influence. Even assuming that women councillors would have been more likely to push the issue than their male colleagues, it would have been an uphill struggle for them within the male dominated committee structure of the city council. Moreover, at the time of the bid there was only one woman officer with an appointment at a senior level within the Education Department. She was strongly committed to promoting equal opportunities, and was later a prime mover in setting up a series of equal opportunities working parties involving officers from across the LEA. In 1987 she was joined by the newly appointed Principal Careers Officer, who at the time was the only woman officer within the LEA appointed at the level of Assistant Education Officer.

As within the broader City Council's deliberations, equal opportunities as a policy issue was largely absent from the discussions of the Education Department prior to TVEI. In bidding for TVEI funding, however, the issue had to be addressed as one of the funding criteria, which involved the senior adviser for secondary education in discussions with each of the headteachers of the proposed pilot schools. The final submission document contained the following statement on equal opportunities:

> It is intended to ensure that the objectives of all courses are equally accessible to boys and girls and the Initiative will be used to explore the ways in which this may be achieved. It is likely that this will include:
> - separate opportunities for boys and girls leading to the same objectives
> - consideration of the titles of courses and activities
> - courses that include content and approaches traditionally regarded as appropriate to boys and girls
> - counselling and guidance
> - inclusion of sex stereotyping as an issue in the core
> - training of senior staff and teachers to make them aware of the issues and how classroom approaches reinforce sex stereotyping.
>
> (City of Masonfield Education Department, 1985).

The actual level of commitment to this particular aspect of the submission at this early stage of TVEI's development is, however, questionable. All TVEI submission documents to the MSC had to include a section on equal opportunities, so in this sense Masonfield was doing no more than any other LEA hoping to secure TVEI funding (see Dale et al, 1990). Certainly, there is little evidence to suggest that this statement grew out of work already in progress, a view reinforced by the assessment of David James on the level of commitment from the five pilot schools:

> I would guess at the time that none of them had any commitment to equal opportunities - I wouldn't guess they did, that was the case - none whatsoever; it was the one issue that I had the hardest time with the five heads over (Central TVEI Coordinator).

With little, if any, lead from the centre, it is perhaps unsurprising to find little evidence of an equal opportunities commitment at the school level. That is not to say that individual teachers were not concerned; undoubtedly, many teachers during this period would have been influenced by the growing interest in gender and education and would have been seeking to develop anti-sexist strategies within their classroom practice. Greenwood High School had also been involved in an action research project to promote the selection of science and technology options amongst girls, whilst Seddon Park High School ran after-school cookery clubs for boys. However, there is no evidence of any *official* policy commitment to the promotion of equal opportunities within the pilot schools.

On the eve of TVEI's launch, therefore, there was little experience of, let alone a strong commitment to, equal opportunities development work either at LEA or school level. Dale et al (1990) developed a typology of 'states of readiness' for equal opportunities work, and Masonfield can best be described in the following terms:

> Had not thought about or investigated the issues to any large extent, if at all, and (was) unresponsive (eg did not recognise a 'problem' and saw current inequities in outcomes as natural or right, or felt that education had little capacity to effect change) (Dale et al, 1990, p.143).

However, David James had moved from a first round TVEI project which had made considerable progress with regard to equal opportunities. He had been personally involved in several initiatives, including work on gender and Information Technology, and the teaching of technology to girls. He was therefore well placed to take the lead in promoting equal opportunities work within TVEI pilot. More significantly, he regarded the promotion of gender equality as a matter of great importance, and expected all involved in TVEI to follow suit.

Why Masonfield as a case study site?

Having provided a brief portrait of Masonfield and the origins of TVEI in the city, this final section will address the question 'why Masonfield?' Why is Masonfield deemed to be a suitable site for a case study of TVEI and its equal opportunities policy? Relatedly, how generalisable are the findings of the specific case study?

Yin (1984) has described a case study as 'an empirical enquiry that investigates a contemporary phenomenon within its real life context; when the boundaries between phenomenon and context are not clearly evident; and in which multiple sources of evidence are used' (Yin, 1984, p.23). The phenomenon under investigation could be, for example, an individual, an organisation or a policy. In the case of this research, the case study as a whole seeks to investigate the impact of a policy, namely TVEI's equal opportunities policy. However, in so doing, a number of units of analysis are incorporated: not only at the global level, on the basis of evidence relating to its national impact, but at the level of an individual pilot project. This level in turn can be sub-divided into the levels of Masonfield's TVEI Central Team, the five pilot schools in Masonfield and the young people who were involved in TVEI pilot in those five schools. By incorporating several units of analysis in this way, the research design can be described as an embedded, as opposed to a holistic, case study.

Critics of case studies often raise the question of the extent to which generalisations can be drawn from a case. Platt notes that, 'the question is not whether it can be done at all, but from what one can reasonably generalise to what' (Platt, 1988, p.17). This is particularly pertinent if, as in this study, only single cases are examined (that is, one policy and one specific project). However, TVEI's equal opportunities policy during the pilot phase should be viewed as an 'exemplar' policy: it was accorded a high profile within TVEI; it was initiated at central government level, which was of course unprecedented in the context of pre-16 education; and progress on equal opportunities within TVEI was considered to be an important measure of the success of TVEI more widely (Weiner, 1990a). Moreover, given TVEI's commitment to vocationalism, theoretical arguments concerning the social reproductive role of education were brought to the fore, bringing the tensions between vocational education and gender equality into sharp focus. On these grounds, the policy is not so much representative of other equal opportunities policies within education, but is rather an example of an extreme case against which other schemes can be measured. Thus, TVEI pilot represented the point at which the greatest concentration of resources for promoting equal opportunities was concentrated on the smallest number of students, and can be seen as the point at which equal opportunities were potentially likely to have their greatest impact (albeit on limited numbers of pupils). This also justifies the focus on TVEI pilot rather than the extension phase, as by then TVEI funding was considerably diluted and was less likely to make a distinct impact.

The extent to which findings from Masonfield TVEI can be generalised to other

TVEI projects is a different matter. Again, though, I would argue for the choice of Masonfield not so much on grounds of typicality, but on grounds of a combination of factors which make Masonfield a particularly salient case. Firstly, as we have seen, Masonfield's commitment to equal opportunities prior to the introduction of TVEI was negligible, rendering the 'TVEI effect' more readily (but, admittedly, not unproblematically) amenable to evaluation. Secondly, despite a lack of prior commitment within the LEA, it will be demonstrated that the central project team was strongly committed to the equal opportunities element of TVEI (a commitment which was by no means typical across all projects). Thirdly, Masonfield's school-led approach allowed for a number of different approaches to be adopted at the micro-level, yet a number of common themes nonetheless emerged across the project. Fourthly, Masonfield became involved in TVEI in the fourth round, at the same time that the national equal opportunities advisers began to make some significant breakthroughs in the approach they took (the advisers' observations about the greater commitment from fourth round authorities was noted in chapter 3). Finally, and by no means least importantly, Masonfield's TVEI project was closely involved in trialling the 'Information System Strategy' mentioned at the end of the previous chapter, and consequently was closely in tune with the national approach to equal opportunities.

Taken together, these factors suggest that Masonfield's Pilot project was likely to give equal opportunities a 'best shot', benefitting both from local and national developments. Moreover, given the general apathy toward equal opportunities prior to TVEI, it would be less difficult to disentangle other possible influences on change. These factors may well apply to other pilot projects, in which case Masonfield is more widely representative, but even if it is a unique case these conditions still need to be taken into account when considering the likely success of TVEI on a wider scale.

The strength of any claim to generalisation, however, whether based on a single case or on multiple cases, ultimately rests on the quality of the data used and the interpretation of that data:

> If there is a rich and detailed account of many features of the case(s), it may be a considerable achievement to devise an interpretation which can deal with all of them, and this may pose a greater challenge than the fitting of superficial generalisations to larger numbers (of cases) (Platt, 1988, p.19).

Yin's definition of a case study, with its emphasis on multiple sources of evidence, also implies that a variety of methods will be utilised in a case study. The following case study accordingly draws on what Denzin (1970) has termed 'methodological triangulation' (as opposed to other forms of triangulation, such as investigator triangulation, theoretical triangulation or time triangulation). In so doing, it uses both quantitative and qualitative methods, regarding them as different yet complementary ways of examining the same research question from alternative standpoints. Cohen and Manion (1985) have further argued that triangulation is a particularly useful method within educational settings when the following conditions pertain: when a more holistic view of educational outcomes is sought; when a complex phenomenon requires elucidation; and when a controversial aspect of education needs to be evaluated. All three of these conditions apply to this case study.

Cohen and Manion also argue that one of the strengths of triangulation is derived from the vulnerability of a single-method approach. They suggest that a multi-method approach, whereby different methods yield substantially the same results, allows the researcher to say with greater confidence that their results are not simply an artifact of a particular research method. However, triangulation rarely produces 'the same results' from its different methods. Rather, different methods and data sources will uncover different facets of social reality and by such means a more rounded picture is likely to be built up (Finch, 1986; Mason, 1996). Similarly, although Bryman (1988) has pointed out that a researcher's claim for validity is enhanced if both quantitative and qualitative methods *do* provide mutual confirmation of conclusions, he also notes that inconsistencies between data sources are not at all unusual. Fielding and Fielding (1986) have also argued that the outcomes of quantitative and qualitative methods are most unlikely to be confirmatory. This does not necessarily mean that one set of outcomes is 'right' and the other 'wrong', but rather that they generate 'different answers to different questions' (Mason, 1994). This is an important distinction to make, as whilst 'it is in the spirit of the idea of triangulation that inconsistent results may emerge... it is not in the spirit of triangulation that one should simply opt for one set of findings rather than another' (Bryman, 1988, p.134). Inconsistencies therefore call for an 'imaginative leap' (Cohen and Manion, 1985), in which one uses the differences as the basis for generating and testing further hypotheses. Bryman (1988) agrees with this approach, arguing that discrepancies may prompt the researcher to probe certain issues in greater depth, which may in itself reap benefits for the validity of the final results of the research.

Conclusion

This chapter has introduced the reader to the City of Masonfield, to its education authority and to its TVEI project. It has been argued that Masonfield is an ideal case study site for exploring the development and impact of TVEI's equal opportunities commitment. Further, the case study which follows tries to do justice to the 'spirit of triangulation' as described by Bryman (1988). Different methods are deployed for different purposes, to answer different types of questions with different units of analysis. At many junctures this has resulted in a creative tension between the various sources of data, and the challenge has been to see how the different aspects of the research ultimately fit together to produce a coherent story about

TVEI and its extraordinary equal opportunities experiment.

5 Managing equal opportunities

Introduction

This chapter focuses on a number of key issues surrounding the management of TVEI, each of which had implications for the success of TVEI's equal opportunities commitment. It starts by examining TVEI's own record of promoting equal opportunities amongst its own staff, at school level, LEA level and at the level of the national TVEI Unit. It then focuses on one key area of TVEI management: the management of equal opportunities. For the most part, equal opportunities posts were taken up by women, and the debate that this caused is quite instructive concerning TVEI's underpinning philosophy on equality issues. The chapter then moves on to explore the impact of the 'Information Systems Strategy', the approach to the management of equal opportunities which was widely and vigorously promoted by the national equal opportunities advisers. A key element of the ISS approach was the formulation of hypotheses to explain the inequalities which were inevitably revealed by data on school outcomes, and the chapter finishes by examining the range of explanations which were considered by the individual pilot schools in Masonfield.

The staffing of TVEI

As highlighted in chapter 4, TVEI funding brought with it a wealth of new opportunities for ambitious teachers (Saunders, 1990). At school and college level, TVEI monies were used to appoint TVEI coordinators who often acted largely independently of the senior management teams in their institutions, unusually being accountable for TVEI to the central project coordinator and not to their headteachers and principals. These coordinators worked with teams of other teachers who were in receipt of allowances for coordinating specific elements of TVEI - Records of Achievement, work experience or IT, for example. At the LEA level central coordinators were appointed, alongside teams of subject-related advisory teachers, TVEI-funded careers officers, teaching and learning styles support teachers and education-industry link officers. The structures put in place in Masonfield were outlined in the previous chapter. However, despite efforts to promote positive images of women and men in non-traditional work roles within the context of work with TVEI pupils, the management structure of TVEI schemes at both LEA and school level often tended to be male-dominated, providing relatively few role models of women in leadership roles within the schemes themselves and in itself sending out mixed messages about TVEI's equal opportunities commitment.

At the national level, it was generally difficult to obtain hard evidence of the gender composition of TVEI teams, particularly at the school and college level; there was plenty of hearsay evidence of the extent to which teams tended to be male-dominated, but it was not an issue that was systematically highlighted by TVEI evaluations, even though the gender breakdown of TVEI *pupils* and their activities was regularly monitored. However, an undated TVEI project managers handbook which contained a full list of the names of LEA project coordinators as of November 1988 confirms the dominance of men in coordinator's posts, with men accounting for 82 per cent of all the posts listed at that time (TVEI Unit, undated). Similarly, Bridgwood and Betteridge (1989) also found amongst a sample of 25 projects that whilst it was not unusual for TVEI teams to be all-male, it was very rare to find an all-female team, whilst Dale et al (1990) highlight the male dominance at both school and LEA level amongst the seven projects with which they were closely involved. Masonfield stands out as unusual within this broader context for having a central team at various times either largely dominated by women, or with equal numbers of men and women. This was despite women being very poorly represented in the broader secondary advisory service.

This situation, of course, reflects the dominance of men at all levels of educational management (Mackinnon et al, 1995), yet it is disappointing that TVEI failed to make a greater impact at this level. To a large extent, this could be a consequence of the curriculum bias of TVEI; central teams would have had difficulty in appointing women to assume responsibility for the development of Craft, Design and Technology (CDT) subjects, for example, because of the general non-existence of women CDT teachers at any level. Moreover, the use of the word 'technical' in the title of TVEI could arguably be seen to have projected a male image, which may have deterred some women from applying for posts even in TVEI curriculum areas where there were larger numbers of women teachers. McIntyre (1987) noted that many TVEI projects had in fact highlighted staffing as an important equal opportunities issue, with many projects seeking to appoint women CDT teachers to provide role models to female pupils and expressing the desire to recruit women generally to positions of authority within TVEI schemes, yet he had found little evidence that this was happening to any great extent.

McIntyre felt this might be because of factors such as the need for training and prior experience and the possible effect of reduced promotion opportunities within the teaching profession. He was also concerned that where limited progress had been made, such as the 'exceptional' recruitment of female CDT teachers, it might be perceived as a token gesture rather than a long term policy commitment.

Ironically, the management structure of the national TVEI Unit was remarkably balanced, perhaps due to the fact that the MSC was a relatively new institution in comparison with the education system (although it did of course arise out of the ranks of the male dominated civil service). The undated TVEI handbook noted above also included a diagram of the TVEI Unit's management structure, presumably from the same year, 1988, as the list of coordinators, which shows that there was a far more equitable distribution of women in senior positions within the National TVEI Unit, with the key post of Director of TVEI's Education Programmes being held by a woman, Anne Jones. The handbook also contained information on the make-up of the Regional Teams in 1988: men accounted for 60 per cent of the posts listed, and were to be found predominantly in more senior posts.

Dale et al (1990) argue that the gender divisions within project management structures were gradually reduced over the course of the pilot years, particularly as projects moved into extension, although by no means to the point of eradication. This was certainly so in Masonfield, where women accounted for the majority of coordinators at school level as the project moved into the extension phase in 1989. More generally within the LEA, women remained seriously under-represented in positions of authority: an LEA-wide review of equal opportunities carried out in 1988 found that although the overall male-to-female ratio within Masonfield's secondary schools and sixth form colleges was more or less 1:1, amongst headteachers the ration was 20:1, amongst senior teachers it was 5:2 and amongst heads of department it was 3:2. Men were also more likely than women to be in receipt of discretionary pay allowances (City of Masonfield Equal Opportunities Working Party, 1989). Some headteachers (both in Masonfield and elsewhere) appear to have actively sought to redress this kind of imbalance in their choice of TVEI team members, whereas others felt that this smacked of positive discrimination and argued that they only appointed on merit, implying that they had no women members of staff of merit (Bridgwood and Betteridge, 1989). For many of the women who did gain appointments within the TVEI hierarchy, however, TVEI provided an important opportunity to gain management experience, often outside of, and complementary to, the senior management teams of their schools, to which many women often find it difficult to gain access. This was an important spin-off of TVEI, one which should not be underestimated in terms of the effect this had on the careers of individual women teachers. (New [1993] makes a similar point concerning the opportunities for women teachers of gaining invaluable experience outside of a school's hierarchical senior management structures by serving on school governing bodies.)

The management of equal opportunities

Against the wider trend, one area of TVEI management was consistently dominated by women: equal opportunities. Most TVEI schools appointed an individual either with specific responsibility for equal opportunities or as part of their wider brief for, say, careers education and guidance. At the central team level, both full-time and part-time secondments or permanent appointments with specific responsibility for equal opportunities were not uncommon. Bridgwood and Betteridge (1989) found, however, that the brief given to equal opportunities coordinators, both in central teams and in TVEI schools, often tended to be vague and indeterminate in comparison with other areas of TVEI coordination (see also Hughes, 1989). Moreover, appointees tended to lack direction in their work, a situation not eased by the fact that they were often accountable to an LEA officer or headteacher with no particular brief for, or even interest in, equal opportunities as an area of policy. At the school level, the success of equal opportunities work was often highly dependent on the support or otherwise of the headteacher and, to a lesser extent, the senior management team (Dale et al, 1990). It was often the case that coordinators were appointed because they had a personal commitment to equal opportunities, not necessarily because they were particularly influential within the school hierarchy; in such circumstances, the headteacher's sponsorship often assumed crucial importance.

Within Masonfield, it was always the intention to appoint a full-time equal opportunities coordinator to the Central Team, yet this post remained unfilled throughout pilot, despite being advertised internally for two successive years. Although initially the post would have been for one year only, it was hoped to make an appointment at senior teacher or deputy headteacher level in order to signal its importance. However, on both occasions there were only one or two applicants, none of whom were considered to be suitable candidates, and an appointment was never made. It is difficult to ascertain exactly why this was the case, although there are at least two possible explanations. A full-time equal opportunities secondment could have been regarded as an ill-advised career move, as some potential employers might have subsequently regarded the secondee as a personal 'crusader': specialists in other aspects of secondary education are rarely considered to have an 'unhealthy' zeal with regard to their area of expertise, whereas for equal opportunities specialists such suspicions are common (Acker, 1988; Kenway, 1995). However, it is more likely that potential candidates were reluctant to apply for *any* seconded posts at that particular time, as teachers were well aware of the pressures on schools to pare their senior management teams in the face of financial constraints: a teacher on a year's secondment might find that their previous post could not be guaranteed on their return.

By default, equal opportunities remained the specific responsibility of David James and he regularly attended regional equal opportunities meetings as Masonfield's representative, even though many pilot projects consistently sent more junior personnel, without regard for the signals this gave out about the priority equal opportunities was accorded within their projects. Towards the end of pilot, however, the day to day responsibility fell increasingly to the TVEI advisory teacher for Business Studies, who acted as convenor of the central team's own equal opportunities working group, which was responsible for planning and providing INSET to equal opportunities coordinators in the TVEI schools, and chaired the meetings of the project-wide working group. This working group provided a coordinating role for the development of the Information Systems Strategy within the pilot schools, as well as a forum for disseminating good practice. Equally important, though, was the group's support function: those involved in equal opportunities developments in the pilot schools had soon encountered the antagonism and suspicion which is often directed towards teachers concerned with gender equality (Ruddock, 1994), and the group provided an invaluable 'safe space' for the confidential airing of grievances and concerns.

Within the individual pilot schools in Masonfield, equal opportunities was originally one of the many responsibilities of each school's TVEI coordinator, none of whom had much, if any, prior experience in this area. In the third year of pilot four of the five schools became involved in the Information Systems Strategy, which is fully described later in this chapter. This necessitated the establishment of an equal opportunities working group in each school and careful thought went into the membership of these groups. Firstly, it was considered important that the membership should represent a broad cross-section of curriculum areas. Secondly, membership included at least one member of senior management in order to give the group legitimacy. Thirdly, the schools tried to ensure gender balance in the groups' membership: two schools achieved an even split, whilst the other two recruited slightly more women than men. In one school at least, there was also a conscious effort to include as wide a range of views as possible, 'in order that all viewpoints would be aired no matter what the person's personal prejudices were' (Seddon Park's second annual report). When asked how successful this move had been, the school's TVEI coordinator felt that it had been a positive advantage to co-opt the potential 'opposition':

> We had the male chauvinist, we had the lot. A real cross-section - we covered nearly all the different areas of the school, but we mainly looked at personalities as well, because we felt that was important... we had some good debates - one or two people will never change, but ... the good thing was that these people could then be given reasons for why we're doing it (TVEI Coordinator, Seddon Park High School, February 1992).

Beyond these criteria, however, lay other important factors in terms of who was likely to have been selected for membership of the equal opportunities working groups:

We have, in the group of us, consciously stressed the fact that confrontation would actually be counter-productive and that a small group of people had to do something gradually... nothing upfront, nothing overt - and this we felt was the best way to work, to work quietly, slowly, and persuade people and talk to people, rather than take up a big strident posture... the whole thing had to be played very low key...' (TVEI coordinator, The Croft High School, June 1992).

The people in the working party are very good in the sense that they are not the sort of upfront shouters; they are quiet workers, almost to a person, and very diplomatic... They have good credibility, good relationships, and that has helped enormously, very much so - they're not just people on a soapbox, shouting at everybody, they are the people who work with people and get on with them, and that's helped a lot (Equal Opportunities coordinator, Mosslands High School, January 1992).

Given the controversy associated with equal opportunities initiatives within many schools there is certainly no argument with the need for diplomacy. However, it is interesting to note the images which are invoked by the use of words such as 'strident', 'confrontational', 'upfront shouters', 'people on a soapbox' and 'shouting at everybody', words which conjure up a spectre of extremism which is often associated with feminism in the media and in the popular imagination (Faludi, 1992). In the course of their efforts to develop anti-sexist education in a London school, for example, Ord and Quigley wrote of being 'forever conscious of the danger of being dismissed as strident, male-hating and humourless' (Ord and Quigley, 1985, p.110; see also Kenway, 1995). Ord and Quigley were open about their feminist commitment, and resented the association of negative attributes with feminism; for women who do not identify themselves as feminists, to be labelled as such can in itself be interpreted as an insult precisely *because* of these negative associations. Within project-wide equal opportunities meetings, for example, throwaway comments were occasionally made by coordinators from the pilot schools about the 'risk' of being labelled a feminist. One of the pilot equal opportunities coordinators actually spoke on one such occasion of the problem of being 'accused of being a feminist'. Thus, feminism was constructed as being an essentially negative and destructive ideology. (Interestingly, in the early 1990s Ord briefly served as the national equal opportunities adviser, before the post was subsumed into a broader advisory role.)

It would not be surprising if the use of such labelling acted as a check on the behaviour of women involved in equal opportunities work in the pilot high schools. For the equal opportunities coordinator at one of the pilot schools this was undoubtedly the case:

There certainly was a little element, at one point, of 'oh, it's her and her hobby horse', but I was very careful to try and militate against that, because I thought that was a very destructive way of looking at things, and I've been very low key in the way I've operated, deliberately, because I do feel that there is an element in every institution that waits for that and tries to make you look like you're an extremist, and in fact I've perhaps in some cases held back because I didn't want to give people that kind of ammunition...

It could be argued that this fear of extremism effectively kept the focus of equal opportunities work on 'safe' issues such as option choice and career planning, rather than issues such as sexual harassment which would automatically conjure up images of extremism in many people's minds. Anecdotal evidence suggests this might be the case, but without more detailed investigation of the nature of the opposition faced by equal opportunities coordinators in the pilot schools it is difficult to draw any firm conclusions. The point is, however, that the fear of being branded an extremist does seem to have led to a 'softly, softly' approach, regardless of whether such caution was actually warranted.

The spectre of extremism could also explain the general unease over single sex provision which was widespread across the pilot schools (see chapter 6). This may possibly have been due to a misunderstanding of what was permissable under the Sex Discrimination Act, with schools understandably wanting to avoid any accusations of discrimination (as opposed to positive action) on grounds of gender. However, it is more likely that it was a further manifestation of the strongly negative reaction within Masonfield to the perceived militant extremism of many 'new left' authorities during the early 1980s, including that of a neighbouring authority. In particular, Masonfield's elected councillors sought to disassociate themselves from authorities which had tried to tackle issues such as sexuality and sexual harassment in schools. The caution displayed by the pilot schools suggests that this was a fear widely shared within Masonfield, with serious implications in terms of who was considered best suited to promote equal opportunities within the pilot schools, and how best that was to be done.

By the end of the pilot period, the equal opportunities working groups had largely ceased to exist, at least in terms of their original function of developing the ISS. Greenwood High School excepted, responsibility for equal opportunities was by the end of pilot in the hands of someone other than the TVEI coordinator. At St Catherine's and Mosslands, it became the responsibility of two female deputy heads, both of whom were English teachers with broader responsibilities for pastoral matters, even though equal opportunities within the pilot schools had developed a strong curriculum-based slant (the two curriculum deputies were both men). At Seddon Park, the equal opportunities coordinator was the female head of English, whilst at The Croft the coordinator was yet another female English teacher (main professional grade, but in receipt of a small TVEI allowance for her equal opportunities work). At Greenwood High School, equal opportunities had fallen by default to the female TVEI coordinator (*not* an English teacher!).

These five women exercised varying degrees of power within their schools: the two deputy heads wielded quite considerable influence; the TVEI coordinator had only limited influence, as had the head of English; and the main professional grade English teacher had virtually no influence in her school's hierarchy. This can be interpreted in different ways. Firstly, to the extent that equal opportunities work, in three out of five schools, was the responsibility of teachers with relatively little influence within their schools' overall power structures, it could be argued that it was thereby treated as a relatively marginal issue. Weiner (1986), however, contends that gender reform policies are potentially more subversive of the status quo if they come from the 'grassroots' level and do not require the stamp of approval from senior management. The implication is that policies originating from the power holders in a school will inevitably be watered down compromises, as power is rarely given away lightly (Ord and Quigley, 1985). Deem (1987) has criticised Weiner on this point for being too simplistic, as the further implication is that feminists who achieve senior management status within education will inevitably sell out on their principles. Jones (1988) criticises a similar argument made in relation to women in positions of authority in local government more generally, whilst Watson (1990) and Yeatman (1993) both highlight criticisms made of 'femocrats' within national and local government in Australia. They all argue that to accuse feminists in senior positions of 'selling out' is to deny the positive influence of 'infiltrators' and to render them effectively powerless.

That these equal opportunities posts were all in the hands of women, rather than men, could similarly be interpreted in a number of ways. Liberals might have argued that equal numbers of men should have been involved in the process, although this would depend on whether or not such appointments were made as a sop to women or as positions of real responsibility. If the latter, it might have been seen as a good thing that the posts were in the hands of women, as this helped to redress the imbalance in the general distribution of positions of authority within schools. However, given the male domination of positions of 'real' power and influence within education, it might similarly have been argued by liberals that, by giving these posts to women, equal opportunities was being marginalised as a 'women's issue'. Thus, these posts were actually of little significance within the wider structures of the schools: if they were truly influential posts, they would have been offered to men, not women.

Len Jones and Joan Gray, the national equal opportunities advisers for TVEI, were very keen to see *equal* representation here as in other areas of TVEI management. Thus, even though most of TVEI's equal opportunities efforts were concentrated on boosting opportunities for girls rather than boys, it was somehow considered to be a weakness that at a management level equal opportunities responsibility was devolved largely to women. A radical approach, by contrast, would have applauded the fact that responsibility for equal opportunities rested exclusively in the hands of women. From this perspective, it would have been regarded as entirely appropriate - not a source of disappointment, which some TVEI coordinators clearly felt it to be - that the cross-project equal opportunities meetings were largely women-only forums (by default, not by design), thus providing a valuable source of strength to the women concerned and providing a unique opportunity to put the needs of girls and women at the top of the agenda. Further, even though there might have been some truth in the suggestion that equal opportunities positions were actually marginal positions, the possibility always existed to subvert the position to the benefit of girls and women.

The Information Systems Strategy

Reference was made earlier in this chapter, as well as in chapter 3, to the Information Systems Strategy (ISS). The ISS was vigorously promoted by the national advisers as a model for monitoring equal opportunities which went beyond a ritualistic collection of data, towards encouraging a constructive debate on the gender differences which existed in student outcomes and then moving towards change in those areas. The basics of the ISS were these: a school would set up a cross-curricular working group, led by a member of the senior management team, which would then collect quantifiable data on various 'outcomes' in the school, highlighting any gender differences. These outcomes most commonly included examination results, option choices in the upper school and post-16 destinations. The data would then be presented to the wider staff in conjunction with a series of hypotheses which sought to explain the differences in order to generate discussion of the problem and to develop a common framework for future target setting in these areas. This would then become a cyclical process, with each year's outcomes being fed back to staff, and new targets set accordingly.

The ISS was trialled amongst schools from the region in which Masonfield is located, and four of Masonfield's pilot schools were heavily involved in its development. In many schools, this was the first time that data relating to gender had been collected systematically and many people were genuinely surprised by the stark differences which invariably emerged. However, schools often had difficulty in moving beyond the data collection stage. This was certainly the case with the schools who trialled the ISS in Masonfield, particularly at Greenwood High School, where the debate following the gathering of data had been far from constructive, as discussed below. David James, the central TVEI coordinator, had the following to say about the ISS:

> What it taught us was the importance of data, of information, of being rigorous, and I think we can still see that. The problem we had with the strategy itself was that... nobody cracked what you did with all this data and what the linking mechanism was between knowing what the problem was and actually doing something and if Joan Gray had stayed in post longer and had worked on it longer we might have got more - but that was always the obstacle that people came up against (David James, 1992).

A further obstacle was that the ISS was underpinned by a rather naive faith in the power of 'hard data' to act as an awareness-raising tool and impress on staff the need for change. The collection of quantifiable data was characterised as being essentially a neutral process which offered incontrovertible evidence of the existence of a problem. The minutes of one of the cross-project equal opportunities working groups, for example, include the point that hard data 'deflected the possible accusation that the group were merely working with subjective opinion rather than with established fact'. The further assumption was made that the inequalities thus identified would, of necessity, be regarded as a 'problem' by teaching colleagues; many teachers did not of course regard the differences as a problem and were happy in their belief that the differential uptake of subjects and post-16 routes not only reflected, but was indeed evidence of, the natural order of things (Whyte, 1986, describes how such attitudes affected GIST).

An associated problem was that the ISS working parties were regarded by some teachers as groups of ideological purists who were piously claiming the moral high ground. As such, the working groups were keen to stress the neutrality of their work but, inevitably, some members of staff interpreted their work as an implicit criticism of their own practices. Greenwood School experienced particular difficulties, for example, when its working group moved on from analysing data on options, examination results and destinations to data relating to the high truancy rates within the upper school. They were surprised to discover that, contrary to common assumptions within the school, girls were absent far more than boys. Furthermore, they found that pupils were not necessarily absent from school for whole days, but were selective in which lessons they chose to attend, and the data that the group had obtained allowed them to identify precisely which lessons girls were missing. Some members of staff understandably felt very threatened by the group's focus and as a consequence were extremely resistant to subsequent work produced by the working party. Further, it was hypothesised that the main reason why girls were absent was because they were expected to care for younger siblings and sick parents, but rather than providing the incontrovertible evidence of discrimination that the working party thought they had uncovered, the data was actually used by certain teachers as a legitimation of the status quo. This was not seen as an important issue concerning the value placed on girls' education; rather, it was argued by some that such absenteeism was unavoidable and, whilst not actually condoned, was far more acceptable than male truancy. Largely because of this incident, Greenwood's working group made slow progress in tackling equality issues, and there was a strong feeling that the insensitive use of data had actually set back the cause of equal opportunities within the school.

Clearly, the monitoring of quantifiable outcomes was extremely important; progress could be monitored over time and improvements sought, and it was important that schools were faced with their record in areas such as option choice and examination results. However, the pilot schools were very disappointed to find that measurable progress tended to be extremely slow, if not negligible. This had important repercussions at the school level. Firstly, it had a negative effect on the morale of equal opportunities sympathisers: to see little or no tangible progress was extremely discouraging. Secondly, detractors used the 'hard evidence' to point out the futility of equal opportunities initiatives: in spite of best efforts, nothing seemed to change. Even more seriously, because tangible results were not forthcoming, certain initiatives were in danger of actually being abandoned for 'not working', even though at a less tangible level they might have been achieving positive results. The fate of the single sex CDT classes at The Croft High School, described in chapter 6, is a case in point.

Further, whilst the ISS proved to be a useful starting point for equal opportunities work, it tended to focus attention only on areas of school life which were amenable to quantification. Some schools did try to develop more qualitative indicators, but this was a time-consuming exercise which required a level of research expertise which was often lacking. In most schools, therefore, the emphasis of ISS working groups remained very much on quantifiable measures, with the inevitable neglect of issues with which feminist teachers were more concerned: sexual harassment in school, the self-esteem of girls and young women, an exploration of the interaction between racism and sexism, to give three examples. Moreover, the emphasis was on measuring outcomes for *pupils*, not teachers. In this respect, it is important to note the indifference of many women teachers at The Croft High School *vis-à-vis* working towards more equitable pupil outcomes, given the glaring inequalities which existed within the school's staffing structure (see chapter 4). As the school's TVEI coordinator put it, 'They said, what difference does it make? You see, some of these things have been perceived by colleagues as being token gestures which do not really change the underlying philosophy' (June 1992).

Despite these reservations, it should be remembered that in many schools this was the first time that data of any sort on gender outcomes had been collated and then made available to staff, and this in itself represented considerable progress. Joan Gray, one of the two national advisers, had this to say:

> If you know anything about education you know that educationalists are good with words, they can find all sorts of ways of wrapping things up, saying that they're already doing things, and so on. And that's why your question about were there dangers in looking at the outcomes and saying are you only looking at things that can be measured, my answer to that in equal opportunities terms is that I wasn't in the least bit worried, because as far as I'm concerned people can pretend to be doing all sorts of things, until you actually look at what's being achieved, until you look at the outcomes.

Explanations for inequality

The ISS approach placed considerable emphasis on the generation of hypotheses to explain gender inequalities in individual schools, and hence generate staffroom debate. The strategies adopted by schools in encouraging non-traditional choices, as the next chapter shows, appear largely to have been based on the premise that the key to changing the gendered nature of subject and career choice lay with raising awareness of the wider opportunities available to pupils. References were rarely made to broader gendered power relations within schools and how these might affect pupil behaviour. However, most of the schools found that their awareness raising efforts bore little fruit in terms of measurable outcomes, and the pages of the pilot schools' annual reports often shed light on the explanations which were put forward in each school for the continuing existence of inequalities and the relative failure of their intervention strategies. Not surprisingly, most recorded debate occurred around gender differences in option choices, rather than other aspects of school life which lay within the remit of the ISS working parties. Further, most of the debate was generated by girls' low or non-existent take-up of CDT options, not by the relatively low uptake by boys of curriculum areas traditionally dominated by girls. Thus, in the main the schools sought to explain *girls'* behaviour rather than that of *boys*, lending support to Hunt's argument that girls' educational experiences tend to be cast as the 'norm plus' or 'norm minus', in comparison with boys' experiences (Hunt, 1991).

Across the pilot schools, the main influences on pupils' choices were largely seen as being external to the school - home, peer group pressure and wider social factors, including the influence of the media and the priorities of local labour markets. Where schools were prepared to direct criticism inwards, it was generally for their failure to raise levels of awareness concerning the range of opportunities open to boys and girls. Thus, early reports referred to the need for awareness raising measures and each of the schools outlined with some optimism what they hoped to do. However, subsequent reports commented on the failure of their efforts to produce marked change, leading them to conclude that external influences exerted a far stronger influence than their own efforts.

Greenwood High School's second annual report noted, for example, that 'lack of awareness, prompting from the home, and less able pupils who find it difficult to grasp such concepts (of equal opportunities)' were acting against the efforts of the cross-curriculum working party on equal opportunities. The first and the last constraint could conceivably have been tackled by action on the part of the school, by means of greater efforts at awareness raising and by taking time to explain the concept of equality of opportunity. In turn, the influence of the home could have been counteracted to some extent by the success of awareness raising amongst pupils; it is otherwise difficult to see what direct influence the school could have had on parents in a catchment area where they tend to have minimal contact with their children's school. In a sense, therefore, this statement implicated the school itself in the perpetuation of inequality in so far as it had failed to raise pupils' awareness or explain in simple terms the importance of concepts such as equality, but the actual structures or power relations within the school were *not* implicated by this statement.

Seddon Park's second annual report similarly attributed resistance to equal opportunities to factors external to the school: 'parental influence, local culture and image.' This was part of the wider challenge facing the school, to break down 'inbred beliefs' about appropriate sex roles in the area. These comments received an echo in remarks made by the school's TVEI coordinator:

> The stereotyping comes very much from the parents again - there's a tremendous parental influence... We find girls tend to, they've got this image that girls have babies, get married, their position is at home, full stop. The lads, they are the macho men, they go out to the pub, have a beer, they have the money, wife stops at home. They cook the meals and everything - very, very traditional. And again, a lot of parental influence in the community on that (TVEI Coordinator, Seddon Park High School, February 1992).

However, the school was also prepared to examine its own record, and in the second half of TVEI pilot it extensively trialled non-sexist lesson materials in a range of subjects. The option choice booklet was also rewritten, in an acknowledgement that language could play a powerful role in perpetuating stereotypes. The second annual report also noted that the equal opportunities working group was hoping to investigate the relationship between equal opportunities and staff structures, a move in the direction of questioning the school's own responsibility.

Mosslands High School had stated boldly in its original proposal for consideration as a TVEI pilot school that 'the entire curriculum of the school is based on the premise of equal opportunities for boys and girls, both theoretically and practically... an open option system does not deter anyone on grounds of gender.' There were in fact nine subjects in the upper school which had been chosen by pupils of one sex only, and this situation was attributed to ignorance of the nature of the courses on offer, peer group pressure, and 'home and environmental pressures', the first factor being in the control of the school, the others largely out of its control. A number of measures were adopted to raise pupil awareness and to make non-traditional subjects appear more attractive, including attendance at a 'Women Into Computing' event organised for third year girls at the local university. The school also sought to influence the parents of new pupils by highlighting equal opportunities at roadshows for feeder primary schools.

Outside of the 'public face' of the annual report, however, there is some evidence that staffing structures within the school had come in for some criticism. In a meeting of the project-wide equal opportunities working party, it was suggested that media priorities and staffing structures played a role in perpetuating 'gender discrepancies' in option choice at Mosslands High School. In interview nearly three years later, the deputy head who had responsibility for equal opportunities at Mosslands explained that up until her promotion in September 1988 there had been no women in the senior management team of the school, and that she was the only woman with a D allowance. A number of women staff were in receipt of B allowances, but none had a C allowance. At Mosslands High School, therefore, there was a growing feeling that the school itself had some contribution to make to the breaking down of stereotypes, not least within its own hierarchy, although external factors were also seen as crucial.

The annual reports of the Croft High School express an awareness of the school's own critical role in the success or failure of equal opportunities initiatives. For instance, it was felt that it would be necessary to provide 'structured counselling' to third years prior to option choice in order to raise awareness of the full range of options open to them. Ultimately, however, subjects were offered to pupils 'based on their motivation, aspirations and staff recommendations'. The lack of girls opting for CDT, even after a girls' only CDT group was run in the third year, was attributed to a number of factors: the lateness of the intervention; the greater attractiveness of other options; the lack of a female role model; and the greater influence of home and peer pressure. The second annual report concluded that,

> there needs to be a more aggressive marketing policy, particularly in overcoming the gender barrier that appears to have developed... input such as 'Girls Into Engineering' is seen as a prerequisite in the fight to develop equal opportunities, and adequate preparation before selection in the third year.

('Fighting talk' such as this was never used in any of the annual reports in connection with encouraging boys to take subjects like Food Studies.) Staffing structures at The Croft were never publicly implicated in the perpetuation of inequalities within the school, despite the fact that this was a school that throughout the pilot years had failed to include women in senior management. The consequent lack of enthusiasm amongst women teachers for equal opportunities policies aimed at *pupils* was noted above.

Finally, at St Catherine's High School it was, once again, the low uptake of CDT amongst girls which caused staff to reflect on possible causes of differential uptake. The following factors were identified: parental reluctance to consider engineering as a suitable career for girls, the continuing decline in local industry (such that engineering-related jobs should be reserved for the boys), and the girls' lack of prior experience in the first two TVEI cohorts. The efforts of the CDT department to increase girls' participation are outlined in the next chapter, and it is worth noting that they took on a woman student teacher to teach CDT for a term, in acknowledgement of the potentially positive effect of role models on pupil attitudes. This was also an acknowledgement, by implication, of the likely negative effect on girls of being taught CDT by a male teacher within a predominantly male environment.

In sum, the explanations put forward by the schools create an impression of a group of schools which felt that they were doing their best to promote equal opportunities, yet also felt that their efforts were constantly undermined by pressures which were outside their control. These schools arguably regarded themselves as agents for the *widening* of opportunities, with a liberal, progressive outlook with regard to gender equality. There is a strong parallel here with Bowles and Gintis' critique of the meritocratic ideal within liberal education. They argue that class-based inequalities in educational outcomes are similarly represented as the inevitable result of different levels of ability and motivation, thereby giving legitimacy to the social reproductive functions of schooling (Bowles and Gintis, 1976). On this basis, it could be argued that the pilot schools operated as meritocracies, offering boys and girls equal access to equal pathways, and that the system was legitimated by the existence of young people who had subsequently managed to achieve outside the limits of achievement associated with their gender. However, most of the schools reported a distinct lack of success in this project: a measurable legitimation of the system was distinctly lacking and they expressed extreme disappointment at their subsequent failures to combat what they felt to be the stronger influence of external factors.

Conclusion

At the beginning of TVEI pilot in Masonfield, equal opportunities was a non-issue, both in the pilot schools and at the LEA level. However, by the end of pilot not only had equal opportunities become acceptable as a key policy issue, but a commitment to equal opportunities was even considered *de rigeur* for those teachers keen to progress through the TVEI hierarchy. Undoubtedly, a huge shift in attitude had occurred. One key element of this success was the establishment of equal opportunities working groups within individual high schools, working towards the aims and objectives of the ISS. The tasks for which these groups were established represented the first time that data on differential gendered outcomes had been systematically collected within the LEA. In one school, for example, this exercise had highlighted the single sex (male) nature of technology and physical science in the upper school, something of which the majority of teachers in the school had been unaware. Moreover, as we have seen, for the first time schools began to discuss the possible reasons behind the inequalities which they had discovered. Nonetheless, the terms of the debates which ensued reveal a great deal about the interpretation which was placed on equal opportunities both within individual schools and across the LEA.

TVEI was clearly responsible for a considerable shift in attitude around gender equality issues in Masonfield. However, the focus within this chapter has been limited to its impact at the organisational level: staffing issues, monitoring mechanisms, and strategies for change. At the end of the day, the overall success of TVEI's equal opportunities initiative should be measured in terms of the impact it had on individual young people who were involved in the pilot. Accordingly, the following chapters shift the focus towards a consideration of the experiences of the young people who were involved in TVEI pilot in Masonfield.

6 The curricular experiences of TVEI pupils

Introduction

This chapter is concerned with exploring the curricular experiences of pupils involved in Masonfield TVEI in the pilot years. It does so by means of an examination of the dominant equal opportunities emphasis of TVEI: the promotion of non-traditional option choices and career routes. The practical and philosophical implications of this emphasis will be described, the former in terms of the intervention strategies that were developed, the latter in terms of the deficit model of girls' achievements that was thus established. The chapter will then focus on the evidence of the unequal involvement of girls and boys in both TVEI generally, and within specific TVEI options, in the Masonfield project. The chapter will conclude with a discussion of the use of single sex provision in Masonfield, which reveals a great deal about the underlying priorities of TVEI.

TVEI's dominant equal opportunities emphasis

Once TVEI had been launched in Masonfield, it was the responsibility of the central project team to continually stress the importance of gender equality to the pilot schools. In practice, however, each of the pilot schools developed their own approach to equal opportunities, albeit within the general framework agreed as part of the bid to the MSC. Despite the development of five different approaches across the project, a number of common themes nonetheless emerged over the pilot years which shed light on the philosophical underpinnings of equal opportunities work within TVEI. These underpinnings point to an essentially liberal interpretation of gender inequalities in education which led to a narrowing of TVEI's focus and consequently ruled out certain more radical responses to the issue.

Encouraging girls towards the non-traditional

TVEI's equal opportunities funding criterion had a very specific focus - equal access to TVEI courses and the avoidance of sex-stereotyping. Not surprisingly, then, this was a focus which was evident within the pilot schools during the early years of TVEI in Masonfield. St Catherine's second annual report, for example, boldly stated that, 'it was felt that all pupils had been given equal opportunities in their choice of subjects', whilst Mosslands High School's report noted likewise that, 'pupils and their parents are free to choose the option subjects which the pupils will follow in the upper school. Few restrictions are placed on the choice, although guidance is given when a pupil appears not to have a balanced curriculum or where too much overlap of subjects might occur'. To facilitate that choice, some of the schools changed the names of courses or introduced new syllabuses which were supposed to have a broader appeal to both boys and girls. The success of these strategies will be considered later in the chapter.

Across all five schools, however, the greatest challenge was always regarded as the recruitment of girls into Craft, Design and Technology options. The efforts of St Catherine's High School are typical of the efforts made to encourage girls to take CDT. When TVEI was launched in the school, CDT was made compulsory for all lower school pupils, in recognition of the effect that lack of prior experience had often had in preventing girls from taking CDT in the upper school. However, only *six* TVEI girls took CDT across the entire four pilot cohorts, despite efforts to improve its image and popularity amongst girls. For instance, a number of girls attended a 'Girls into Engineering' event; non-sexist lesson materials and careers literature were acquired; and female ex-pupils who had found work in engineering were invited into school to talk to the younger girls. St Catherine's had even acquired a female PGCE student to teach CDT for a term of teaching practice in the hope that this would make an impact on girls' options. The TVEI coordinator felt that these measures had achieved some degree of success in that CDT had been transformed into a subject which the girls now enjoyed, rather than dreaded, in the lower school, yet was disappointed that the broader goal of increasing the numbers of girls opting for CDT in the upper school had not been achieved. Other schools tried similar measures in a bid to encourage more girls to opt for CDT, but experienced similar failure in achieving a more equitable take-up.

This general concern over subject uptake fed into a broader concern about the impact such choices had on post-school destinations, in particular the extent to which young people continued to opt for stereotypical career paths. A number of strategies were introduced in an attempt to broaden the horizons of pupils. Stereotypical images of men and women were challenged by displaying posters depicting non-traditional role models at work, for example, or by purchasing careers literature based on positive images, whilst men and women with non-traditional careers were invited to come into school and talk to pupils about their work. A number of the schools organised their own 'World of Work' days, which were aimed at encouraging pupils to consider occupational areas more traditionally associated with the opposite sex. As with subject choice, greater emphasis was placed within these activities on encouraging girls to consider careers in male occupational areas.

In the fourth year of pilot, however, St Catherine's organised events for boys as well as girls. At the girls' event, women employed in non-traditional occupations were invited into school to meet girls, whilst at the boys' event a small number of male role models (a florist and a nurse, for example) were invited to the school alongside some of the women who had attended the girls' event. The idea behind the boys' event was not just to get boys to think about non-traditional jobs, but to point out that women could be found in areas of employment traditionally regarded as male areas. Apparently, the deputy head who had planned the girls' event had not originally intended to organise a similar event for the boys, as she had organised the event primarily as a means of raising girls' self-esteem. However, the boys had made repeated requests for a similar event and eventually one had been arranged. The following year, in anticipation of a repeated demand from the boys, a mixed event had been organised, effectively undermining the primary reason for organising such an event. However, the deputy head felt unable to do anything else given the protests from male pupils that it was unfair not to include them. This incident seems to tie in with Foster's observation that 'a perceived conflict with the rights and interests of men is created in any educational setting which seems to advocate, in a major way, the needs and interests of women' (Foster, 1996, p.50), as opposed to those of men.

In general, though, there was relatively little concern expressed across the pilot schools over the low uptake by boys of subjects and careers traditionally seen as female domains, and it was certainly never regarded as problematic in quite the same way as girls' low take-up of CDT and related careers. This was a trend repeated across TVEI projects up and down the country, and arose not from any commitment to radical feminist arguments concerning the importance of placing girls at the centre of an anti-sexist educational framework (Weiner, 1986), but from the apparent need to shift increasing numbers of girls from female-dominated areas of employment into two broad occupational spheres. The first of these spheres embraced male-dominated occupational areas such as engineering, the shift being construed as necessary given the projected shortage of male school leavers in the late 1980s. The second sphere embraced the supposedly 'gender neutral' new technologies. In terms of the national interest, the shortage of young men within female-dominated occupational areas was therefore deemed irrelevant, given the existence of a supply of adult women returners prepared to fill gaps in these areas. Such an emphasis had the all too familiar effect of problematising the educational experiences of girls in relation to boys, whose choices tended to go unchallenged.

The inherent danger of this emphasis was that the dominance and assumed superiority of male academic and occupational achievement was thus underlined and reinforced, whilst the greater economic rewards accruing from male-dominated areas of employment were legitimated and shown to be rightly deserved (Wright, 1988).

By implication, areas in which women had traditionally been able to excel - both in school and in the labour market - were further devalued and their subordinate position reinforced (Kenway et al, 1994). The unintended consequence of this approach was to 'tap right back into the gendered dualisms from which escape (was) sought' (Kenway, 1993, p88). Further, this emphasis on the requirement of girls to change their traditional behaviour patterns and attitudes had other worrying implications. For example, Grant and Harding (1987) noted with some concern the following statement taken from a leaflet on TVEI and equal opportunities produced by the EOC:

> Equality of opportunities between boys and girls is essential to the success of TVEI schemes, but unless special measures are taken, the negative attitude towards technology which girls already reveal will *undermine the objectives of TVEI*... Schools should make it clear that you want, *and expect*, as many girls as boys to be involved in the science and technological side of TVEI (EOC, 1985, pp.6-7, emphasis added).

The onus for the success of TVEI - and by implication its failure - was thus placed squarely upon the shoulders of young women within the scheme, whilst boys' achievements became the measure against which girls were seen to 'succeed' or 'fail', a practice with a long history within British education (Hunt, 1991). The possibility that the system itself might be at fault or that young women may have had perfectly rational reasons for rejecting male-dominated areas were discounted in favour of common sense arguments which implied that they were clearly foolish not to take advantage of the increased opportunities available to them in the changing economic climate (Cockburn, 1988). Thus, by ignoring the existence of structural factors militating against the attainment of equality of opportunity, the liberal perspective which largely underpinned TVEI's approach to equal opportunities fell back on a belief that discrimination and inequality were largely the consequences of a lack of awareness of wider opportunities (Stromquist, 1990).

TVEI's equal opportunities commitment tended therefore to operate on the basis of a 'deficit' model, with young women themselves being cast as largely responsible - even culpable - for the stereotyped decisions they invariably made regarding their options and careers. Indeed, a TVEI Unit-sponsored evaluation carried out by the independent National Foundation for Education Research found that:

> There was a noticeable tendency during the NFER evaluation to lay the blame for stereotyping at someone else's door. Frequently it was the fault of that nebulous entity known as 'society', often it was parents, but students themselves were also blamed for not making the 'right' option choices or for deciding on a traditional career (Bridgwood, 1990, p.53).

It would be unfair to suggest that TVEI never attempted to encourage boys to opt for non-traditional subjects and job areas, but such initiatives were far outweighed by the number of strategies designed to encourage girls to follow non-traditional pathways. There were of course (and still are) fewer economic incentives for young men to consider careers in traditional female areas of employment in contrast to the 'obvious' benefits to girls of choosing high status, well paid 'male' career routes: 'We know that we are offering girls a viable future by encouraging them into 'male' areas of knowledge and skill; sadly the same is not true for boys' (Wright, 1988, p.67). Strong ideological pressures towards gender conformity and compliance with hegemonic forms of masculinity would also have been in operation (Mac an Ghaill, 1994; Pye et al, 1996), and it may also have been partly for these reasons that teachers and careers officers were less likely to promote the large-scale movement of young men into female occupational areas. In the eyes of many young men (and, not unimportantly, their parents), there would seem to be no sound reason why they should willingly choose such careers, short of having been the victims of a misguided exercise in social engineering.

TVEI cohort membership and subject choice

Given this concern with a more equal gender distribution of pupils across courses, what were the actual patterns of subject choice amongst Masonfield's pilot pupils? It is important firstly to consider the gender make-up of the overall cohort in each school. Involvement in the TVEI cohort, in Masonfield as elsewhere, was usually determined by the combination of option choice subjects chosen by pupils in their final two years of compulsory schooling. Typical TVEI subjects included Information Technology, Business Studies, Food Studies, Textiles, and various Craft, Design and Technology subjects. A pupil would usually have to choose two or three TVEI options in order to be included in the official cohort and thus qualify for the wider TVEI entitlement curriculum (which included elements such as work experience, TVEI 'residentials' and participation in Records of Achievement). The extent to which young men and women were fairly distributed across TVEI options lay at the heart of TVEI's equal opportunities funding criterion, yet even at the level of access to the scheme in general, TVEI failed to live up to that criterion. Evidence from pilot projects nationwide in the first three rounds shows that within each round there was a slightly higher proportion of boys than girls involved pre-16 and that across the three rounds overall the inequalities in participation were actually greater in 1985-86 than in 1983-84 (McIntyre, 1987). This situation was replicated in Scotland, too, where analysis of the Scottish database revealed that there were always slightly more boys than girls in each pilot intake (Lyon et al, 1990).

These aggregate figures tend to obscure variations in individual projects, and in 1984/85, four out of 57 pilot projects had a greater proportion of girls than boys, increasing both proportionately and absolutely to twelve out of 68 projects by 1985/86 (Tenne, 1987). Hertfordshire and Wirral TVEI projects had the highest rates of female participation, young women accounting for 58 per cent of the cohort in 1985/86. By contrast, they accounted for only 24 per cent of the cohort in Wigan TVEI, one of eight projects where girls accounted for less than a third of the overall cohort. The issue of cohort membership was actually raised on three occasions within Parliament. In May 1984, in response to a question concerning equal access for boys and girls to 'technically based' aspects of TVEI, the Conservative Secretary of State for Employment played down any gender differences in take-up, arguing that 'broadly equal numbers' of boys and girls were involved in TVEI (Hansard, 1984). The late Jo Richardson MP (Labour) asked a similar question in 1985, as did Clement Freud MP in May 1986. Freud was told that 43 per cent of TVEI students at that time were female, even though they accounted for 49 per cent of the total population in maintained secondary schools (Hansard, 1986).

It was noted in chapter 4 that the idea of focusing TVEI only on a selected cohort had proved to be something of a sticking point in Masonfield, but was something which the MSC had insisted upon. Consequently, each of the five Masonfield pilot schools had a maximum of 50 TVEI-funded pupils in each of the four year groups. In the first two years of pilot, the notion of a TVEI Cohort still had some meaning: only Cohort pupils were able to participate in activities such as work experience, Records of Achievement and residential experience. Moreover, information such as the subject choices and subsequent examination results of Cohort pupils was routinely collected as part of MSC-commissioned evaluations by both Trent Polytechnic and the National Foundation for Educational Research. However, by the third year of pilot, the pilot schools began to extend TVEI-style provision to *all* upper school pupils and, if they had selected a TVEI Cohort at all, had done so purely for 'statistical purposes'. In practice, therefore, by the third year of pilot the majority of non-TVEI pupils were reaping most of the benefits of TVEI funding previously associated only with membership of the Cohort. However, for Cohort II, membership of the Cohort still retained its significance, and in fact it is only for this group of pupils - who started out as TVEI pupils in September 1987 - that it has been possible to gather reliable figures for TVEI involvement.

In the second year of Masonfield's pilot project, boys accounted for 52 per cent of all fourth years across the five pilot schools, yet accounted for 60 per cent of all cohort pupils. Boys were therefore over-represented within the TVEI Cohort in Masonfield. Table 6.1 illustrates this further by showing the absolute numbers of pupils involved in TVEI and those same numbers expressed as a percentage of all boys and all girls in the fourth year group in each of the schools. In two of the pilot schools girls were actually more likely than boys to be included in the Cohort, but across all five pilot schools 37 per cent of boys were involved in TVEI compared with only 27 per cent of girls.

These numbers need to be contextualised further, however. As TVEI Cohort membership was dependent on choosing a specified number of TVEI subjects, the gender ratio of the cohort within each of the schools was largely contingent on the perceived gender bias of the TVEI subjects on offer. Indeed, with this in mind,

Table 6.1
TVEI cohort membership in Masonfield by gender: cohort II (1987-89)

	Girls No.	%	Boys No.	%
Pilot schools:				
St Catherines	15	29	16	28
Seddon Park	19	30	31	60
Mosslands	18	21	49	45
The Croft	24	32	21	27
Greenwood	20	24	28	29
All	*96*	*27*	*145*	*37*

Source: Masonfield TVEI Annual Reports

Table 6.2
TVEI subjects available to cohort II and their prior gendered association

| Subject | Association | Pilot High Schools | | | | |
		St C	SP	M	TC	G
Business studies	Girls	✓	-	✓	-	-
Information Technology	Boys	✓	-	✓	-	✓
BS/IT Combined	Boys/Girls	-	✓	✓	✓	✓
Craft, Design & Technology (CDT)	Boys	✓	✓	✓	✓	✓
Media Studies	Boys	✓	-	-	✓	-
Social & Community Studies	Girls	✓	-	-	-	-
Food Studies	Girls	✓	-	-	✓	-
Theatre Arts	Girls	-	-	✓	-	✓
Agriculture/Horticulture	Boys	-	-	✓	-	-
Business French	Girls	✓	-	-	-	-

Notes:
✓ Indicates that this subject was offered to TVEI pupils

Source: Masonfield TVEI Annual Reports

Parliamentary assurances had also been sought in 1984 and 1985 that the take-up of options *within* TVEI schemes was broadly equitable. The official response on both occasions was that take-up 'has *sometimes* tended to follow traditional lines' (my emphasis). Given the evidence that was already available at this early stage of TVEI's development, this is clearly an understatement. An HMI report on the 14 first round TVEI projects had concluded in 1985 that,

> even where the recruitment of boys and girls was well balanced, there was widespread and sometimes almost total division into traditional sex-stereotyped patterns of work when the pupils chose between course options (HMI, 1984, p.10).

Tenne (1987), for instance, noted that 63 per cent of male TVEI pupils in the 1984/85 cohorts of the first and second round projects had opted for a CDT option, compared with only 32 per cent of female TVEI pupils. These figures were reversed for the take-up of Business Studies options, which were often associated in pupils' minds with the female-dominated Typing/Office Studies courses which they invariably replaced. Home Economics courses were taken by nearly half of all female TVEI pupils, compared with only nine per cent of TVEI boys - and most of these young men had opted for courses with an emphasis on catering and the hotel industry, courses 'which have greater commercial application' (Tenne, 1987, p.iii; see also Bridgwood, 1988).

How do these national trends relate to what was going on within Masonfield? Table 6.2 summarises the subjects which were offered as TVEI options in each of the pilot schools in Masonfield. Across the project, ten new subjects were introduced, although no one school offered more than seven of these new subjects. On the basis of earlier research on the gendered appeal of particular subjects (Pratt et al, 1984), five of these new subjects were likely to have attracted greater numbers of girls, four were likely to have attracted greater numbers of boys and one was likely to have had equal appeal. The combinations in which they were introduced into the individual schools meant that in only one school (St Catherine's) was the cohort potentially likely to have attracted significantly more girls than boys - and this is indeed reflected in the gender breakdown of the pupils in St Catherine's cohort, although the difference is only very slight (see Table 6.1). Given the prior gendered associations of the new subjects, it is not surprising that there were more boys than girls in Cohort II overall. Whether the gender balance would have become more even in subsequent cohorts is, of course, impossible to tell because of the jettisoning of the idea of a designated cohort for anything other than statistical purposes. This was in itself a positive step, however; the perceived elitism of TVEI had always been a cause of anxiety in Masonfield, and the extension of TVEI's benefits to the optimum number of pupils at a relatively early stage (albeit only within five schools) was widely seen as a step forward.

Turning to the actual take-up of TVEI subjects by gender, one comes across a

Table 6.3
Uptake of TVEI subjects amongst cohort II pupils in 2 pilot schools

	Girls No.	%[1]	Boys No.	%[1]
(i) St Catherine's				
Business Studies	13	84	11	69
Information Technology	7	47	7	44
Craft, Design & Technology	1	7	6	37
Media Studies	7	47	9	56
Social & Community Studies	8	53	1	6
Food Studies	7	47	2	12
Business French	11	73	4	25
(ii) Greenwood				
Office Studies/ Info Technology	4	20	6	21
Craft, Design & Technology[2]	16	-	34	-
Performing Arts	7	35	5	18
Information Technology	11	55	15	54

Notes:
[1] Percentages refers to the percentage of each sex within cohort II
[2] Not disaggregated by cohort membership

Source: Masonfield TVEI Annual Reports

surprising discovery: despite the supposed emphasis on the careful monitoring of the numbers of pupils taking particular options by gender, it actually proved extremely difficult to obtain reliable figures for each of the pilot schools. In general, the information that was included in the annual reports was inconsistent from one year to the next, whilst there were also inconsistencies *within* reports, with apparent confusion concerning the actual numbers of pupils included in the cohort. The reasons for such confusion are uncertain, but the failure to present take-up data systematically makes the task of assessing the extent to which improvements occurred almost impossible. Arguably, this reflects a wider neglect of the issue: in reporting progress in CDT, for example, the frequent lack of any acknowledgement of the huge gender differences in take-up amounts to a glaring omission.

Given the lack of reliable information, Table 6.3 confines itself to presenting take-up figures for cohort II pupils at St Catherine's and Greenwood High Schools only. There are no figures included for Seddon Park because of the inconsistencies between the numbers supposedly involved in TVEI subjects and the overall numbers supposedly involved in the Cohort, although the text of the second annual report suggests that CDT was taken exclusively by boys in Cohort II, with few boys taking BS/IT. The Croft's annual reports are equally confusing: their text suggests, however, that only one girl took CDT, that more than twice as many girls than boys took the BS/IT option and that very few boys took Food Studies. Media Studies, though, succeeded in attracting equal numbers of pupils. Reliable take-up figures for Mosslands High School are available, but they are not disaggregated by gender: again, the text of the annual reports suggest that Business Studies, Theatre Arts, Agriculture and Information Technology attracted equal numbers of boys and girls, but that no girls in Cohort II took CDT and only a few boys took the double option BS/IT.

Despite the evidence of strong gender polarisation within TVEI, it is interesting to note that only a minority of respondents to the Masonfield Leavers Survey felt that TVEI had been 'mainly for boys' or 'mainly for girls': 14.5 per cent of boys and 2 per cent of girls thought that TVEI had been mainly for boys, whilst 14 per cent of girls and 5 per cent of boys thought that TVEI had been mainly for girls. Interestingly, those who expressed agreement on this issue tended to feel that TVEI was *most appropriate for their gender* and were themselves taking 'stereotypical' options: this seems to highlight the extent to which pupils taking stereotypical subjects would largely be aware only of people of the same gender within those subject areas.

Stereotyped option choice was not of course a phenomenon unique to TVEI, but with TVEI's 'up front' commitment to the erosion of sex-stereotyping within the curriculum, it might have been supposed that the TVEI curriculum would be able to boast a better record than the wider school curriculum. There is in fact some evidence to suggest that in some subjects sex-stereotyping was very slightly reduced within TVEI projects. McIntyre (1987) noted that female TVEI pupils in the first three cohorts spent a larger proportion of their time studying 'technically-based' subjects (not defined) than their non-TVEI peers, both male and female, whilst male TVEI pupils spent a larger proportion of their time on Business Studies and Office Practice courses than their non-TVEI male peers. McIntyre concluded that change, although very slight, was at least in the right direction. Researchers at Trent Polytechnic also noted that TVEI boys and girls were studying 'technological subjects' (again undefined, but presumably referring to CDT options) at a ratio of four to one, compared with a ratio of five to one amongst non-TVEI pupils (Trent Polytechnic, 1988). However, male TVEI pupils were spending less time than non-TVEI males on domestically-biased Home Economics courses (McIntyre, 1987).

A DES report on the first seven years of TVEI concluded that,

> overall, TVEI reduced gender stereotyping. Schools examined both their culture and structures so that, for example, girls within TVEI schemes were more likely to take the more technological courses and boys were more likely to take food courses or media studies than those not involved in TVEI (DES, 1991a, p.19).

Given the high degree of stereotyping within the curriculum prior to the introduction of TVEI, any progress was to be welcomed, whilst one can only concur with the 1984 HMI report mentioned earlier that the criterion of success - equal numbers of boys and girls in all courses - was 'a stringent one' (HMI, 1984, p.11). At the end of the day, however, TVEI was unable to force pupils to take particular subjects (in contrast to the requirements of the National Curriculum), and in many cases young people were choosing their options entirely on the basis of their embryonic career ideas - themselves highly stereotypical. TVEI's explicit orientation towards preparation for 'adult life' may perhaps have meant that pupils who opted for TVEI were more career-oriented than non-TVEI pupils. Certainly, almost a third of respondents to the Masonfield Leavers Survey agreed that 'TVEI was mainly for those who knew what they wanted to do when they left school' (young men were almost twice as likely to agree than young women: 39 per cent and 20.5 per cent respectively). This supports findings from research carried out in Masonfield amongst TVEI Extension school pupils (City of Masonfield, 1991): whereas young women were prepared to opt for some subjects chiefly on the basis of enjoyment or the willingness to try something new, young men tended to have career-related reasons for their choice, particularly when the subject in question was regarded as gender atypical. Indeed, some boys subsequently dropped their atypical subjects on changing their career ideas: once the career plan had changed, the apparent justification for studying a non-traditional subject was gone, and the need to leave a 'feminised' curriculum area became paramount.

The instrumentalism of TVEI pupils is further reinforced by responses to a question in the Leavers Survey which asked ex-TVEI pupils whether or not they had found their involvement in TVEI to be worthwhile. 44 per cent of ex-TVEI pupils said that their involvement had been 'very worthwhile', whilst a further 46 per cent said that it had been 'worthwhile in some ways'. When asked to give a reason for their response, over a third commented on the relevance of TVEI to the 'real world', whilst a further 10 leavers made similar points when invited to comment more generally on TVEI. Such comments were made predominantly by ex-TVEI pupils who had moved straight into the labour market on leaving school, and many felt that the skills they had acquired as TVEI students were directly related to what they were now doing. For example, one young woman wrote that 'I thought the Business Studies and Information Technology courses were extremely good. Everything I learnt has been very useful in my work at present.' Other comments highlighted the usefulness of IT-related skills, which may have been acquired in Business Studies and Information Technology courses, but equally may have been picked up within other TVEI courses, all of which attempted to utilise new technologies whenever possible. The fact that so many young people found these skills useful is also a reflection of the high concentration of school leavers in junior clerical positions (see chapter 8).

These responses add weight to the argument that TVEI pupils viewed their involvement in TVEI in highly instrumental terms. TVEI subjects were, however, related in young people's eyes to a distinct set of potential careers - business and commerce, catering, computing and engineering, for example - and it is likely that only young people specifically interested in such careers would have opted for TVEI. Those interested in other occupational areas were probably no less career-oriented than their TVEI peers, but the subjects which they felt were related to their career plans were not available as TVEI-funded options; if they had been, they too, presumably, would have been TVEI students. Thus, although Blackman has argued that the introduction of TVEI 'may heighten the pupils' scramble for occupational identity and currency' (Blackman, 1987, p.42), *most* upper school pupils are probably well tuned in to the need to make their subject choices in line with their career aspirations.

So, pupils' career aspirations may have played a large part in producing polarised curriculum experiences. However, further evidence suggests that the organisation of the TVEI curriculum in many schools tended to facilitate rather than challenge sex segregation in the curriculum in a number of important ways (McIntyre, 1987). Firstly, as we have seen, TVEI funding was often used to enhance existing courses that already had a strong in-built bias towards one or other gender (Hopkins, 1986) or, if new courses, were associated in pupils' minds with existing male- or female-dominated subjects. The combination of a subject that was not only associated with members of the opposite sex but was also totally new to a school was likely to have represented a formidable choice, posing a double risk to pupils. It should be noted, however, that TVEI funding was often used by single-sex schools to furnish and equip 'non-traditional' classrooms; a number of girls' schools used TVEI funding to build technology suites, for example, where previously there had been no such provision (HMI, 1985).

Secondly, there were often inherent problems in the timetabling of TVEI subjects. Teachers often complained that even though they offered an 'unlocked door', pupils continued to opt for traditional subjects. Putting aside more complicated considerations such as the social pressures to conform to a stereotyped curriculum (Ryrie et al, 1979; Pratt et al, 1984; Weiner, 1985c), there was often a simple structural explanation: inept and ill-conceived timetabling, whereby 'boys' subjects' were directly timetabled against 'girls' subjects' (Millman, 1985; McIntyre, 1987; Bridgwood and Betteridge, 1989), leaving pupils with an 'either/or' decision to make. This is a practice with a long history and reflects the extent to which many schools in the past expected such subjects to be more or less single sex, if they did not actually explicitly make them single sex subjects.

Further, in many projects TVEI subjects were only available as double options - Business Studies and Information Technology, for example, or a double CDT option. The Croft High School, for instance, timetabled a Business Studies/IT option against the only opportunity to study physics and chemistry on the timetable, whilst the double CDT option was timetabled against the only opportunity to study Home Economics, Art and Textiles. Leaving aside the considerable determination that would be needed in the first place for pupils to opt for non-traditional areas, pupils were also having to make choices which would deny them access to the security of a traditional option alongside a less traditional one. McIntyre (1987) actually noted that, in some projects, many girls had refused outright to consider CDT options if they could not study more traditional options alongside.

Thirdly, in many projects young people were inadequately informed about courses, or the information they were given tended to perpetuate gender divisions within the curriculum. Stoney and Froud (1986) studied TVEI publicity materials and option choice booklets from nearly one hundred TVEI schools. Whilst only five options booklets failed to mention TVEI's equal opportunities commitment, most booklets managed to undermine this commitment by the use of female-exclusive language, stereotypical cartoons and illustrations, or by stipulating certain entry criteria which effectively acted as a barrier to equal accessibility (prior use of tools, for example, as a condition of entry to CDT options in schools which did not have CDT as a core element of their lower school curriculum). Some schools sought to make certain subjects more attractive by simply renaming them. This was clearly likely to be counterproductive if course content remained the same, and so many projects took the logical step of introducing a range of new syllabuses. A good example of this is the replacement of 'Home Economics' with courses such as 'Food and Nutrition' or 'Food Studies', courses which deliberately emphasised their scientific and exploratory character in an attempt to avoid obvious associations with domestic circumstances (McIntyre, 1987, p.11). Whilst these new courses invariably succeeded in attracting greater numbers of boys, this was arguably at the price of a clear downgrading of traditionally female areas of knowledge in order to increase their attractiveness to boys.

The place of single sex provision

Despite the shared concerns of the pilot schools with encouraging the uptake of non-traditional subjects, there was extreme reluctance across the project to adopt any measures which might be interpreted as positive discrimination in favour of girls, the most obvious measure being the provision of single sex classes in certain subject areas. The national TVEI equal opportunities criterion implied that single sex classes would be the exception rather than the norm (boys and girls 'should normally be educated together on courses within each project'), yet the equal opportunities statement in Masonfield's original proposal to the MSC gave the schools *carte blanche* to provide single sex classes where necessary: ways of achieving equal opportunities, it stated, were likely to include 'separate opportunities for boys and girls leading to the same objectives'. David James, the central coordinator, was undoubtedly in favour of single sex provision in certain areas:

> What I was very concerned about was to get schools to understand that equal ops wasn't just the open door policy, that somehow girls and boys came equally to the starting line... but that they actually came with a whole repertoire of skills and background experiences and expectations and so on, and very early on we bought Val Millman's book on teaching technology to girls... and I used that - that was very soon after I came here - really as a way of starting, to get them to understand that people need to be prepared differently, particularly to succeed in technology and technological areas... there is evidence of (single sex provision) around the place, but people are very cagey about it' (David James, Central coordinator, 1992).

Indeed they were. The pilot schools were primarily concerned with encouraging integration rather than further segregation, which was reflected in some of the early gains in the pilot schools. Four of the five pilot schools changed their system of class registration, for example, ending the practice of listing pupils by gender and instead introducing alphabetical listings; pupils no longer had to sit in assembly according to their gender, but could sit where they wished; school uniform rules were changed in four of the schools to allow girls to wear trousers (and boys to wear earrings); St Catherine's changed their practice of appointing a head boy and a head girl and instead appointed two 'head pupils' chosen on merit alone (and in the first year of the change, both head pupils were girls); three of the schools introduced mixed games lessons in the upper school. These changes, which sought to alter the nature of the signals given out by elements of the hidden curriculum, were made fairly early on in the pilot phase and strove to make as little differentiation as possible between the educational experiences of boys and girls. It is not difficult to see, therefore, that single sex provision would have marked quite a departure from this integrationist trend.

The one exception to this in the early days of pilot was the decision of The Croft

High School to introduce single sex CDT teaching for third year pupils. This example will be examined in some detail because it highlights a number of the dilemmas and contradictions that the TVEI schools were forced to face up to in making single sex provision. The rationale behind the experiment was to 'try and overcome the reticence that girls would have towards the subject in the presence of boys' (second annual report). In recognition that a male CDT teacher was likely to aim lessons more at boys in a mixed environment, it was noted that a male teacher faced with an all-female class would be forced to modify his classroom practice towards 'a more neutral approach'. Greater attention was also paid to the suitability to girls of the design briefs and one of the first was to make a clock, as it was thought (apparently without irony) 'that perhaps the design of military vehicles and heavy articulated lorries was possibly not attractive to girls' (taken from a paper presented to the TVEI Consultative Committee, December 1988).

According to the second annual report, the girls had appreciated the benefits of single sex teaching, 'not distracted by what they consider to be immature behaviour patterns of the boys', whilst they felt that they were receiving far higher levels of individual attention than they would have done in a mixed environment (graphical descriptions of the attention-seeking strategies of boys in the CDT classroom are provided in Dixon, 1996 and 1997). However, none of the girls subsequently opted for CDT in the upper school, to the surprise of the teachers concerned, and a number of factors were felt to be important in explaining the apparent failure of the experiment. Some teachers felt that the intervention had come too late to have any serious impact on the girls' attitudes and that other options had been more attractive, whilst others felt that peer group and parental pressure were influential factors. No one appears, however, to have commented on the possible impact of the timetabling of CDT in the upper school. CDT, as noted above, was only offered as a double option subject and, whilst taking a double option in a traditional area would undoubtedly require high levels of commitment to the subject area, taking a double option in a non-traditional area would conceivably require even greater levels of determination and commitment. Moreover, by choosing a double option in CDT the girls would have been deprived of the security of choosing a more traditional option alongside, as CDT was timetabled against the only two columns in which Home Economics, Art and Textiles were to be found.

Another factor that was considered by The Croft High School was the possible impact of the lack of a female CDT teacher with whom the girls could identify. In a paper presented to the TVEI Consultative Committee in December 1988, this aspect was considered further: 'Compulsory redundancy did not allow the school to enter the open market (to recruit a new CDT teacher) - and would it have been 'equal opportunities' for the male applicants if the school had deliberately homed in on a female applicant?' Although hypothetical, this suggests that whilst the school was prepared to provide a girls-only group for CDT (which was unlikely to have harmed the educational chances of the boys in this subject area who, from the fourth year, were taught in single sex groups by default), it was not prepared to be seen to favour women at the *staff* level. (The Croft, it should be remembered, was the pilot school without any women in senior management). Legally, of course, the school would have been in breach of the Sex Discrimination Act if it had openly advertised for a female CDT teacher or had chosen a woman teacher purely on the basis of her sex, but Section 48 of the SDA does allow for 'special encouragement' to be given to the minority sex 'where there have been comparatively small numbers of persons of one sex in particular work for the previous 12 months'. The school could legally have taken positive measures, therefore, such as retraining existing female staff or giving positive encouragement to applications from women (EOC, 1991). However, even though the view was expressed that the appointment of a female CDT teacher might be a positive advantage to the girls in the school, their potentially enhanced position would have been 'sacrificed' in order to maintain the 'equality' of the male teaching staff, thus benefiting male pupils, who were already 'more equal than others' within the context of CDT teaching.

In spite of the success of the girls-only course in creating an enhanced learning environment, the experiment did not meet its stated objective of encouraging a greater number of girls to opt for CDT in the upper school. As a result of this 'failure', single sex teaching was discontinued - although CDT continued as a virtually single sex boys' subject by default. However, when interviewing the TVEI coordinator four years later, it became clear that the CDT teachers involved had had little commitment to teaching CDT to girls:

> The biggest problem was the fact that the people who are trying to do something have to have belief in what they are trying to do, and they've got to be convinced that they feel it's right and proper, and one or two individuals I believe didn't seem to think that CDT rooms were places for ladies - its got nothing to do with girls - along with a lot of other problems... (TVEI Coordinator, The Croft High School, June 1992).

Later in the pilot phase, two other schools experimented with single sex maths groups for lower school pupils. In both cases this was not strictly a TVEI initiative, but it sheds light on the conditions under which single sex provision was considered permissable. At St Catherine's, it was decided to teach the first years in single sex classes because of the tendency for boys to dominate classroom interaction (which was construed as a problem with girls and maths, rather than a problem with boys). However, the experiment was abandoned after one year when it transpired that the top group for the second year would be almost entirely female, the boys having failed to do as well as expected. At Seddon Park, a similar experiment was carried out with third year pupils, with the girls being taught by a woman and the boys being taught by a man. The TVEI coordinator remarked that,

> The interesting thing will be when we start looking at the results, because from what I've heard so far, the girls are absolutely bombing along, they've made

tremendous improvements. The lads - typical lads, you know - I wouldn't say they've digressed or gone worse or anything - pretty much the same. But it's certainly helped the girls, because in maths it's a subject where girls are very frightened to put their hand up and say, oh I know it, I've done this, with lads watching, because of the stick they get - a lot of peer pressure (TVEI coordinator, Seddon Park, February 1992).

When asked if it would continue in future years, the coordinator commented on the futility of the experiment if it *wasn't* continued, given its apparent popularity (although popularity of itself was no guarantee of single sex provision being continued at The Croft High School). He also noted, however, that the female maths teacher would be leaving the school that year, and he doubted whether the experiment would be such a success if the girls were taught by a male member of staff.

At the heart of this discussion of single sex provision lies a question which strikes at one of the essential differences between the radical and liberal approaches to gender inequality: 'what should be done about the boys?', a question which has attracted considerable attention in the last few years due to the much-publicised trends in GCSE performance. In general, the pilot schools shared a belief that single sex provision was not really fair to the boys, that this in itself constituted unequal access and was therefore discriminatory. Rather, it was felt that equal opportunities practice should be seen to be scrupulously fair to the boys as well. This attitude is consistent with a liberal feminist approach to gender inequality, and is an approach which tends to ignore the very different starting points for boys and girls, thus denying the power dimension of gender inequalities. The needs of girls and boys with regard to gender inequalities are cast as being essentially the same, with any attempt to differentiate between those needs constituting an act of discrimination in itself. For proponents of a more radical, anti-sexist approach, single sex events and teaching groups are a key element in bringing about change in the educational experiences of young women, and are seen to compensate for the otherwise male dominated educational experiences of girls. Thus, it is not a case of girls being offered something extra and boys being neglected, but rather of girls being given the same treatment that boys have effectively enjoyed throughout their educational experiences (Mahony, 1985).

Conclusion

There was possibly more time spent on finding ways of encouraging non-traditional option choice than on any other aspect of equal opportunities within TVEI. It was the major focus of both of the two main TVEI equal opportunities reports (McIntyre, 1987; Bridgwood and Betteridge, 1989), whilst the pages of the National Equal Opportunities Network abounded with case studies on this theme. Moreover, it was a closely monitored aspect of equal opportunities. During the Pilot years both the National Foundation for Educational Research and Trent Polytechnic were commissioned to establish databases on TVEI participation, whilst a TVEI Extension Database was set up by the Training Agency, with annual returns required from individual projects providing data on subject take-up by gender. This focus is hardly surprising, given that the original TVEI equal opportunities statement focused on this very issue, whilst TVEI's success in encouraging young people to pursue non-traditional careers and courses post-16 was almost entirely dependent on its success in encouraging young people to choose non-traditional options pre-16 by way of preparation. Given this concern, it would have seemed essential for TVEI projects to ensure that any efforts to promote equal opportunities within individual schools should be brought together to form a cohesive whole in the eyes of the pupils involved, thus avoiding the dangers of sending out mixed messages. That this was invariably not the case will become evident in the next chapter, which examines the often counter-productive initiatives which were initiated under the auspices of the overtly work-related curriculum which TVEI introduced into schools.

7 TVEI and the 'world of work'

Introduction

The development of close links with the 'world of work' was an integral part of the broader TVEI project. TVEI's *raison d'être* was the preparation of young people for their post-school adult lives, and great emphasis was placed on ensuring that pupils developed a keen awareness of the opportunities that were potentially open to them. The provision of good quality careers education and guidance, therefore, was clearly a crucial element and under the auspices of TVEI's own careers education and guidance programme a number of special events were held. However, without a doubt the 'jewel in the crown' was surely TVEI's extensive programme of work experience, which rapidly spread across the secondary sector, beyond the boundaries of TVEI. This chapter considers the centrality of careers education and guidance within TVEI's broader brief, and then explores the impact of work experience. In particular, it focuses on the difficult problem that work experience posed for TVEI's effective promotion of equal opportunities.

Careers education and guidance for TVEI pupils

At the time of TVEI's launch in 1986, the Masonfield Careers Service had a team of school-based careers officers, each working with a small group of high schools, and the bulk of their time was spent working with final year pupils. Each final year pupil had at least one vocational guidance interview with a careers officer; they would be encouraged to think constructively about the options open to them, and would be provided with any additional support needed, such as the provision of relevant literature, the organisation of interviews with prospective employers or training agencies, or indeed a further careers interview. Each school also had a careers teacher, whose efforts were also invariably concentrated on fifth year pupils, although they also had an important role to play in the upper school option choice process. In addition to in-school careers work, upper school pupils attended the annual cross-LEA careers convention, where they could meet with representatives from local employers, training providers and post-16 educational institutions.

Under TVEI, this 'standard' provision was enhanced with the appointment of a centrally-based careers officer, whose role was to provide a direct link between the careers service, the central team and the TVEI schools. In the early years of pilot, though, the TVEI careers officer tended to take on the standard workload of the school's careers officer amongst TVEI pupils, rather than supplementing the latter's usual work. By the third year, however, the TVEI careers officer took on a more strategic role within the wider programme of careers education and guidance within pilot schools. At St Catherine's, for example, she began to provide 'more individual guidance of a continuous nature' for fourth year TVEI pupils, complementing the work of the school's careers officer (Second Annual Report).

The work of the careers officer was also supplemented by a series of special one-off careers events, such as the 'Women in Industry' event which was organised in the second year of pilot. Representatives from local firms and colleges offering 'non-traditional' employment and training opportunities were invited to this event, which was aimed at young women in their final two years of high school. The girls were encouraged to talk to the representatives about opportunities in these areas and an evening session, with input from women speakers, was also organised, to which parents were invited. The event was generally considered to have been a success by all involved. An equally successful girls-only event was organised the following autumn, 'Different Sex, Different Future?', a one-day conference for year nine girls. The workshop sessions were led by women who were either employed in non-traditional occupational areas or who were in senior management positions in local firms, and the workshops covered topics such as learning to recognise stereotyping, the implications of the Sex Discrimination Act, balancing home and work, and identifying skills. Again, there was an evening event aimed at parents, teachers, careers officers, local employers and governors. Individual schools also ran similar events, such as St Catherine's 'World of Work' days for boys and girls. Events such as these tended to benefit whole year groups, rather than TVEI pupils alone, but were made possible by TVEI funding.

Young people who had been involved in TVEI tended to have strong views on the subject of careers education and guidance. Respondents to the Leavers Survey had had, on average, three careers interviews in their final two years in school, and the vast majority of leavers valued the advice they had received, feeling that their careers teachers and officers had done their best to be helpful in the face of a difficult job. Even so, with hindsight many were critical of the way in which advice had been given. The comments of many of the respondents suggested that they felt that certain options had been pushed to the exclusion of others: either particular jobs or schemes, particular colleges or particular courses. These sentiments received an echo in the fuller comments of ex-TVEI pupils interviewed in the follow-up study:

> They tried to push you into something... we all thought it was a waste of time at first, because if you had made up your mind, it was as if (careers officers) were pushing you or something (Paul).

> They tried to shuffle us off into jobs they wanted us to have. I said I wanted to be a draughtsman and the careers officer at the time said, 'actually, there's not much call for that at the moment... why don't you try this, that and the other?' (John).

These comments raise a critical issue in the provision of careers guidance - the extent to which an interventionist approach should be adopted. In an interview in August 1991, the principal careers officer stressed that a non-interventionist approach, which failed to ask pupils to justify their career ideas, had the effect of reducing careers officers to little more than providers of information, and not providers of *guidance*. However, she argued that it was often extremely difficult to 'encourage' pupils to consider alternative careers (even alternative 'traditional' careers) if they had already made up their minds, and it was perhaps not surprising if the attempts of careers officers to encourage young people to widen their horizons met with some resentment.

The positions that individual careers advisers adopted on this question clearly had serious implications for the promotion of non-traditional occupations as, if left unchallenged, most young people would have been considering careers traditionally associated with their gender. Respondents to the Leavers Survey were asked whether they had ever been encouraged by either a careers officer or by any of their teachers to think about pursuing a career or a post-16 course more commonly followed by someone of the opposite sex. Overall, only one in five of the leavers said that they had been encouraged to think in terms of non-traditional careers or courses - not that they were necessarily interested in this advice. However, young women were *five times* more likely than young men to have received advice of this kind, confirming Coles and Maynard's view that careers officers are mainly concerned with promoting opportunities for women in predominantly male occupational areas, rather than the reverse (Coles and Maynard, 1990). In contrast, one young woman commented that,

> The Careers Officer (male) kept trying to change my mind and offering me information on things I had no interest in... A careers officer once said to me, after I'd explained that I wanted to join the police, 'have you ever thought about nursing?' ('A' level student two years after leaving high school).

The young women were also asked about the 'Women in Industry' event held in the second year of pilot (when they had been in year 10). All those interviewed could remember the event, although not all had attended. The message of the event had been clear to them, however; Jane said it was about 'women doing men's jobs', whilst Karen had 'got the impression that they was trying to like push women into the kind of areas that men had just been'. Although she didn't feel that the day had been relevant to her personally, she felt that some young women did benefit from the event's message: 'you got the odd girl that would just be different, and say well I'm definitely going to do this now, after going to something like that...' The idea that some girls were considering non-traditional careers 'just to be different' was echoed by David, who commented that 'I know some people wanted to copy off Kylie, you know...', (a reference to the singer Kylie Minogue who at the time was portraying a female car mechanic in the Australian soap 'Neighbours'). Even if 'Women in Industry' had achieved its goal of raising awareness, young women who subsequently opted for non-traditional careers were therefore likely to have their motivation questioned by their peers. As both Cockburn (1987) and Stafford (1991) have found, many people appear to find it hard to believe that young women will choose non-traditional careers without having ulterior motives for doing so.

The comments of the young people involved in TVEI suggest that they had mixed views about the value of some of the careers advice they had received, or the manner in which it was given. Some pupils had been encouraged through their careers interviews to broaden their horizons, but most felt that the guidance they were given in this regard was irrelevant to their plans, which were already firmly set. The Principal Careers Officer was in favour of events such as 'Women in Industry', but was aware that they highlighted a general lack of support for young people with non-traditional career plans. She believed that more needed to be done to provide ongoing support to such young people, and that the onus was on the Careers Service to ensure that any potential obstacles were removed from their paths. She also acknowledged that there was a fine line to be drawn between ensuring that young people were aware of the discrimination they were likely to face if they opted for non-traditional careers and providing this information in such a way that they were not deterred from their chosen career.

Her main concern, however, was that careers education and guidance throughout most of the TVEI Pilot period tended to exist in a vacuum and was not sufficiently grounded in the curricular experiences of pupils more widely. As a consequence, equal opportunities work under the auspices of careers education and guidance tended to be somewhat tokenistic. In particular, the lack of an integrated cross-curriculum careers education programme meant that pupils were liable to receive mixed messages about appropriate gender roles. Clearly, the message of an event like 'Women in Industry' could easily be undermined by injudicious remarks made by classroom teachers, but this would be hard to monitor, let alone control. However, it was also clear that the message of such an event could be easily undermined by *legitimate* aspects of the curriculum, and one of the chief concerns of the Principal Careers Officer was the negative effect of work experience within a broader equal opportunities framework. The provision of 'appropriate planned work experience as an integral part of programmes' (TVEI Unit, 1985), was actually another of the key funding criteria for TVEI projects, alongside the equal opportunities criterion. Yet it was here that the inherent problems of promoting equal opportunities within a vocational context were foregrounded:

> If all these things only happen in isolation... then you actually haven't got a whole, you've got a lot of piecemeal bits, that each could be working against the other, so you're actually running to stand still... Nobody actually makes the connection between work experience and curriculum experience and their decisions beyond 16, because it's not seen as a whole approach, it's not seen as having an influence; it's short-sighted (Principal Careers Officer, August 1991).

Work experience under TVEI

Work experience - described by HMI as the 'jewel in the crown of a programme of industrial and economic understanding' (HMI, 1990) - was by no means unheard of before the launch of TVEI in 1982, but it was under TVEI that it became widespread, soon being extended beyond the boundaries of the TVEI cohort (Fuller, 1987). By Spring 1986, 80 per cent of TVEI pupils had had at least one week of work experience (Sims, 1987); by 1991/92, 91 per cent of *all* year eleven pupils had been on work experience, an achievement which has been linked to TVEI's influence (DTI, 1994).

Work experience, by definition, involves a close engagement with the needs of local labour markets (Stronach, 1984), yet TVEI projects were ultimately reliant on a source of supply which was outside their direct control. Moreover, they were faced with the task of finding placements with employers whose recruitment practices were not generally informed by the equal opportunities ideals espoused in TVEI's first funding criteria. This left schools in a double bind: trying to fulfil the equal opportunities criterion, yet simultaneously having to introduce pupils to a 'world of work' characterised by gender inequalities (Howieson, 1990). Thus,

> a vocationalist view of work experience linked to the labour-power needs of industry, and resting on industrial and commercial realism, ultimately degenerates into support for gender and race inequalities when viewed in a recruitment context (Ribowski, 1992, p.20).

For these reasons, throughout TVEI's existence work experience represented a major site of struggle and contradiction for educationists committed to gender equality.

The DES had viewed work experience primarily as an educational activity, but under TVEI's influence there was a gradual shift towards a view that work experience was an important way of moving the curriculum closer to the needs of industry (Shilling, 1991). By 1984 the MSC were claiming that it was integral to providing an 'early' and 'permanent bridge between school and work' (MSC, 1984), a phrase which was also used to describe the Youth Training Scheme, which included a work experience element. However, despite the importance attached to work experience, the MSC failed to provide clear guidelines, leaving individual TVEI projects with considerable latitude to develop customised approaches. Some projects created work simulation centres, others opted for work shadowing programmes, but the majority developed programmes in which pupils spent one or two weeks on a placement within local workplaces, engaged whenever possible in 'real work' (McIntyre, 1988).

In many projects, work experience was organised through 'Project Trident', a privately sponsored agency responsible for recruiting, allocating and monitoring work experience. However, Trident operated to the benefit of participating employers rather than schools. For example, Trident allowed firms to participate on a trial basis, but it was clear that it was the education system which was on trial, rather than employers (Dale et al, 1992). Employers were given the final say in selecting pupils, with Trident information booklets often describing placements in terms of their suitability for boys or girls (ibid). Further, there was no obligation on participating firms to comply with TVEI's equal opportunities commitment. Thus, Trident acted as a broker for employers in mediating pre-existing social divisions within the labour market.

Other projects organised work experience through their LEA Careers Service or left the organisation to individual schools. Either way, efforts to promote equal opportunities were continually thwarted. The unwillingness of employers to provide non-traditional placements was not the only obstacle, however. Firstly, many pupils equated work experience with job-sampling, with few expressing preferences for non-traditional placements (Cross, 1987; McIntyre, 1988). Secondly, parental consent was needed before a placement could be confirmed, and parents were often unwilling to expose their children to non-traditional workplaces. Thirdly, many teachers similarly sought to protect pupils from 'bad experiences' within non-traditional environments (Bridgwood and Betteridge, 1989). These factors all tended to reinforce stereotypical patterns in the labour market, a cause for concern which was highlighted on numerous occasions (HMI, 1985; Bridgwood and Betteridge, 1989; Sims, 1987; McIntyre, 1988; Barnes et al, 1989a and 1989b; DES, 1991). Tables 7.1 and 7.2 reproduce the findings of Sims (1987), typical of all the surveys in this area, showing not only the gender differentiation in terms of workplace location of TVEI students, but also differentiation in terms of the activities engaged in within those workplaces. It was not uncommon, for example, for girls to be given placements in engineering firms, only to find themselves based in an office. Dale et al (1990) also argue that a small minority of the TVEI pupils who did manage to secure non-traditional placements were subjected to sexual harassment whilst working in environments dominated by the opposite sex.

Table 7.1
Occupational location of fifth year students' TVEI work experience

Type of occupation	% of total respondents	% of students citing each occupation	
		Boys	Girls
Admin., clerical & office work	19	42	58
Manufacturing, assembly & processing	14	81	19
Caring, community, education & health	14	15	85
Retail & sales	14	49	51
Installation, maintenance & repair	10	96	4
Food preparation & service	5	32	68
Computers & electronics	5	86	14

N=2616, excluding 715 non-respondents
Other types of work experience were each cited by less than 5% of respondents, who could record more than one work experience location.

Source: Sims (1987)

Table 7.2
Fifth year students' activities in TVEI work experience

Activity	% of total respondents	% of students citing each activity	
		Boys	Girls
Admin., clerical & office work	30	43	57
Retail & sales	13	46	54
Installation, maintenance & repair	11	98	2
Caring, community, education & health	11	11	89
Manufacturing, assembly & processing	10	90	10
Computers & electronics	7	80	20
Food preparation & service	7	32	68
General (low-level/ 'dogsbody')	6	59	41
Variety/ range of tasks	5	65	35

N=2605, excluding 726 non-respondents

Source: Sims (1987)

Work experience was actually relatively uncommon in Masonfield before TVEI's launch. Under TVEI funding, work experience was organised by each individual school, although the LEA's Careers Service was responsible for ensuring the quality of placements and provided training for work experience coordinators in each of the participating schools. Work experience was typically available to pupils at the end of year ten for a period of one week, although some students arranged to return in their holidays for a further period. Initially, only designated TVEI students were offered placements, but provision soon spread not only beyond these students, but to schools outside of the Pilot scheme.

Masonfield's work experience policy statement noted its value in easing the transition from school to work, but sought to translate any vocational lessons learnt straight back into the educational experiences of pupils. The benefits of involvement in work experience were seen to include the provision of insights into work, increased awareness of the relevance of study, the acquisition of greater self-confidence, improvements in powers of expression and the ability to assess careers advice in a more purposeful way. Despite the best efforts of work experience organisers, however, these wider insights often went unnoticed. A survey of TVEI pupils in Stockport, for example, found that 46 per cent of pupils could not think of any subject areas in which they had 'used something I learnt or experienced during my placement' since returning from work experience, whilst 45 per cent felt that they had learnt more about the world of work from their paid part-time jobs than they had from their placements (Tapp, 1990).

For students, work experience was widely viewed as an unprecedented opportunity to 'sample' occupational areas of interest, to the point that the success or failure of an individual placement was judged almost entirely in terms of its relevance to their career plans. Amongst respondents to the leavers survey, 52 per cent of young women and 59 per cent of young men said that work experience had provided the opportunity to try out a job of interest. Further, 28 per cent of young women and 30 per cent of young men said that their placement had helped them to make up their minds about the jobs they wanted to do. A minority of young people were dissatisfied with work experience, and their comments suggested disappointment at the lack of a 'relevant' placement. For example, one young woman had wanted experience of accountancy, but ended up 'doing the work of a secretary'. The follow-up interviews found further evidence of the link between dissatisfaction and occupational irrelevance. Jane had wanted to gain nursing experience, her preferred career at that time:

> Mine was a waste of time, it really were. I mean, they tried their best, but I said I wanted to go on a ward... so they sent me to a dentist! ... I ended up like typing the odd bit of typing - they wouldn't even allow me in the dentist's surgery!... I mean I wouldn't have minded if I could have gone in and observed

Table 7.3
Work experience placements amongst a sample of cohort II pupils (numbers)

	Girls	Boys	All
Clerical work	16	16	32
Retail	2	3	5
Service/caring[1]	12	3	15
Catering	3	2	5
Engineering	0	6	6
Maintenance/construction	0	2	2
Factory/warehouse	1	4	5
Drawing office	0	2	2
Other[2]	3	0	3
Total	37	37	74

Notes:
[1] Includes placements in hospitals, schools, sports centres and cleaning work
[2] Security guard, library assistant and vetinerary assistant

Source: Masonfield School Leavers Survey

the dentist... but they wouldn't let me in, full stop.

Karen related a similar tale of disappointment:

> It was at Tesco, you know. I mentioned at the time that I wanted to go into personnel management, so it was a bit of a shock really, it was silly, but you know, you have all these visions, you know, walking round in a suit and everything. So anyway, I turned up, they took me to this room, filled out a bit of paper and that - right, you'll need this hat and this coat - I thought, coat? A white hat and a white coat - I was in the bakery department!

Karen had soon realised that her own expectations had been unrealistic - 'when you think about it they're not exactly going to put me in a situation where you're personnel manager, are they?!' - and, although 'a bit annoyed', she had actually enjoyed the experience. Both these examples, however, highlight that it was often impossible to find placements in pupils' chosen career areas because of their age and inexperience. So what kinds of placements were young people given? The next section addresses this question.

The nature of work experience placements

In a circular to schools in 1988, the DES acknowledged the dangers of giving pupils a free choice of placement:

> (Schools) should consider how far they should allow their pupils an unfettered choice in placements - when these choices may reflect unduly narrow horizons - whilst being sensitive to the risk that pressing pupils into fields in which they feel uncomfortable may be counterproductive (DES, 1988).

If the placements given to TVEI pupils in Masonfield were based on their career plans, they would certainly have tended to reflect 'unduly narrow horizons', given the high degree of stereotyping surrounding their career plans. Table 7.3 illustrates the nature of work done on placements by respondents to the postal survey. It highlights the extent to which young men and women were indeed gaining experience of quite different occupational areas, confirming the impression received from work experience coordinators and the often sketchy data provided by the Pilot schools in their annual reports. Interestingly, equal numbers of both male and female respondents had been allocated to clerical placements, although this probably reflects the popularity of Information Technology and Business Studies (both TVEI subjects) amongst both boys and girls, and the desire of this group of pupils to sample work in related areas. Table 7.3 also highlights the extent to which young men were spread more evenly across a fuller range of placements, whilst young women were concentrated within a narrower range of occupational areas.

Work experience providers in Masonfield were required to sign an undertaking which included a commitment to 'offer places to male and female students' and to provide 'the opportunity for them to sample work normally undertaken by the opposite gender'. Thus, even within the bounds of an apparently traditional placement there should have been scope for innovation, yet this latter undertaking was rarely fulfilled. Indeed, in some instances employers did not even fulfil the first part of the undertaking. One coordinator noted, for example, that 'problems have been encountered with certain employers who refuse to accept pupils of a particular gender in certain work areas'. Another coordinator highlighted the difficulties she had faced in finding non-traditional placements for girls. She spoke of employers who were taken aback when the young person for whom a placement had been arranged 'turned out' to be female and not male, prompting comments such as 'bring her down and I'll vet her over and then I'll make my decision.' Other employers had argued that their premises lacked suitable toilet facilities for women, that the working conditions were unattractive, or even that they would distract male employees. She had, however, managed to organise a small number of successful non-traditional placements, as had the coordinator at a third school:

> It's not easy, but we find it's not as if 20 or 30 kids all want it, we just get a few - if there's only a few, there's a chance of sorting it. I think a few years ago, when we got our first mechanic down at the district garage, a lot of the garages were very apprehensive - not because 'we don't want girls' - it was how their staff would react to the girl - is it fair putting a girl in a situation with, say, 20 lads? and that was more a concern for the girl's welfare than the equal ops side. But one or two have been very good - like hairdressing, we had a lad into that.

Ultimately, however, pupils rarely sought non-traditional placements. In the majority of cases, work experience organisers were merely responding to specific requests for placements in traditional areas, as these were the occupational areas in which they hoped to pursue careers on leaving school. The shortcomings of this approach, given TVEI's wider equal opportunities commitment, was not lost on work experience coordinators. One noted for example that,

> Our present work experience system, which allows pupils to specify the nature of their employment placement may serve to reinforce stereotyping by failing to introduce pupils to other careers possibilities.

This is not to argue that efforts were never made to encourage pupils to choose non-traditional placements. However, it was undoubtedly far easier from the point of view of the organisers' workloads to place pupils in traditional placements, in line with the expressed wishes of the majority of the young people themselves. Given the link in pupils' minds between successful placements and their career relevance, a propaganda war would have needed to be won before convincing the majority of pupils that they should choose a placement for reasons other than its career-relevance.

One of the greatest ironies of work experience from an equal opportunities viewpoint was that some young people who expressly indicated an interest in a non-traditional or slightly unusual career pathway on leaving school often ended up being allocated to some of the most traditional of placements. This was partly by default, as by the time it was clear that in most cases such placements were impossible to negotiate, the most exciting but nonetheless stereotypical placements had been snapped up by other pupils. This left only placements such as clerical or caring work which were always plentiful and relatively straightforward to arrange. It is particularly regrettable that pupils who were prepared to innovate were not given the opportunity to put their ideas into practice. Moreover, it seems disingenuous to argue that work experience was not about job sampling, and that young people should not have been disappointed if appropriate placements proved impossible to organise, when the majority of pupils *were* able to have placements in their chosen (traditional) field. The group who often seemed to miss out under this system were precisely those who wished to challenge the status quo.

In some cases, coordinators tried their best to find non-traditional placements, only to see their efforts backfire. For example, young women were occasionally placed in engineering companies, but ended up in the general office. Amanda, one of the TVEI leavers interviewed two years after leaving school, had such an experience. She had wanted to be a policewoman, and was accordingly placed at the Regional Police Training College - where she spent most of the week engaged in ironing and cleaning. She said she had enjoyed the week, but made it clear that the best feature had not been the work itself:

SH You enjoyed it? What made it for you?
A   The policemen!
SH They were all young police cadets were they?
A   I don't know what they was, but they were very nice!

Amanda had undoubtedly learnt a great deal about the social relations of waged labour within the police force from this placement, but not in ways that her teachers had anticipated! Her comments were made somewhat tongue-in-cheek, but a serious point lies behind them. Despite the rhetoric concerning the educational value of work experience, all too often the most important lessons that young people appeared to be learning were reinforcements of gender-appropriate behaviour, both in terms of social relations and the sexual division of labour.

These are criticisms of which the central coordinator in Masonfield was acutely aware but, given the high rates of adult unemployment in the city, he remained a strong defender of work experience for pragmatic reasons. For many young people, he argued, it represented their only real link to the contemporary labour market:

> (T)he traditional sources of employment and information about employment in the home and in the extended family and in the community weren't there, and work experience therefore did at least give kids a real taste that very often their parents denied. That's a very important experience, even if it's a bad one, in that sense.

He stressed work experience's potential for generating debate about traditional gender roles, but admitted that briefing and debriefing were often carried out inadequately and failed to include the issue of equal opportunities 'as part of the totality of the experience'. He also re-emphasised the economic climate in which work experience in Masonfield operated:

> It's a difficult problem; certainly in the mid-80s, we had a period in 86/87 when more girls were getting jobs than boys, but in traditional occupations. The problem is there's a strong economic logic to traditional gender roles; you're much more likely to get a job as a typist or a shop worker than you are anything else in Masonfield, and you're more likely to get it if you're a girl than you are seeking to get an industrial training or whatever...

The deterrent effect of work experience

Work experience had the potential to produce a strong 'deterrent effect' amongst some pupils, as they found that the reality of the job to which they aspired differed considerably from their expectations. Amongst respondents to the postal survey, for example, 28 per cent of young women and 30 per cent of young men said that work experience had 'helped me make up my mind about the job I wanted to do', yet a third of both young men and women agreed that 'work experience put me off doing that type of work when I left school'. For many pupils, work experience had actually thrown them into uncertainty about the future. In at least one of the pilot schools there was an explicit acknowledgement of the way in which this deterrent effect could be harnessed to equal opportunities ends:

> The banks request that only students of 'average-plus' ability are sent out to them on work experience. As a result the most able Business and Information Studies students are often placed in banks. They have returned disillusioned, feeling that the new skills they have acquired have not been utilised whilst on work experience. Often able girls in school are sent out, who are not considered to be achieving their full potential, in a concerted effort to encourage them to be more ambitious in their career choices.

In some cases, therefore, traditional placements served an equal opportunities function, by highlighting the drawbacks of certain careers and by encouraging young people to raise their aspirations.

Conclusion

TVEI pupils were acutely aware of the adult 'world of work' during their final two years of compulsory schooling. In part this was due to the careers education and guidance which they received in school, but also the additional events in which they were involved, the most influential of which was work experience. It cannot be ignored that work experience remained extremely popular amongst TVEI pupils. The vast majority greatly enjoyed their placements and expressed the view that it had been of value to them both socially and educationally (Sims, 1987; Barnes, 1989b). The enthusiasm with which it was thus greeted tended to serve as a 'common sense legitimation' for TVEI's work experience programme, even though the very nature of work experience tended to undermine TVEI's wider policy commitment to equal opportunities. It could also be argued that work experience was actually of negligible value to TVEI's new vocationalist agenda, never mind to its supposed commitment to equal opportunities. TVEI aimed to facilitate a smooth transition into the 'changing world of work', yet it is hard to understand how the placing of young people into stereotypical placements, invariably engaged in low level tasks, could in any way have contributed to the acquisition of both specific and generic skills and the development of a flexible work force (Dale et al, 1990). (It is, however, relatively easy to imagine how this process served the needs of a sexually divided labour market.) Ribowski (1992) goes further, and questions whether work experience could in any sense be regarded as essential to the process of transition, given that employers place little value on the experience. Its only value to employers, he argues, may lie in providing evidence of a prior interest in a particular area of work, which places at a disadvantage those young people who are directed into placements which are unrelated to their career plans. As we have seen, these are often young people with non-traditional aspirations. Mizen (1992) has also argued that work experience programmes presuppose that pupils are inexperienced with regard to the 'world of work', thus denying the importance of 'the very real cultural competence' most young people gain from widespread child labour.

So how successful was TVEI in affecting pupils' post-school destinations? The next chapter examines this issue by means of secondary analysis of Masonfield Careers Service annual destinations data. The chapter starts with an overview of ethnographic literature which has sought to explain the experiences of young people as they move from school to the youth labour market, and it highlights the experiences of young people in both traditional and non-traditional occupational areas.

8 Post-16 destinations: A 'touchstone' for measuring progress?

Introduction

One of the key policy objectives of TVEI was to encourage the development of a flexible workforce. One strand of this objective was the fostering of a willingness amongst young women to consider non-traditional occupations in response to the projected national shortage of school leavers available for recruitment into traditionally male-dominated occupational areas. Following on from this theme, an editorial in the newsletter of TVEI's National Equal Opportunities Network noted that 'we have been focusing in on the importance of post-school destinations as a 'touchstone' for measuring real progress in outcomes terms of EO development work' (NEON, 1989, p.6). The post-school destinations of TVEI leavers were clearly seen, therefore, as one of the key outcome indicators of the success or otherwise of TVEI's equal opportunities policy. In this and the next chapter, a detailed analysis is provided of the actual destinations of leavers from the TVEI pilot schools and their experiences once in the labour market. To provide a broader context to the Masonfield data drawn upon in these two chapters, however, this chapter begins with an overview of research findings drawn from a number of key ethnographic accounts of gendered transitions from school to work. In line with TVEI's own emphasis, the focus is on studies of young women moving into female- and male-dominated occupational areas, and considers some of the chief factors which appear to influence young people in their post-16 career decisions.

Ethnographic accounts of gendered transitions

The publication of Willis' *Learning to Labour* back in 1977 paved the way for a tradition of ethnographic studies of young people in transition from school to work. Willis' work was concerned with the way in which young working class men - the 'lads' - effectively reproduced their own working class identity through their resistance to middle class forms of education, and his work highlighted the importance of hard physical labour to the lads' sense of masculine identity. However, his work was widely criticised for its attempts to develop a model of transition which could be applied to other sub-sections of the youth population, including young women, even though the focus of his research was concerned solely with the transition of young white working class *men* into the labour market. Moreover, their transition was characterised by a deeply ingrained and oppressive sexism, which Willis largely failed to address, even though it was a central theme in much of the material he presented in support of his arguments.

In the twenty years since Willis' study was first published, a number of studies have attempted to fill the gaps left by his work. Many of these studies have been written from a feminist perspective and have either looked at the experiences of young women alone or, in looking at both young men and young women, have not assumed that their experiences will be identical. More recent work has also considered the very different experiences of black young women. This section provides an overview of the feminist riposte to Willis' work, highlighting the experiences firstly of young women moving into traditional areas of employment, particularly into office and clerical work, and secondly of young women moving into non-traditional areas of employment. Central to both sets of experiences are the concepts of 'glamour', 'romance' and 'reputation', concepts which it is argued effectively police the decisions and behaviour of many young women on leaving school, such that the vast majority will opt for traditional areas of employment. The use of such concepts sits comfortably with contemporary interests in schooling and the making of masculinities and femininities, and highlight the importance of image, desire and identity as important concerns in young people's decision making processes.

Moving into traditional women's work

Office work remains one of the most popular occupational areas to which young white women aspire (Sharpe, 1976; Griffin, 1985; Cockburn, 1987). It has been argued that central to the appeal of work in an office is the (invariably unfulfilled) notion of 'glamour', as well as notions of appropriate, acceptable forms of femininity. Sharpe's early study, for instance, found that young women believed that office work represented a 'nice job for a girl'. Not only did they feel that office work would be intrinsically interesting, but that it would pay good money and give them the chance to travel and meet people, a point noted too by Sheratt (1983). Griffin (1985), Hollands (1990) and Gaskell (1992) have similarly found that many young women are attracted to office work because they feel it offers them a very real chance to 'get on' in life. Hollands, for example, has argued that office and clerical work (particularly within the context of youth training) represents a 'glam transition', offering a clear distinction between 'respectable' work and less respectable work, such as factory work, even though young women on clerical YTS placements are often performing extremely mundane duties. Central to the 'glam' transition is the notion of 'careerism', which promises individual opportunity and success to young women who wish to 'get ahead'. Thus, office work is thought to offer the possibility of a glamorous lifestyle and the prospect of promotion and success: 'A job in an office conjured up a picture of clean modern rooms, full of 'nice' smartly dressed and made-up young women; a polite and middle class image of femininity' (Griffin, 1985, p.102).

This last point is critical to the appeal of traditional female occupations. It is argued that they offer an idealised, unambiguously heterosexual version of femininity at a time when young women are feeling extremely vulnerable about their sexual identity. Griffin (1985) and Cockburn (1987) have both clearly shown that young women in transition from school to work are not only having to manage the economic and social pressures of finding and keeping a job, but are also having to manage the pressures of 'finding a man'. Thus, they are having to compete in both the labour market and the 'sexual market', the latter being characterised by 'compulsory heterosexuality' (Rich, 1980): 'Seen in this light, the fact that offices have clear-cut masculine and feminine roles makes them positively attractive to heterosexual young women' (Cockburn, 1987, p.118). The importance of self-image is also supported by recent research conducted by the Health Education Authority (Boseley, 1995), which found that teenage girls' placed a very high emphasis on being liked, on being seen as good company, as confident and outgoing: looking attractive was, however, considered fundamental to being liked.

The working class young women in Griffin's study felt that office work offered them the chance to escape from their expected lower status, not least through the opportunities they believed it offered to better themselves through meeting men of higher social status. Moreover, the full-time wage gave them access to more exciting and expensive leisure activities, thereby providing an alternative forum for finding potential boyfriends. Although office work invariably failed to live up to the young women's expectations, at least it was a 'respectable job', in contrast to factory work, which apart from being monotonous and unpleasant with regard to working conditions, was tied up with very different notions of femininity, with the risk of being seen as 'vulgar' and 'not nice' (Sharpe, 1976; Griffin, 1985; Wallace, 1986).

Mirza (1992) notes that office work is becoming increasingly attractive to second generation black women, particularly those from working class backgrounds, yet she is dismissive of the relevance of the above arguments to the desire of young black women to work in this area. On the contrary, she argues that young black women regard office work as providing them with the opportunity to acquire status and prospects in an occupational area which has previously been denied them because of racism. Mirza argues that office work is regarded very much as an upwardly mobile choice, particularly amongst young women whose parents are located within unpleasant, poorly paid, unskilled and semi-skilled occupations. Indeed, she argues that young black women are effectively redefining the meaning of women's work: they do not see office work as degrading, or as a temporary position before marriage, but rather regard it as an opportunity for career advancement within the constraints placed upon them by racism in other occupational areas.

Whilst office work is becoming increasingly popular amongst young black women, Mirza notes that jobs within the caring professions are by far the most popular choice. It has often been argued that caring occupations serve as a form of 'domestic apprenticeship' (Deem, 1978; Hollands, 1990; Bates, 1993a), but Mirza argues that for black women this is to deny the complications of the process of black occupational choice. She argues that the appeal of caring work is not based on black young women's subjective perceptions of their femininity (in contrast to Bates' 1993a arguments concerning white female care workers), but is based on rather more pragmatic and rational reasons: as a means of maximising occupational mobility. Thus, the caring professions, most notably social work and nursing, have historically offered black women the opportunity for social mobility, not least because of the opportunities to obtain higher educational qualifications which go hand in hand with the choice of such careers.

Bates (1993b) has made similar comments about the choice of fashion design as a career amongst upper working class and lower middle class young women. She notes that the fashion industry is undoubtedly based on notions of female dependence on 'attractiveness', but argues that the choice of such careers also represents a form of resistance to stereotypes of traditional feminine behaviour, as they are seen as offering a means to achieving *in*dependence, mobility and emancipation from domestic responsibilities. Bates describes the young women in her study in the following terms:

> Out of the traditional female domain of dress-making they were making post-feminist, 'cosmopolitan' woman, blending sexual power and career power, and magically free from childcare... it offered all the attractions of a Post-Fordist, individualistic, enterprise career path which could be carved out in an international arena, transcending the generally more fettered forms of female labour (Bates, 1993b, p.72).

In reality, however, only a tiny number of the students in Bates' study could expect to find work in fashion design at the end of their course, and even then in rather less exotic locations than they had anticipated. Most, however, were more likely to find work in shops and factories, principally because by choosing a fashion design course they had foregone the opportunity to gain qualifications which would equip them for more prestigious jobs which they might otherwise have been able to consider.

If office work and caring work are seen to be relatively safe environments for women, what does this imply about young women who break away from traditional expectations and actually dare to opt for the non-traditional? The work of Cockburn (1987) on equal opportunities within the Youth Training Scheme deals with this issue as a central theme, as does the work of Stafford (1991) which explores similar issues in relation to the earlier Youth Opportunities Programme (YOPS) in Scotland. Cockburn draws on Lees' concept of 'reputation' as a key factor in determining young women's sexual behaviour (Lees, 1986). Cockburn notes that if young women in male-dominated environments show an interest in their fellow male workers, they are accused of being sexually promiscuous, whilst if they choose to ignore the men, they are accused of being lesbians - within a predominantly heterosexual culture, both accusations are considered to be slurs on a young woman's reputation. Consequently, Stafford notes that young women in non-traditional environments can only fit in if they act in a sexually neutral manner, assuming the identity of a 'daughter' to the supervisors and a 'sister' to the male trainees. It might be thought that the safest route would be to act 'like a boy', yet Stafford found that even this was fraught with difficulty, as behaviour which was deemed acceptable for boys - chasing around in the workshop, for example - was deemed *unacceptable* for girls, and if young women did act in such ways, sexual motives were assumed.

Given the delicate balancing act young women are therefore expected to perform within male-dominated environments, Cockburn argues that it is hardly surprising that young women prefer to remain within the security of traditional areas of employment which do not pose quite the same threat to their sexual identity. She found that young women in a light engineering workshop were assumed by the male instructor to be there *only because they wanted to be with the boys*, and he (like Stafford's instructor) was waiting for these 'real motives' to come to the surface. Cockburn's instructor felt his views were confirmed when the young women left the scheme after only a few weeks, whilst the fears of Stafford's instructor were confirmed when one of the young women started going out with one of the male trainees. The other trainees in the scheme in Cockburn's study (which covered both traditional and non-traditional areas) had been universally supportive of the young women's original decision to opt for a non-traditional area (although they were unwilling to innovate themselves), yet nonetheless felt that their behaviour needed *explaining*. It was thus assumed that they were tomboys, who wanted to be *like* boys, which seemed to provide an adequate explanation for such unusual behaviour. In non-traditional environments, therefore, young women are not only having to handle the pressures of coping with new forms of knowledge (of which young men will invariably have had prior knowledge), but are also having to handle gendered sexual relations which, although often represented as 'harmless fun', all too often become a form of harassment.

Griffin (1985) echoes some of these themes in her comparison of young women engineers in a mixed training environment with those in a single-sex training environment. The female trainees in the mixed setting felt isolated and were often treated in a patronising manner by the male trainees, whilst the young women in the women-only setting had gained a sense of collective confidence and support from each other and were not content to be patronised or to become 'one of the lads' (see also Chiosso and Tizard, 1990, and Greed, 1990): 'This was not a mark of their conservative views, but a pragmatic decision made in a situation of limited available options: an affirmation of the value of female friendship groups' (Griffin, 1985, p.191). Stafford (1991) similarly notes that the young women in her study were strong and articulate when on their own within their single-sex workshop, yet when young men impinged on that space they were left feeling silly and weak.

Is it really, surprising, therefore, that few young women opt for non-traditional occupations? On the contrary, Cockburn argues that it is perhaps more surprising that some young women *do* decide to do so. Thus, in spite of the greater economic rewards which are often held out as an incentive, Cockburn argues that, on the whole, young women are not interested:

> It is important not to bury away this embarrassing fact, but rather to acknowledge it. There is a good reason for women's reluctance. It is not that women are set against the idea of non-traditional fields of work... They are simply aware, however, of the high social costs that we all pay if we disobey gender rules. The gendering of jobs... advertises loudly where women are not to enter. If we ignore the message we are made to feel silly, pushy, unnatural - all by turns. There is a relentless low-level noise of harassment. We become unloveable (Cockburn, 1988, p.40).

Resistance and accommodation

The question which needs to be raised, however, is the extent to which young women are active or passive within the processes described above. Do young women not offer any resistance to their expected roles? Are they as preoccupied with 'romance' as these accounts suggest? Stafford, for example, notes that the young women in her study went as far as creating fictitious fiancés in order to impress their workmates (although it could be argued that this was actually a defensive strategy). The following statement is pertinent:

> To say that girls are preoccupied with romance is not simply to perpetuate an old slander. There are by now many studies of teenage girls which detail the obligatory and demanding nature of heterosexual culture, the extent to which girls are compelled to devote their energies and skills to competing with and 'succeeding' in the sexual sphere and the adverse effect this has on their educational and vocational achievement (Cockburn, 1987, p.39).

One such study was conducted by Lees (1986). Her work highlights the extent to which girls' lives are circumscribed by virtue of being female, and the way in which girls tend to be defined by boys in terms of their sexual reputation. She argues that sexuality constantly impinges on girls' lives, 'not so much in terms of their sexual experience but in their day to day social life where their gender (is) a constant source of comment and often abuse' (Lees, 1986, p.10). Above all, Lees argues, girls must avoid the label of 'slag', and the only antidote, once labelled, is to find a steady boyfriend. Given that 'reputation' is arguably given such a high profile by young men, and serves to effectively 'police' the behaviour of young women, it is perhaps not surprising that writers such as Cockburn and Griffin have found the concept of romance and 'appropriate' behaviour to be a guiding principle in the lives of many young women.

In contrast, Mirza (1992) argues that young black women do not share the cultural orientation of young white women towards the centrality of 'romance' as a guiding principle. She argues instead that the young women in her study, unlike their white counterparts, reiterated time after time their commitment to full-time work and their desire for economic independence: they expected to work throughout their adult lives, in the same way as their mothers and grandmothers had before them, and potential relationships with men were not seen as an inhibiting factor. Similarly, Mirza notes that young black women are more likely to opt for non-traditional occupational areas than young white women (although still in relatively small numbers). Whilst this could be seen as a form of resistance, Mirza argues that it is more likely to be due to the lack of cultural constraints on such choices and the notion that black women are primarily motivated in their aspirations by the prospect of upward mobility and are not therefore gender-bound in the same way as white women, who are arguably more conscious of 'gender rules'.

Cockburn does not, however, regard the young women in her study as victims, in the sense that they are powerless and unresisting when faced with the apparent constraints of 'gender rules'. Both Cockburn and Griffin note that young women do not necessarily accept unquestioningly the 'rules' of appropriate behaviour and they both describe incidents in which young women acted in ways which subverted the conformity to gender rules expected of them. Moreover, Griffin noted that some of the young women clerical workers in her study were being encouraged by supervisors to use their femininity to their own advantage within a career structure which stressed the importance of appearance and manner. However, far from challenging the reproduction of existing gender relations, such behaviour invariably reinforced the *status quo*. Some of the young women in Stafford's study, for example, deliberately made tea for the supervisor in order to keep in his favour, yet by so doing served to reinforce notions of female domesticity (see also Bates, 1993a and 1993b).

These are strategies that many young women have learnt to deploy within the classrooms. Riddell (1989) notes, for example, that many pupils draw on exaggerated forms of masculinity and femininity as a form of resistance, but a form which ultimately serves to reinforce traditional gendered assumptions. She argues that,

> Much of the parodying and contradiction of gender codes supported rather than undermined patriarchal relations. In their exaggerated displays of masculinity and femininity, pupils were locking themselves into restricted gender roles. Even girls who deliberately rejected the conventional notion of femininity in their opposition to schooling were strengthening gender divisions by uncritically adopting male modes of behaviour, and sometimes oppressing other women (Riddell, 1989, p.196).

Similar conclusions have been drawn by McRobbie and Garber (1975), McRobbie (1978), and Skeggs (1991), all of whom have focused on the use of an assertive sexuality in the classroom to intimidate male teachers.

Labour market transitions in Masonfield

The impact on Masonfield's economy of industrial decline from the 1970s onwards was noted in chapter 4. This was a period characterised by very high rates of both short-term and long-term male unemployment, but of a rapid growth of job opportunities in the female-dominated service sector. At the time that Cohort II pupils were preparing to leave school in 1989, the largest numbers of job vacancies notified to Masonfield job centres (representing about a third of all vacancies) were to be found in nursing, clerical work, cleaning and personal service occupations (Masonfield TEC, 1990). This suggests that TVEI's nationally-prescribed objectives were out of step with the recruitment needs of the local labour market as, far from there being a shortage of school leavers (whether male or female) to fill vacancies in male-dominated engineering and manufacturing industries, the demand was for recruits into occupational areas traditionally dominated by females. Despite efforts, therefore, to encourage girls to consider occupations such as engineering, such jobs were few and far between in Masonfield.

During the 1980s, Masonfield LEA had one of the lowest participation rates in the country for full-time post-16 education (DES, 1991b), and it was hoped that TVEI would encourage greater numbers of young people to stay on in full-time education by demonstrating the labour market currency of further qualifications. Throughout the 1980s the proportion of young people entering full-time employment remained relatively constant in Masonfield (a low of 13 per cent, a high of 17 per cent, but mainly hovering around 15 per cent), whilst there was indeed an increase in the proportion of young people entering full-time education at the expense of participation in YTS (staying on rates rose from 32 per cent in 1984 to 47 per cent in 1990, with YTS participation rates dropping from 42 per cent to 25 per cent over the same period). Following national trends, young women were more likely than young men to stay on in full-time education, with 49 per cent of all

Table 8.1
Destinations of 1989 pilot school leavers six months after leaving school (%)

	TVEI pupils (n=244)	Non-TVEI pupils (n=622)
Employment	18	17
Youth Training Scheme	43	35
Full-time education	28	30
Unemployment	3	7
No information	8	11

Source: Masonfield Careers Service Database

Table 8.2
Destinations of cohort II leavers by gender[1]

	Females		Males	
	No.	%	No.	%
Job/Youth Training Scheme	47	55	100	77
College of further education	14	16	6	5
Sixth form college	25	29	23	18
All	86	100	129	100

Note:
[1] Excludes leavers for whom no information was available

Source: Masonfield Careers Service Database

female leavers staying on in full-time education in 1990, compared with only 37 per cent of male leavers. In contrast, 13 per cent of female leavers and 20 per cent of male leavers found employment, and 22 per cent and 28 per cent respectively entered YTS (Masonfield Careers Service, 1991).

Table 8.1 compares the destinations six months after leaving school in 1989 of all TVEI and non-TVEI pupils from the pilot schools. Leavers who were involved in the TVEI cohort were more likely than non-cohort pupils to enter YTS schemes and permanent employment. The figures might initially suggest that TVEI pupils were slightly less likely to be unemployed on leaving school, but this cannot be substantiated without finding out the precise location of the 7 per cent 'unknown' TVEI leavers. None of these differences were statistically significant, however. Neither were there any significant gender differences between TVEI and non-TVEI leavers, although very significant gender differences did emerge between the 215 male and female TVEI pupils who entered the labour market or remained in full-time education. As Table 8.2 shows, female TVEI pupils were far more likely to remain in education (particularly at a college of further education) than their male counterparts. These differences can be attributed at least in part to the slightly higher academic potential of the young women who were involved in TVEI, compared with male TVEI pupils, there being a strong relationship between academic achievement and post-16 destinations.

Leavers in employment, YTS and on vocational courses

So what kinds of jobs and training schemes did TVEI pupils take up on leaving school? This final section is based on secondary analysis of 1989 Careers Service destinations data for *all* leavers, both TVEI and non-TVEI, from the five pilot schools - a total of 866 leavers. Of these, 540 were either in employment, in YTS or on a vocational course by December 1989. Detailed information is available for all of these leavers on the 'Occupational Training Family' (OTF) of their job, placement or course. Occupational Training Family classifications were developed by the Training Agency as a means by which jobs could be grouped according to broadly similar training needs. Whilst they were not developed specifically for the purposes of statistical analysis, rather as an administrative convenience, OTFs are widely used by the Careers Service for analysing the specific post-16 destinations of school leavers (Cockburn, 1987).

In general terms, the major differences between the leavers from the TVEI cohort and those who weren't involved in TVEI were that the former were more likely than the latter to move into office and clerical-based jobs (OTF1), jobs in install-ation, maintenance and repair (OTF4) and manufacturing and assembly jobs (OTF6). This could in part reflect the nature of the TVEI courses offered in the pilot schools: the choice of courses like Business Studies, Information Technology and CDT would suggest a prior interest in those areas of employment.

Table 8.3 shows the distribution of the 540 leavers across the eleven OTFs by

Table 8.3
Occupational Training Families of 1989 pilot school leavers by gender (%)

	Females (n=253)	Males (n=287)
OTF1: Office and clerical	38	15
OTF2: Horticulture and agriculture	1	6
OTF3: Craft, art and design	4	3
OTF4: Installation, maintenance and repair	0	30
OTF5: Scientific and technical	1	3
OTF6: Manufacture and assembly	2	12
OTF7: Processing	7	4
OTF8: Food preparation and service	8	4
OTF9: Personal service and sales	18	3
OTF10: Community and health services	18	11
OTF11: Transport services	3	11
All	100	100

Covers all leavers in employment, YTS or taking vocational qualifications

Source: Masonfield Careers Service Database

gender - and illustrates the stark differences in the destinations of young men and young women. The picture amongst 1990 leavers was broadly similar, although in 1990 slightly more young men were to be found in OTF3 (craft, art and design), whilst there was also a more equitable spread of young men and women entering OTF5 (scientific and technical). Amongst 1990 leavers, the gender gap was also lessened amongst young people entering food preparation and service jobs (OTF8), whilst it was increased amongst young people in processing jobs (OTF7). A further point to note in comparing 1989 data with 1990 data is that the proportion of young women entering OTF10 (community and health services) rose from 18 per cent to 24 per cent, at the apparent expense of fewer young women entering OTF1 (office and clerical): 38 per cent in 1989 compared with 32 per cent in 1990.

Cockburn's 1987 study of sex-stereotyping within YTS at the national level found that all but one of the eleven OTFs (OTF8: Food Preparation and Service) were sex-typed: that is, they had a gender imbalance of 70:30 or more. In Masonfield, amongst both cohort and non-cohort leavers, eight of the eleven OTFs were sex-typed. Amongst TVEI leavers alone five of the sex-typed OTFs were *exclusively male* and one was exclusively female, compared with three all-male and no all-female OTFs amongst non-TVEI leavers from the pilot schools. Thus it appears that TVEI leavers were choosing their YTS placements in a far more stereotypical way than non-TVEI leavers. Once again, this could be due to the nature of the TVEI subjects on offer and the high degree of stereotyping within those subjects.

One of the major drawbacks of the OTF classifications, however, is that the eleven categories tend to be very broad and actually cover a very wide range of (often disparate) occupations. As broad categories, therefore, OTFs can be very misleading: although the title of an OTF might suggest a traditional male or female bias, the categories each contain both traditionally male *and* traditionally female occupations, and they do not give enough detail to show that even within an OTF there is often a very high degree of gender segregation. By examining some of the eleven categories in greater detail, the true extent of gender segregation amongst leavers from the pilot schools can be demonstrated.

OTF1: Office and clerical

142 of the 540 leavers were to be found within the bounds of OTF1 six months after leaving school: 98 young women (38 per cent) and 44 young men (15 per cent). If non-TVEI pupils are excluded, this OTF accounted for 53 per cent of female TVEI leavers. At first sight the numbers of young men within what would appear to be a 'female' OTF seem to be quite encouraging, particularly as young men who had been in the TVEI cohort were slightly more likely to have entered this OTF than their non-TVEI counterparts. Moreover, there seems to be a gender balance in terms of the proportions going into employment, YTS or into vocational courses. However, the actual nature of these jobs, placements and courses differed quite significantly by gender. Whilst over three quarters of the women and only a

third of the men were found within clerical and secretarial positions, a further third of the men were working in the computing industry, compared with only five per cent of young women. The remaining leavers were scattered across a variety of courses and jobs, including insurance, contract control and accounts, jobs which although of a clerical nature, have traditionally been associated more with men than women, particularly in terms of who progresses to management positions. Cockburn (1987) has also highlighted the way in which young men on clerical YTS placements are more often than not regarded as trainee managers, unlike their female counterparts.

OTF7: Processing

This OTF contains a wide range of occupations, from unskilled manual jobs such as general process work, through to semi-skilled/skilled jobs such as printing and bookbinding. There were 43 young people in this OTF, all in employment or YTS. The 17 young women were clustered in sewing machining YTS placements and process work, whilst most of the 26 men were general labourers or process workers. Young men were slightly more likely than young women to be in permanent employment rather than on YTS placements.

OTF9: Personal service and sales

58 leavers were to be found within this OTF six months after leaving school. A broad range of retail and leisure-based occupations are included within this category, as well as jobs such as cleaning and hairdressing. There were 12 young men in this category, none of whom were on vocational courses, whilst 8 of the 48 young women were on FE courses (six were studying hairdressing, one was on a 'hair and beauty' course, and the eighth was on a 'sports and recreation' course). Within the retail sector, which accounted for nearly all the men in this category, young women were concentrated in food-related retailing, whilst young men were concentrated in retail outlets such as sports shops and electrical suppliers.

OTF10: Community and health services

There were 52 leavers within this category, only seven of whom were male, reflecting the tendency for most of the occupations within this OTF to be female-dominated areas of employment, such as nursing, nannying and other 'caring' occupations. All of the young women were to be found within these very traditional areas. This OTF also includes jobs in the police force, the fire service and the armed services, and four of the seven young men were in the army. However, the remaining three young men were in non-traditional occupations: one was studying Family and Community Care at an FE college, and the other two were on YTS Community Care placements. A further 21 young men had expressed an interest in

OTF10 occupations whilst at school; only two of these had shown an interest in non-traditional employment (nursing and care work), yet both had ended up in traditionally male-dominated areas of employment.

A detailed exploration of the remaining Occupational Training confirms the trends revealed in these four OTFs: far from generating an interest in non-traditional areas of employment, there is no evidence to suggest that TVEI had anything more than minimal impact on the stereotyped career choices of young people. Table 8.4 summarises the destinations of the few 'gender innovators' amongst the 1989 leavers from the pilot schools, adopting a very generous definition of what can be counted as 'traditional' or 'non-traditional'. Out of a grand total of 540 pilot school leavers who were to be found in YTS, employment or full-time vocational training six months after leaving school, only 31 young people (5.7 per cent) had opted for non-traditional career pathways post-16, and only 13 of these young people had been involved in TVEI. Interestingly, all but 2 of these TVEI 'non-traditionalists' were *male*; thus, TVEI did not enjoy mass success in encouraging young women into non-traditional occupations, but it may have had a *tiny* measure of success in encouraging some young men to respond to the demands of the local labour market for personal service workers. Of course, whether this is attributable to TVEI is impossible to know, but certainly they were entering occupational areas (catering, clerical work) which had close links to TVEI subjects (food studies, business studies). Amongst 1990 leavers, only 4.8 per cent of leavers entered non-traditional occupations and courses. There were, however, more female 'innovators' than the previous year, with ten women in jobs such as painting and decorating, computing, motor vehicle maintenance and engineering. Only 4 of the 10 had been involved in TVEI.

13 months on, updated destinations data showed that 72 per cent of young women and 71 per cent of young men who had been involved in TVEI were found to be in exactly the same job or course in January 1991 as they had been in December 1989. There was little overall change in the distribution of young men and women across the 11 OTFs, although the biggest change was found in the proportion of women in OTF1 (office and clerical): in December 1989, 53 per cent of all female ex-TVEI pupils were located within this category, whereas by January 1991, *60 per cent* of all the female TVEI leavers had jobs or were on courses within this category.

Of the 13 ex-TVEI pupils who in December 1991 were reported to have been in vaguely non-traditional occupational areas, 10 were still to be found in the same job or placement, including both of the female engineers. The remaining 3 young men had shifted towards jobs and courses which had a more traditional bias to them: one of the caterers was working as a repairer of domestic appliances, and of two clerical workers one had joined the RAF, whilst the other had started a BTEC in Business and Finance. The loss of these three young people from the non-traditional end of the spectrum was not compensated for by other young people entering non-traditional jobs during the course of the year; indeed, not only were there no

Table 8.4
Non-traditional destinations of 1989 pilot school leavers

Nature of work/course	Location	TVEI status
Females: (8)		
Building studies course	FE college	Non-TVEI
Computing (x2)	YTS	Both non-TVEI
Horticulture	YTS	Non-TVEI
Engineering apprenticeship (x2)	YTS	Both TVEI
Butcher's assistant	Job	Non-TVEI
Warehouse assistant	Job	Non-TVEI
Males: (24)		
Community Care course	FE college	Non-TVEI
Clerical work (x19)	YTS	7 TVEI, 12 non-TVEI
Catering (x2)	YTS	Both non-TVEI
Hairdresser	Job	TVEI
Kitchen assistant	Job	TVEI

Source: Masonfield Careers Service Database

additional young people in non-traditional areas, only one young person had had such a job over the course of the year - a young man who had worked as a cleaner for two months in between working as a joiner and a warehouse assistant.

Conclusion

Despite a rhetoric which stressed the centrality of equal opportunities to its wider criteria for success, it should be clear from this and the previous two chapters that TVEI's equal opportunities policy had little impact in Masonfield, as elsewhere, *in terms of measurable outcomes*. Girls were under-represented within successive TVEI cohorts, whilst specific TVEI options were subject to strong sex-stereotyping in uptake. Careers education and guidance tended to operate in a vacuum, disconnected from pupils' wider curriculum experiences, most evident in the way in which work experience tended to undermine the equal opportunities push in other aspects of TVEI. Finally, at the end of the day TVEI appeared to make little impact on post-16 destinations, not least because local labour market needs were out of step with the objectives of nationally-developed policy.

So, was it a strategic error to have concentrated so much on horizontal segregation when the vast majority of school leavers were not even remotely interested in non-traditional employment? In terms of measurable outcomes, the equal opportunities emphasis ultimately appeared to benefit only a tiny minority of (mainly male) pupils, offering little to the majority of pupils who moved into very traditional forms of employment and training. The following chapter, however, explores a range of equal opportunities-related issues which apply as much to 'traditional' as to 'non-traditional' forms of employment. Through exploring material taken from interviews with school leavers from Masonfield's pilot TVEI schools, it considers the wider relevance of TVEI's equal opportunities emphasis within the context of young people's early experiences of the youth labour market. It will also consider the extent to which young people were aware of TVEI's equal opportunities emphasis, regardless of whether or not they acted on it, and therefore seeks to assess whether there were any less tangible benefits to pupils of TVEI's equal opportunities policy.

9 Into the labour market: Preparation for life?

Introduction

Previous chapters have demonstrated that Masonfield TVEI's equal opportunities policy had minimal impact in terms of measurable outcomes such as the wider take-up of non-traditional examination subjects and career paths, and that these were trends which were also evident at a national level. The model of equal opportunities development which was often used within TVEI regarded the promotion of equality of *outcomes*, as distinct from equality of *access* (as enshrined in the equal opportunities criteria), as the pinnacle of success (Chambers, 1988; Rees, 1992). In the context of Masonfield, however, it seems to have been an entirely unrealistic goal: by their actions, pilot pupils appeared to belie the very existence of an equal opportunities policy. This, however, begs further questions: were the young people aware of an equal opportunities emphasis? If so, did it have an impact on them in less tangible ways? And did they perceive it as having any relevance to their post-school lives? This chapter explores these questions, by drawing on material from the interviews held with pilot pupils two years after leaving school.

In these interviews, twelve young people - all of whom had been involved in TVEI as cohort II pupils - reflected upon their experiences of schooling and of the transition from school to work, and their comments raise a number of key issues concerning the applicability of TVEI's narrow focus on the non-traditional. All twelve - five young women and seven young men - had responded to the Leavers Survey conducted in the summer of 1990 and at the time of the interviews were either 18 or 19 years old. Eight of the young people were in full-time employment, one was a YTS trainee, one was studying for 'A' level resits, and the final two were both studying at university. Between them they had a wide range of experiences and views, and accounted for just under 5 per cent of the young people who had been involved in cohort II. However, their claim to representativeness lies not in their statistical significance, but in their commonality of experience in secondary school.

Regardless of how they might be compared on other measures, all twelve had been closely involved in the pilot phase of a major curriculum innovation, and had been exposed to its centrally-endorsed equal opportunities policy. As such, they each had important observations to make about TVEI and its relevance to their post-16 experiences. A brief biography of each of the young people is included in Appendix 1.

Equal opportunities as an identifiable policy strand

The extent to which pilot pupils could reasonably be expected to be aware of equal opportunities as a dimension of TVEI is perhaps debatable; it could be argued that they did not need to be aware, as equal opportunities should have permeated the whole curriculum and should not have been treated as a discrete topic. However, previous chapters have shown the extent to which equal opportunities concerns tended to crystallise around particular aspects of TVEI, most notably around subject and career choice, and that specific events and strategies were organised which had overt equal opportunities messages. Consequently, if young people were unable to pick up the message behind these events, then it is unlikely that the more subtle aspects of equal opportunities dissemination would have had much impact on them.

Kenway et al's insights concerning young people's 'readings' of gender reform are of particular relevance here. As outlined in chapter 2, post-structuralist feminism stresses the constantly shifting meanings surrounding gender reforms in school:

> Whatever the moment or the level, the meaning of gender reform will be constantly contested, negotiated and appropriated... the moment of production will never have a direct correspondence with the moment of consumption because of the range of social, political and cultural factors and relationships of power which have an impact along the way (Kenway et al, 1994, p.193).

Previous chapters have highlighted the ways in which individual schools placed their own meanings on TVEI's equal opportunities policy: whatever the intentions of TVEI's architects, those responsible for its implementation were invariably able to place their own stamp on the policy. By implication, TVEI pupils were just as likely to interpret the policy in the light of their own experiences and viewpoints, despite the 'preferred reading positions and privileged meaning systems' within their schools (ibid, p.193). Indeed, Kenway et al argue that a failure to take on board these subjective readings has fatally weakened many gender reform programmes.

The twelve young people involved in the follow up interviews were asked whether they had been aware of TVEI's promotion of equal opportunities and, if so, in what ways they felt this emphasis had manifested itself. No attempt was made to define the term 'equal opportunities', so the responses were based very much on the young people's own understandings of the term. Seven young people stated unequivocally that they had been aware of the emphasis, largely on the evidence of non-traditional subject choice. Keith, for example, commented that boys were able to take home economics subjects, which 'I think formerly you weren't allowed to do', whilst David noted that not only did girls do CDT, but 'they actually did better than me!' As Karen put it,

> It was very strong... They definitely got that across... they kind of had girls doing the same thing as boys. I mean, its sub-conscious really, you didn't think 'oh that's weird, she's doing the same' - but you kind of got used to accepting it, you know what I mean.

Four of the seven leavers also noted an emphasis on non-traditional career choices, including one young man who described the way in which his own preconceptions had been challenged in a classroom discussion:

> This girl, Carla, said 'I want to be a car mechanic', and everyone went 'you're a girl - *car mechanic?* And it set off this big discussion, and by the end of it everybody had different opinions. I was saying, yeah, I could be a cook, there is men cooks... so I thought, well, I could do that, and then there was a few girls in Tech Drawing and that's not normally a lady's job either... obviously it was such a shock, because Carla - I don't know if she was prompted to do it, 'I want to be a car mechanic' - and everybody said, 'wait a minute, its all wrong, we've all been totally clouded, it isn't right'... and everyone thought, 'yeah, it should be equal rights for everybody'.

Karen also commented on the way equal opportunities was manifest in the content of her TVEI subjects, through the use of material in Business Studies lessons which included business*women* as well as men:

> I mean, they could have had all men doing it, but they had women - it was probably just coincidence, I don't know, but I think it probably was something to do with the fact that they were trying to bring it to people's attention.

Three leavers who had initially said that they had been unaware of TVEI's equal opportunities emphasis later qualified their responses. Jennifer suggested that the reason she had been unaware was largely because at the time she had not been conscious of the problem it was seeking to address, whilst Andrew and Tina both felt that their lack of awareness actually highlighted the strength of the policy. As Andrew said,

> I wasn't *aware* of it, but that probably wasn't a bad thing... it wasn't put forward as, 'oh we're doing this, we're trying to get equal numbers of people to do it', they just said anyone can do it... so by default then it was, you know, equal

opportunities.

Overall, only two leavers had been totally unaware of the equal opportunities emphasis, and were surprised to discover that it was supposed to have been an important element, given that TVEI subjects had been dominated by one or other sex. In general, though, the leavers were aware that TVEI sought to promote non-traditional choices, and felt that this represented a very real change, albeit one without widespread success. Prior to TVEI, such choices were strongly circumscribed; TVEI made those choices acceptable, even though few pupils exercised that choice. Thus, for some, the idea that it was 'okay' to take a non-traditional subject had been very novel, and appeared to have affected their thinking, if not their actions.

Most of the leavers had mixed views on the *rationale* behind the equal opportunities emphasis. Four leavers argued that its inclusion was related to the pursuit of equal rights and social justice. Keith, for example, argued that 'its not really fair to say to a girl, "well no, you can't do that because you're a girl"'. Three others argued further that the policy was linked to the needs of the labour market, including Keith who noted that 'if the world ever runs out of carpenters, then there is women who can do it as well!' and Jennifer, who reflected that,

> Perhaps they were worried that too many girls were going into jobs like secretaries and jobs that were supposed to be for girls... I don't know, they were trying to get over that its not just for the lads to get on in sciences and doctors and mechanics and engineers and so on.

These are both arguments which support the recurring view that equal opportunities was an issue primarily affecting women. However, three leavers questioned the *prima facie* case for an equal opportunities emphasis. At the time Jennifer 'didn't see what the fuss was about - I didn't think there was much to change', and Karen similarly argued that she personally did not feel that certain jobs were more suitable for one sex rather than another: 'That idea wasn't in my head - I thought I can do any job I want to do and it didn't matter to me whether I was female or male or whatever.' With the benefit of hindsight, both young women agreed that there probably had been a need for an equal opportunities policy. Mike, however, had not changed his mind:

> I was aware of it, but there was no need really, I don't think. Maybe five or ten years ago, but nowadays, you had a woman ruling the country, how can you go on about equal opportunities? Maybe in some cases they do, but I think nowadays employers don't bother about sex any more, it's just if you can do the job, you do it... I think they were going a *bit* too paranoid about (discrimination), really, cos it *is* around, but not as much as they put it out to be; they thought it was around every job, you know, you have to be a man or

you have to be a woman, you can't swap around, but I think that those days have gone now...

Mike's comments highlighted the need for an approach towards the promotion of non-traditional occupations which did not unnecessarily deter young people from following careers in those areas nor cause others to dismiss the whole concept of discrimination as 'paranoia'. His views echo comments made by St Catherine's equal opportunities coordinator, that several women representatives at the school's 'Women and Work' event had been 'a bit annoyed' that so many of the questions asked by pupils related to sexual harassment and discrimination in the workplace. They did not deny its existence, but felt that it had been overplayed, causing unnecessary apprehension amongst some pupils.

Paul was the only one of the leavers to have actually taken a non-traditional subject at school (Food Studies), whilst John had taken a typing course in his own time. None of the others, however, had seriously considered moving outside of traditional boundaries. David, for example, said that he had not considered Business Studies because 'it sounds quite girlie, actually - not being sexist or anything... it sounded like secretarial stuff, and I wasn't in to that at all', whilst Keith noted that the reason he had not taken Food Studies (which he had enjoyed in lower school) 'wasn't because it was a girls' subject or anything'. Most were at pains to point out that if they had wanted to take a non-traditional subject, they would have done so without hesitation; they just did not choose to do so. Thus, whilst they could appreciate why equal opportunities intervention was necessary and were happy for *other people* to make non-traditional choices, they clearly felt that such choices were not for them personally - even within the relatively sheltered environment of the school.

It is important in this context to remember that TVEI's equal opportunities commitment was largely based on the assumption that social aspiration, mobility and achievement were very much a question of individual access and motivation, and that once barriers to access were removed boys and girls would compete as equals. The reality appeared to be that even when access was granted and awareness of opportunity was raised, few young people chose to step across the non-traditional threshold. Non-traditional career pathways, far from being seen as personal escape routes from humdrum 'traditional' occupations, as the rhetoric seemed to imply, were just not attractive to these young people. They genuinely held no intrinsic appeal for them, whilst the young people may also have been aware of the high personal costs likely to be incurred by working in an environment dominated by the opposite sex (Griffin, 1985; Cockburn, 1987 and 1988). By underestimating the importance of a secure and strong sense of gendered identity, which is offered to many young people by employment in traditional occupational spheres, the non-traditional discourse offered little to the majority of leavers, and in particular was weakened by a failure to take on board the importance to young people of factors such as desire and pleasure in their choice of post-16 pathways, seeking refuge instead in a rather rationalist model of career choice.

However, labour market discrimination was clearly not confined solely to young people in non-traditional working environments, and issues such as equal access to training and promotion prospects, sexism and harassment in the workplace were issues which were likely to affect all young people, regardless of their specific labour market location. The next section explores the way in which the early labour market experiences and longer-term aspirations of TVEI leavers were indeed strongly shaped by their gender.

Into work: Issues of equality and difference

Two years after leaving school, nine of the twelve leavers were either in full-time employment or nearing completion of Youth Training. Most were working in occupational areas which were not particularly unusual for their sex. Reflecting the dominant focus of employment amongst female TVEI leavers, all four young women were engaged in some form of clerical or administrative work, although Jane, who worked for a mail order company, noted that her particular administrative post was more usually held by a man. Two of the young men worked in retail sales, another was a building surveyor and a fourth worked as a bank clerk. The fifth young man was employed as a travel agent, an occupation which tends to have a greater proportion of women than men working in entry-level jobs.

Experiences and expectations

Many school leavers assume that, having chosen examination subjects in line with their aspirations, they will unproblematically find work in their chosen field. This may have been a safe assumption in times of low youth unemployment (Ashton and Field, 1976), but the reality during a period of recession is rather more complicated. Many leavers, of course, change their minds about their choice of career (Ryrie, 1981), but even if their aspirations remain intact, many discover that the concept of occupational *choice* is rendered meaningless in the local labour market context, where supply and demand do not necessarily complement each other (Furlong, 1987). Of the nine leavers in work, only one had moved directly into a job which had actually matched their earlier aspirations, whilst the remainder moved into jobs in which they had expressed no prior interest. So why did they take them?

Few felt that they had exercised a positive choice when deciding on their jobs; rather, they knew that they had to find work of some kind and could see no reason *not* to take the jobs they were offered. Mike, for example, had ideally wanted to work with computers, yet when a Careers Officer had suggested that he consider working as a trainee travel agent, his response had been 'Oh, why not? Sounds okay...', and he was now extremely content in his second such post since leaving school. Similarly, Karen had been keen to establish financial independence from her parents and on approaching a clerical YT Managing Agent shortly after leaving school had been offered work as a purchase ledger clerk: 'I just picked it because it was relatively near home, so I thought I'll get that one, its ten minutes on the bus.'

Tina, Jane and Amanda were also in clerical or administrative jobs two years after leaving school. Tina had originally started a foundation course in Art and Design, but had left the course after falling out with her tutor. She had eventually taken a secretarial job at the local university, and although she enjoyed it, her artistic aspirations remained, and she talked of moving into the university conference office, which would allow her to use her design skills in creating publicity materials. Tina justified her decision, therefore, by arguing that her clerical job might prove to be the means of achieving a more attractive career goal. This is consistent with Sheratt's finding that young women who drop out of further education often argue that the jobs they then 'choose' still provide a means to their desired end, although this may not be immediately obvious to observers (Sheratt, 1983).

Both Amanda and Jane were less enamoured of their jobs. Amanda had wanted to become a police officer, but on leaving school had joined British Rail's in-house clerical training scheme because 'it just seemed good', but she had soon decided that 'its a bit boring, office work, I don't want to do it for the rest of my life, I mean I only did it from school because it was something to do...' Jane also regarded her first job as a stopgap: 'I had it in my mind that I wanted to go into nursing very soon, so I never thought, oh well, I've got to get into like a *good* office environment... it doesn't matter if I don't enjoy it, 'cos I'm going into nursing.' As will be discussed below, Jane was still half-heartedly considering a nursing career, but now wished she had shown greater discernment in choosing her 'temporary' job.

Paul, a sales assistant in a sports shop, and Keith, a bank clerk, had also chosen their jobs as stop-gaps, until they were old enough to apply for the Fire Service and the Police Force. Unlike Amanda and Jane, both enjoyed their jobs, but would have no qualms about leaving when the time came. Finally, whilst John's second job (as a building surveyor) had been in line with his long-term career plans, his first job on leaving school had been in sales, a job he had not previously considered, nor particularly wanted. However, 'I thought I'll give it a shot, because I was quite desperate at the time.'

In most cases, therefore, the jobs done by the young people two years after leaving high school, far from being the result of rational career planning, appeared to be largely attributable to vagaries of circumstance (Hollands, 1990). It is hard to see any sense in which they had exercised genuine choice; their actions were constrained by more compelling factors such as the need to avoid unemployment, the need for financial independence, the need to fill time before making further career decisions and the ready availability of work in other occupational areas. Nonetheless, it is also striking that the jobs they moved into, with the exception of Jane, were all highly gendered; gender therefore appeared to be as strong a constraint on opportunity as the other factors noted above, even if they were unconscious of this (see Gaskell, 1984). Further, even if they had originally aspired to non-traditional careers, they would still have found that the majority of openings on which they could *realistically* 'fall back' without having to face undue competition would have been highly traditional in nature (Ashton et al, 1987).

Unequal access to training

Regardless of whether their jobs were products of genuine choice, the young people were nonetheless keen to avail themselves of training opportunities. Interestingly, this was not necessarily out of a sense of commitment to their current employer but, on the contrary, because they wanted to be in a strong position to apply for other jobs. The provision of employment-based training opportunities for young people over the last fifteen years, particularly those entering full-time employment at 16, has been consistently poor and, in many cases, non-existent, especially for young women (West and Newton, 1983; Wickham, 1985; Cockburn, 1987; Courtenay, 1989a and 1989b; Rees, 1993; Furlong and Cartmel, 1997). The Leavers Survey found that only 65 per cent of leavers in employment or YT had received *any* form of training in their first year (including minimal training of the 'sitting by Nelly' variety). Of these, only 58 per cent of young women, compared with 70 per cent of young men, were receiving structured off-the-job training. Moreover, fewer women than men were studying for widely recognised qualifications such as BTEC or City and Guilds courses (this was before the introduction of GNVQs), whilst the courses taken by young men covered a much wider range of topics. Again, this is a trend confirmed by recent research (Arnot et al, 1996).

Most of the young people who were interviewed were receiving some form of training, either in-house or externally, but their perceptions of its value varied greatly. Tina, Amanda and Keith all worked for organisations with large internal training departments, so most of their training needs were met in-house. Tina was able to apply for any courses which appealed to her, whilst Amanda and Keith's training needs were dictated by their superiors. Paul and David's training as sales assistants was conducted chiefly on-the-job, and appeared to be fairly minimal. Indeed, they both spoke of their frustration at the lack of training in the first few months of their jobs.

Many had also been enrolled at some stage in college-based training, but only three were still studying: Tina was taking a book-keeping course in her own time, Mike was taking a computing course by day-release, and John was studying in his own time for ONC Building Studies resits. All the others had abandoned their college courses, in many cases with only a few months left to run. Amanda, for example, had left a day-release course in Business Administration with only two modules outstanding. Keith, the bank clerk, had been studying for a BTEC in Business and Finance for two evenings a week, but after 18 months 'I'd had enough! It bored me silly!' To compound matters, it transpired that he had deliberately chosen to do a BTEC in his own time, rather than internal banking exams on a day-release basis, because he had felt a BTEC would render him more marketable should he leave the bank. By failing to complete the course, he could impress neither his current employer nor any future employers. Karen had started the same course as Keith, albeit by day-release, but she too had abandoned the course due to stress, which eventually cost her her job.

West and Newton (1983) have argued that although women are often far more enthusiastic about training than men, they are also less likely to receive any. All four young women expressed a desire to pursue further training opportunities. Tina and Amanda were working for organisations with a strong training ethos, and were satisfied that any future training needs would be met. However, both Karen and Jane felt let down by their employers' unwillingness to train them. Karen was very unhappy with this situation and planned to take 'A' level evening classes, partly out of interest, but also as a possible stepping stone to a career change. Jane's employers were totally unsupportive, insisting that the Business Studies course she wanted to take be done at her own expense, both in terms of time and money. Moreover, the college she had in mind was situated in a particularly unsafe area of the city, and this also acted as a deterrent. Hollands argues that 'young women are still highly constrained from using the street to construct alternative identities outside work and the home' (Hollands, 1990, p.138); in Jane's case, the male monopoly on public space was denying her an important opportunity to carve an alternative identity in the context of her working environment.

In contrast, only one young man was actively seeking further training. John, the building surveyor, hoped to start an HNC on completion of his ONC in Building Studies, possibly with a view to subsequently studying for a degree. The others were remarkably casual about future training: either they did not see the need for it or they regarded their current jobs as temporary. Neither did any of the young women envisage following the same line of work indefinitely, yet this had not prevented *them* from seeking further training opportunities. They were arguably far more realistic concerning their likely futures: being aware that circumstances might conspire against a career change, they were keen to acquire as much training as possible to increase their marketability both externally and internally. Conversely, the young men were more optimistic concerning their chances of a change of career, even though their optimism may have been misplaced. These contrasting attitudes could also reflect the extent to which they were aware that employers often attach different value to training and experience according to an employee's gender: a woman can often only prove her commitment to paid labour through acquiring further qualifications, whereas men's on-going commitment to paid labour is taken for granted (Crompton and Sanderson, 1990).

Hopes for the future

Another striking feature of the youth labour market (and indeed the wider labour market) is that jobs undertaken by men tend to have greater promotion or career chances than women's jobs. This is not unrelated to the growth of female employment in low paid, often part-time, service sector jobs, but is also the case more widely. Ashton et al (1987), for example, found that even within semi-skilled or unskilled occupations, only 24 per cent of young women felt that their job offered them promotion opportunities, compared with 62 per cent of young men. West and Newton (1983) also found that young women were significantly less likely to be interested in promotion or in changing jobs than young men, even though they also felt less settled in their jobs than men. Male respondents to the Leavers Survey did tend to be more positive than young women about their jobs: they were almost twice as likely to agree that they liked their job 'very much', whilst three times as many women expressed ambivalence concerning their job or YT scheme. West and Newton argue that these attitudes do not reflect a lack of ambition, but the lack of real promotion prospects for women.

Whilst few of the young people found their jobs particularly fulfilling, most nonetheless felt that their promotion prospects were good. Tina, for instance, was confident that if she stayed in her current post for 'about three years', then she would automatically be promoted to 'bigger and better things, still in the university'. Karen felt that there were plenty of promotion opportunities within British Rail, and 'if I wanted promotion I'd go for it in BR, but like I'm happy at the moment, its not that I want to get to the top straightaway...' John made similar comments: 'When I started here there was a lot of opportunity, that was what I liked, there still is, there's eight different jobs I know I can take up if I carry on.' Although these three were happy to remain with their current employers, the others felt that their next promotion was likely to come about more quickly by changing their jobs. For Karen and Jane, however, this was chiefly because there was no obvious promotion route for them. In Karen's case, the only possible promotion route would be to take over her supervisor's job ('unless you shove her out, there's nowhere to go!'), whilst Jane had already had quite a substantial promotion, and felt it unlikely that she would progress any further with her current employer.

The young people were also asked what they hoped to be doing in ten years time. All five young men had quite definite ideas in mind, and felt that their aspirations were realistic. Paul and Keith both hoped to have left their current jobs to have joined the Fire Service and the Police respectively. David hoped to have left retail sales to become a sales executive, Mike's plan was to start his own travel agency, whilst John hoped to be a departmental head. In contrast, the young women were less certain about their longer-term plans. Tina envisaged a future still with the university, either as a 'highly paid secretary', or in a job which would utilise her artistic talents. Amanda could also see herself staying with her current employer, BR, but was quite keen on a move into an administrative post in the Transport Police. Amanda, it should be remembered, had aspired to police work whilst at school; the police force still attracted her, but she no longer imagined herself as a police officer. Karen was desperate for a change of occupation but found it difficult to imagine what she might be doing in ten years time. She clearly bitterly regretted having left school at 16.

Jane was most uncertain of all about her future, even though Jane's overriding ambition since the age of fourteen had been to pursue a career in nursing. To that end, on leaving school she had enrolled at a local college to take additional GCSEs and a City and Guilds course in Health Studies. At the end of that year, she had still needed an additional GCSE before she could apply for nursing, and so had looked round for a job to fill time until she could apply: that is why, as noted above, she had not been particularly 'choosey' about the job she had taken, regarding it as only a stopgap. However, as time went by she had found her attitude towards nursing changing, despite clearly disliking her current job. She had not enrolled for the extra GCSE in time to take the exam in her first year of employment, but perhaps more significantly, she was beginning to have doubts about the whole idea, not least for financial reasons: 'now like I'm on quite a bit of money and its gonna be like a bit of a step down when I'm on £80 a week training as a nurse... I want to do it in every other way, I've wanted to do it since I was 14, the only thing's that stopping me is the money... don't know if I can afford it.' On this basis, Jane could not predict what she would be doing in ten years time, as she genuinely did not know her own feelings on the matter.

In most cases, the longer-term career plans of the young people were linked to long-standing aspirations so far unsatisfied by the local labour market. This confirms Furlong's argument that in the context of declining employment opportunities young people will adopt a variety of 'image maintenance' strategies 'to enable the retention of a self-concept which had been developed under different structural conditions. In other words, their aspirations (are) not simply modified to take account of existing opportunities, but continue to be pursued' (Furlong, 1987, p.62). One such strategy he identifies as 'role distancing' (Goffman, 1961), whereby young people regard their current work as a temporary situation only, and consequently feel no commitment to remain within that job.

It is significant that none of the young people spoke of future domestic roles in the context of their long-term plans. This may have been due to the 'vocational' focus of much of the interview, but many previous studies have argued that girls in particular place great emphasis on this aspect of their lives when talking about their longer-term career plans. Burnhill and McPherson (1984), however, conducted a study of girls' aspirations in 1971 and then in 1981, and found that less emphasis was placed on marriage and family commitments in the later study. Given that questions were not specifically asked about this aspect of their lives, it is difficult to generalise, but it does at least suggest that in their late teens these young men and women shared a similar commitment to the labour market and did not anticipate an immediate change in their circumstances.

Differential treatment in the workplace

The discussion so far has highlighted both similarities and differences between the experiences of the young men and women. The rather random nature of job selection appeared to be applicable in virtually all cases, regardless of gender, whilst many of the young men and women shared a general dissatisfaction with their current positions, which they rationalised by reference to longer-term or temporarily deferred plans. However, there do appear to be subtle differences with regard to the confidence and certainty with which the young men and women faced their futures, as well as differences in the level of training they could reasonably expect to receive, which in turn affected their ability to transform their situations. These are differences of which the young people themselves may well have been unaware. In other areas, though, they were all too aware of the differential treatment accorded to men and women in the workplace, and this final section considers the young people's responses when asked to consider gender differences in relation to their own workplaces, relating to their awareness of both horizontal and vertical segregation; discrimination in recruitment and promotion; and their attitudes towards 'gender innovators' at work.

Horizontal and vertical segregation

The Leavers Survey highlighted the degree of horizontal segregation amongst pilot school leavers. When asked whether there were any members of the opposite sex doing a similar job to their own, half the young women said that they worked alongside men doing the same type of work, whilst only 35 per cent of young men worked alongside women doing a similar job. Thus, male occupational areas tended to be subject to greater overall segregation than predominantly female areas. Of the 27 young people who did not work alongside members of the opposite sex, five (including four ex-TVEI pupils) thought that members of the opposite sex could not actually do their job. All five were young men: a computer engineer, a motor mechanic, a joiner, a labourer and a trainee manager.

In interview, most of the leavers made reference to horizontal segregation, even if only to argue that it did not occur where they worked. Keith, for example, argued that: 'I'd say there was no discrimination between men and women where I work... jobs that I do, a girl could do, and there's jobs that all the girls could do that I could... if we're all the same grade then we can do all the same jobs.' In contrast, David initially claimed that men and women were treated equally where he worked (an electrical goods retailer), but as he described the work that each tended to do he began to change his mind: 'The girls do a lot of filing, whereas the men don't do it, we do all their shifting about for them and so I can't say it's equal opportunities there... everyone shares the cleaning... but we do have our own filing sometimes, so I don't just leave it up to them all the time.' So, although both men and women shared identical job titles, there were actually considerable gender differences in the allocation of duties. The other leavers talked about horizontal segregation within BR ('We've got one woman train driver!'), within surveying, within the travel industry ('When I was in my first job there was me - and about fourteen women - which I wasn't complaining at, you know!'), within secretarial work and within sales work.

Karen described how, in the places she'd worked, 'the people in the offices have been women, and the salesmen have always been men'. She suggested two possible explanations for this, one to do with status, the other to do with the qualities needed in sales work:

> Sales, to me - well, it *is* - is the most important part of the company, and all the sales are men... it's a man's kind of thing. I mean, it's this daft idea, and you'd think it would have gone away, but (women) are supposed to be soft, whereas salesmen, you know, you've got to con people, and I suppose they think, well, a woman won't be able to get on the phone... you imagine a woman to be saying 'Oh I can't tell lies!'

Jane agreed that horizontal segregation was often based on different expectations of male and female behaviour. Her own job, for example, was considered to be a man's job because 'you've got to be really aggressive with the suppliers and that, but I can be aggressive anyway, cos I'm bad-tempered, it don't really make any difference if you're a woman or a man.'

Although all the young people made reference to horizontal gender segregation, the existence of vertical segregation was noted *only* by young women. Amanda noted that whilst in her office there were more or less equal numbers of men and women, the higher one went up the hierarchy the fewer women there were. However, Amanda did not view this as a problem, but felt that it was a question of individual motivation rather than a structural problem: 'I don't think anything of it, me; I just think you'd apply for it if you wanted it.' Jane was less sanguine about vertical segregation, however, partly because she already felt herself to be affected by it:

> I'm the youngest supervisor there is, and I'm one of the only women supervisors there is as well... I find it annoying, I really do, because I think they should have more women supervisors - there's only me and another woman... according to our company I'm doing a man's job anyway! Shouldn't be a man's job, but it is: I just think it's not fair.

Discrimination in recruitment and promotion

Two leavers spoke of their awareness of discriminatory recruitment practices in their workplaces. David, for example, recalled the recent appointment of a new YT trainee in his electrical shop: 'When (the boss) was looking for the YTS that we've got now, he'd rather like a boy because obviously he can do all the lugging about... the girls never got a look in.' David gave the impression that this had been a reasonable decision, given the nature of the job. Tina, on the other hand, accepted that both men and women could work as secretaries, yet was aware that it was extremely unlikely that anyone would ever be given the chance to prove this in her department: 'Its just the old-fashioned idea that the boss has - he would never employ a male secretary, and he's told me that.' She went on to describe the circumstances of her own appointment. Apparently, a young man had also applied for the job, which had caused a dilemma for her boss, as he was acutely aware of his obligations to abide by the SDA in making appointments, not least because the University's equal opportunities officer sat in on the interviews!

In contrast, John believed that horizontal segregation arose because few women applied for 'men's' jobs, rather than because they were discriminated against in recruitment. Thus, any stereotyping that existed at his firm was 'from no fault of theirs, they're offering the jobs to both sexes, its just that the lads are all taking the jobs.' This was despite the fact, as he later noted, that women who sought to enter surveying were often far better qualified than their male counterparts; there were three women on his Building Studies course, and they had all done better in their exams than the men. John's views concerning their recruitment prospects confirm the conclusions of Greed's research into women surveying students: 'Even if women survive this stage intellectually intact, their future career prospects are often not as rosy as they might have been led to believe' (Greed, 1990, p.49).

John's comments also highlight the need for women to 'out-perform' men in order to prove their competence, particularly within occupational areas traditionally regarded as male preserves. Jane considered herself to be in just such an area within the mail order company she worked for. Her earlier comments noted her frustration at the lack of promotion prospects within the company, and initially she gave the impression that the chief obstacle was her age. However, gender was clearly playing a much more critical role, as it transpired that a young man had been promoted at the same time as Jane, against whom comparisons were constantly being drawn by her immediate boss:

> He seems to treat this other trainee totally different because he's a lad; like, he looks down on me... cos I'm a woman and like cos I'm young... he really makes you feel like that big, and he really notices the bad things you do... he seems to talk to the other trainee as if he really knows what he's doing, talks to me as if I'm thick and stupid... it makes me feel really uncomfortable, I feel like as if he's looking over my shoulder all the time to see if I'm doing anything wrong... he's noting all the bad things, and noting all the good things about the other trainee.

Jane was convinced that her boss was deliberately 'grooming' the other trainee, even though they did identical work, which she felt she did as well as he did. The boss constantly took him aside 'for chats', for example, and frequently praised him in front of the other office workers. Jane was particularly angry that a promised review had not yet materialised; in fact, the day of the interview she had demanded that her review be held soon, 'cos I feel as if he's getting ahead more than me, which isn't fair, cos it's the boss that like notices the good things about him and like overrides them on me.'

Thus, at eighteen, Jane already felt that she had hit the 'glass ceiling', and her employer's refusal to sponsor any external training courses denied her the opportunity to distinguish herself from the other trainee. Moreover, the reason given by Jane for not studying in her own time - the difficulties associated with physical access to a poorly situated college - was unlikely to have had quite the same deterrent effect on the male trainee if he had decided to pursue training in his own time.

Attitudes towards 'gender innovators'

Although the majority of the leavers were themselves working within traditional boundaries, a few made comments during the course of the interview which hinted at the attitudes which 'gender innovators' in their workplaces could expect to face. The impression received was that, despite their exposure to, and awareness of, TVEI's equal opportunities ethos, some of the young people were still surprised to find women in non-traditional roles.

It was noted above that John had studied alongside a handful of women on his ONC Building Studies Course. His view was that the course was 'more of a challenge to them' because of their need to out-perform the male students: 'they see it as like this is lad's work, we're in alien territory here, we've got to watch our backs.' John had earlier commented on the recent appointment of a new surveyor, and described his surprise at discovering that 'he' was in fact a 'she':

> Today for instance, they're taking a new surveyor on in another department and I had to get his name - and shock, horror, it was a *she*. It was the first time, it had really hit home today that we'd not got any female surveyors, and I said 'what's his name', and they said 'its a she' - 'ooh, a *she*?'.

Paul had been equally surprised to find himself working for a woman in his sports shop. Earlier in the interview he had referred to 'the manageress', and had immediately broken off to laugh and say 'I'm working under a woman!' When asked later why he had expressed surprise, he revealed that,

> Well, its just that all me mates, you know, they all work over (women)... I got used to that, I'm not really bothered... but I didn't really like it at first - I thought I should have been doing it, not her! But its not too bad.

Thus, even as a 16 year old YTS trainee fresh from school, he had felt that it was somehow inappropriate for a man to take orders from a woman, and his comments suggest that his unease had not disappeared totally.

Only Jane could provide an 'insiders' view of being a woman in a male-dominated working environment. Some of the obstacles in her path have already been highlighted, but she also spoke of her strategy for coping with the male environment in which she worked:

> They seem to keep themselves to themselves, anyway; its not as if they all like go out in a big group and I can't get in... its like, they're all men, like I've had to find myself adapting and that to the way they are, try and act like them, otherwise I wouldn't fit in like; they all talk about men, you know, they swear a lot and things like that. I've grown like a hard skin to that now...

In order to cope on a day to day basis, therefore, Jane had to adopt what she considered to be male behavioural traits, but even her attempts at assimilation did not lead to equal treatment by her boss: for some purposes, she would always be seen first and foremost as a woman in a man's world.

Conclusion

In as much as the young people who were interviewed were aware of an equal opportunities emphasis in their schooling, TVEI could be said to have achieved some measure of success, particularly as the young people recognised that the main thrust of policy was in the direction of encouraging pupils, and in particular young women - to consider non-traditional subjects and careers. However, despite this awareness, it is clear that such a message had little practical impact: whilst the young people were perfectly happy, if somewhat surprised, for other people to make non-traditional choices, they were very rarely interested in making such choices for themselves - quite possibly for some of the reasons outlined in the previous chapter. If this emphasis on horizontal gender segregation had been only one aspect of a wider equal opportunities concern, this would not particularly matter; however, earlier chapters have shown that the bulk of time and effort with respect to equal opportunities under the auspices of TVEI was concentrated on this one theme.

An equal opportunities policy originating from within TVEI was bound, of course, to have had a vocational bias, and given that its origins lay partly in the need to respond to the 'demographic timebomb', it is not at all surprising that horizontal gender segregation came under scrutiny. However, TVEI could quite legitimately have developed an equal opportunities emphasis which was of relevance to the vast majority of school leavers, whilst still remaining true to its vocational bias, by tackling the sort of issues which affected all young workers - or, more to the point, the sort of issues which adversely affected all young *women*, some of which have been described in this chapter. It is at this point, however, that the central contradiction of TVEI emerges most strongly. TVEI claimed to be concerned with questions of gender equality in the workplace, and tended to concentrate on the impact of horizontal segregation on women; however, because its underlying philosophy tended to underplay the prior disadvantages of gender, assuming that both girls and boys competed on equal terms, it was constrained from developing an emphasis which might be interpreted as prioritising the needs of young women over those of young men. This is highlighted, for example, in the dilemma over the question of single sex provision: TVEI could identify the problem, but felt unable to provide the logical solution.

10 The legacy of TVEI

Introduction

TVEI was the first educational policy initiative to include an equal opportunities brief as a built-in contractual funding obligation, thus establishing progress with respect to this criterion as a legitimate measure of TVEI's success or failure. Prior to the launch of TVEI, a wide variety of grassroots gender initiatives had flourished in 'unofficial spaces' within schools. Feminist teachers and researchers had highlighted the existence of gender inequalities in education and, with varying degrees of success, had sought to develop strategies for change. With the advent of TVEI, gender equality issues moved mainstream, providing a unique opportunity to assess the impact of a centrally-legitimated equal opportunities intervention, as opposed to the *ad hoc* and, more often than not, informal interventions of feminists. Would TVEI enjoy any greater success, by virtue of being an 'official' policy? Or was its official nature likely to have serious implications for its interpretation of the nature of the problem, thus weakening its impact? These were important questions: if TVEI ultimately proved to have a negligible impact on gender inequalities in education, despite a huge investment of time and money, would its philosophical underpinnings be able to provide an adequate explanation for its lack of impact, or would its failure have implications for the future of equal opportunities work more generally?

This final chapter addresses these issues by considering the implications of the impact of TVEI within two key areas: school and LEA organisation, and student outcomes. The cumulative evidence presented in this book suggests that its impact was greater in the former rather than in the latter, even though TVEI was *primarily* concerned with equal opportunities outcomes amongst young people in transition from school to work. There are important underlying reasons both for TVEI's success in changing the culture of school organisation and for its failure to have much of an impact on pupils, and these reasons will be explored in the first sections of this chapter. The chapter will then consider the longer term legacy of TVEI's equal opportunities experiment, particularly given the ongoing emphasis on vocationalism within secondary education. It will end with some tentative thoughts on a feminist way forward.

TVEI's impact at the organisational level

Both the evidence of this book and the findings of other studies indicate that TVEI's equal opportunities policy did in fact have a major impact on the context of educational policy making. Under TVEI, equal opportunities as a policy issue was effectively transformed from a taboo subject into a mainstream educational concern. Ruddock (1994), for example, has noted the way in which the influence of TVEI emerged as a recurring theme within schools renowned for their equal opportunities good practice, whilst Weiner (1994) has pointed to TVEI's positive role in bringing about changes to discriminatory curriculum structures. More recently, a series of EOC-sponsored evaluations of the impact of educational reform on issues of gender equality in England, Scotland and Wales has underlined TVEI's impact. The report for England and Wales, for example, found that TVEI was cited as an impetus for introducing an equal opportunities policy in 37 per cent of the 223 secondary schools surveyed (Arnot et al, 1996). This made it the fourth most cited factor, after 'groups of interested teachers' (50 per cent), 'a group of headteachers' (47 per cent) and 'the LEA' (39 per cent). TVEI was also cited by a quarter of LEAs as an impetus for the introduction of LEA-wide policies (again, in fourth place to other factors). In both cases, the National Curriculum was viewed as having a negligible impact. It was also reported that in 19 per cent of secondary schools, a TVEI coordinator had been responsible for initiating change with respect to equal opportunities policies. Similarly, the Scottish report, whilst highlighting a number of negative features of TVEI, concludes that 'TVEI was generally seen to have been the most important development in drawing schools' attention to gender equality matters' (Turner et al, 1995, p.62).

In Masonfield, typical of many LEAs, neither officers nor elected members had shown much, if any, commitment to equal opportunities as a policy issue in the period prior to TVEI's introduction. In part this was because of the extremist stance with which they associated such concerns, but also because the particular emphasis which TVEI was to acquire - encouraging girls into predominantly male curricular and occupational areas - was deemed to have little relevance in a city where there were insufficient jobs for young men in traditional areas, let alone for young women. By the end of pilot, however, it appeared that a huge shift had occurred in the culture of the LEA's schools:

There was a sea-change going on, which you don't immediately observe when its going on - I can look back now and it's a sea-change in everything that's happened as a result of that TVEI Initiative. Is TVEI deemed to have been a success? Yes, it is, it has been deemed to be a success (Mrs Lewis, Chair of Masonfield's Education Committee).

Many of the changes which were made in the early days of pilot were seemingly minor - the listing of class registers alphabetically rather than by gender, the re-writing of school uniform regulations to allow girls to wear trousers, introducing mixed games lessons - yet even these changes would have been unthinkable in the years immediately preceding the launch of TVEI:

> In 1986, if we'd suggested that... boys and girls shouldn't line up separately, that they needn't be listed separately, and that you really didn't need different sets of uniforms - we would have been considered insane, quite insane, and the fact that by the end of pilot these things had happened and had been implemented in some of the most right wing schools... there were clear signs that people had looked at the issues and were beginning to look at some of the nitty gritty. So, yes, I think we did achieve quite a lot with the pilot scheme (David James).

The establishment of equal opportunities working groups within individual high schools was another success of TVEI. The four pilot schools where working groups were formed were able to harness the concerns of individuals who, in many cases, had been interested in equal opportunities issues for some time, but whose interests were now given official sanction under the auspices of TVEI development work. Moreover, the tasks for which the working groups were established represented the first time that data on differential outcomes according to gender had been systematically collected in the pilot schools. As David James noted, 'there were just no monitoring procedures; people had never looked in those terms'. It was also during this period that the cross-LEA TVEI working party on equal opportunities was set up to provide support and encouragement to the pilot schools. The group was perhaps at its most active in the final two years of pilot, which were also the first two years of TVEI extension funding, and the working group was able to flag up equal opportunities as a key issue for extension schools.

As the influence of TVEI widened, a commitment to equal opportunities gradually became recognised as one of the essential prerequisites of teachers applying for TVEI posts. David James was convinced that this had filtered through to other key appointments in the LEA, and he drew a comparison with a shift in attitude towards racism within education:

> I think teachers are far less racist than they were ten or fifteen years ago, far less racist, and much more aware of youngsters' cultural needs and ethnic identity... for a very simple reason, I think, that most authorities you couldn't

get promotion if you maintained old fashioned integrationist philosophies... and that could happen again, and I think is very slowly beginning to happen on gender issues, that as people are pressed and it becomes clear that you can't be appointed as a headteacher or a deputy if you think everything is hunkydory and you don't have to do anything, then things will change. As long as there's money behind it or promotion behind it, things will happen (David James).

In 1995, TVEI funding finally came to an end in Masonfield. The wind-up report to the Training, Education and Employment Department provided an extremely honest assessment of both the strengths and weaknesses of TVEI, and captured something of the excitement of being involved in such a ground breaking initiative (City of Masonfield, 1995). The report pointed out that 'undeniably the best work of TVEI took place in the pilot phase or the first three years of extension' (the latter coinciding with the last three years of pilot). TVEI was of course about much more than equal opportunities alone, and on a broader front the report declared that 'the Technical and Vocational Initiative in Masonfield has been a success', which it undoubtedly was. With respect to equal opportunities work in Masonfield, the report concluded - if anything, rather modestly - that,

> Much progress has been made over the last nine years in developing equal opportunities policies and practices in schools. However, a number of issues remain to be addressed: the project researcher's work reveals that there is still some distance to be travelled in overcoming stereotyping in option choices and career paths; established policies need monitoring and evaluation on a regular basis; the loss of the working group will inhibit future sharing of information and strategies; there remains a considerable amount of work to be done on issues of ethnicity (City of Masonfield, 1995, pp.50-51).

Although as this statement admits there was clearly still much to be done, it was also evident that TVEI had wrought a huge change in Masonfield. It is deeply ironic that a government policy which had initially been so unpopular with councillors because of its perceived threat to equality of opportunity *vis-a-vis* class and ability should by the end of pilot have had such an impact on the policy agenda with regards to the promotion of *gender* equality in education. This was of course a concern that was far from the minds of most officers and elected members in the years immediately preceding TVEI. Indeed, the changing climate had not only affected practice in the schools and the way in which policy was being generated - equal opportunities was at least given lip service in all policy documents emerging from the LEA by the end of pilot - but had made an impact on the composition of the council. Increasingly, a new 'breed' of Labour politicians were being elected who, following the lead given by Mrs Lewis, the Chair of the Education Committee, were keen to promote issues such as gender and race equality quite visibly.

Much of this success at the organisational level can be attributed to a number of features which were actually central to TVEI organisation more generally. The overall approach to educational innovation which was adopted by the MSC was based on the model of contract compliance and categorical funding,

> a strategy which can be used to facilitate a policy where the policy makers or their initiating agency, under existing conditions, have neither the statutory right nor the means to implement change without the cooperation of those who have both. They do, however, have the resources and proceed to use the normal processes of contract to implement their policies (Harland, 1987, quoted in Saunders, 1990, p.178).

Contract compliance was potentially a powerful tool for bringing about rapid change. Logically, it required a system of accountability and monitoring, and the development of appropriate performance indicators increasingly became a concern of the Training Agency. However, given that the criteria were non-negotiable, it was also essential that those involved in TVEI adapted to the particular philosophy of TVEI. Consequently, a programme of awareness-raising and in-service training was integral to TVEI's model for the management of change (Lines and Stoney, 1989; Sims, 1989), with much of it conducted under TRIST funding (TVEI-related In-Service Training). The application to equal opportunities work of these three elements of TVEI's broader organisation - contract compliance, accountability and awareness raising - had fundamental implications for the success with which change could be achieved in this area, and each of these elements will be considered in turn.

Contract compliance

Given that equal opportunities was the first funding criterion of TVEI, a commitment to equal opportunities was clearly deemed to be a prerequisite, although LEAs came to TVEI with a variety of 'states of readiness' in this respect (Dale et al, 1990). Nonetheless, the acceptance of resources was effectively equated by the MSC with acceptance of TVEI policy in all areas and with the ability to 'deliver', regardless of whether this was in fact the case (Harland, 1987). In Masonfield, David James was convinced that contract compliance was the key to getting schools to tackle gender issues:

> One of the things I'm quite convinced about (is) that had it not been on the agenda, then certainly we in Masonfield would never have been able to have tackled the schools. The fact that the schools were getting tens of thousands of pounds for a project where it was the first thing on the agenda meant at least we were in a position to force them to tackle it - which they would not have done, I'm absolutely convinced of that, without TVEI (David James).

Equal opportunities was a recurring theme in annual reports to the Training Agency, and was a theme which was invariably picked up in annual review meetings between projects and the Training Agency. However, many projects appeared to get away with a bare minimum of effort year on year. Indeed, Dale et al claim that some of the projects with which they were involved as evaluators did not even include a section on equal opportunities in their original submission documents:

> The fact that the MSC accepted even those submissions with no mention of gender may have shed doubt on their own level of awareness or the extent to which LEAs would be held accountable for equal opportunities within the contractual arrangements (Dale et al, 1990, p.145).

So how successful was contract compliance as a strategy for 'enforcing' a commitment to equal opportunities in pilot projects? As noted above, there is evidence to suggest that involvement in TVEI led to a genuine shift in attitude towards gender issues across many pilot projects. Such success was, however, highly dependent on the personnel who were appointed to key TVEI posts. Committed coordinators, by means of their own personal power base, were able to 'accelerate' progress even within LEAs which had had no previous track record on equal opportunities (ibid). Conversely, LEAs whose TVEI projects were headed by someone with minimal commitment to equal opportunities were unlikely to achieve much sustained progress, even despite the existence of highly motivated and committed teachers within the pilot schools.

Of all TVEI's criteria, equal opportunities was arguably the criterion towards which it was easiest to pay lip service. Failure to progress in other areas would be highly visible - the existence *or not* of records of achievement, the placement *or not* of pupils in work experience. Equal opportunities work was rather more subtle, and unlikely to result in dramatic, overnight change. Consequently, it would have been relatively easy for a pilot school - or an entire pilot project - to claim that it was addressing the issue, but finding progress slow, when in fact they were paying no more than lip service. But what if a pilot project was blatant about its lack of commitment? Certainly, the national advisers were only too well aware of pilot coordinators who had a scant regard for the issue. How realistic was the threat of the withdrawal of funding? It would appear that, in practice, as with potential breaches of the TVEI contract in other areas, contract compliance was an empty threat:

> It may be that 'contract' is a misnomer for the kind of deals struck between LEAs and the MSC. Despite a good deal of bluster on some occasions, no project has had to give up any funds on the basis of not having kept to original proposals. Indeed, no project has kept to original plans, and even more so, no school has kept to the deal. Despite elaborate and extensive monitoring, the control that 'contract compliance' may imply has been a sheep in wolf's

clothing. Writers (for example, Harland) were mistaken in assuming that control might be achieved through the mechanism of a contract. TVEI has colonised schools, there is no doubt, but not because of any monitoring procedures. Its influence has more probably derived from the attractiveness of several other factors - funds, progressive educational ideology and speed of delivery, and the resultant complicity of the teachers themselves' (Saunders, 1990, p.180).

The MSC were of course forced to rely on contract compliance as a means of control given that it had no legal basis for its control of schools. Saunders concludes that 'in comparison with legislation, categorical funding is a weak form of control' (ibid, p.187). This may well be true with regard to curriculum change and in comparison with the power of the National Curriculum, yet one only needs to consider the negligible impact of the Sex Discrimination Act on education policy to begin wondering whether legislation has been any more successful in the area of equal opportunities. On the contrary, contract compliance within TVEI, whilst ultimately of limited usefulness in influencing schools who were persistently resistant to the need to address gender issues, arguably resulted in greater progress with regards to equal opportunities in secondary education than the power of the law. This is particularly significant when we consider that the TVEI influence in many, if not most, projects extended well beyond the confines of the pilot schools alone. Under the terms of the SDA, schools received advice from the EOC on equal opportunities good practice, but the majority of pupils would have been unaware of their rights with regard to equal access and treatment. Moreover, a compromise deal between the EOC and the DES meant that any equal opportunities complaints had to go through the DES in the first instance (Rendel, 1985) and, as we have seen, the DES was hardly a leader in the field (Carr, 1989; Amos, 1990). In contrast, under TVEI, a government quango with no formal powers over education managed to bring equal opportunities issues to the attention of key players in LEAs and schools, as well as to pupils themselves, and in many schools wrought considerable change. (More recently, Weiner et al (1997) have pointed to the similar effect on schools arising from OFSTED's requirements for equal opportunities information prior to inspection visits.)

But why was action not taken against those schools and projects which failed to deliver on their contractual obligations? One possible explanation is that such action would have reduced the MSC's influence within education at a time when it was hoping to extend TVEI to every LEA in the country. In order to maintain and increase that influence it would have needed to persuade the Treasury that its huge programme of expenditure on TVEI pilot had been worthwhile, particularly given that intervention within compulsory education was formally outside of the MSC's brief. Under such circumstances, it is unsurprising that funding was never withdrawn from individual projects, because the MSC would have been keen to demonstrate to the Treasury the universal success of TVEI. Indeed, Dale et al (1990) argue that 'only the supportive was disseminated' by the national TVEI Unit and that 'as a result any less auspicious developments within the scheme did not become widespread knowledge' until well after TVEI was established in the majority of LEAs (Dale et al, 1990, p.178). So what role did monitoring play within TVEI, and what were its implications for equal opportunities work? This is the focus of the following section.

Monitoring equal opportunities

From its earliest days, TVEI evaluation was accorded a high priority. Indeed, at the time, TVEI was arguably the most intensively evaluated and researched British education initiative ever (Bell and Raffe, 1991; Dale, 1992), although National Curriculum evaluation has by now undoubtedly appropriated this honour for itself. The use of terms such as 'cohort' and 'pilot project' implied that TVEI was being promoted as a serious 'experiment' in vocational education, from which lessons would be learned for future developments. That the announcement that TVEI was to be extended beyond the original ten pilot schemes came only three months after its original launch largely gave the lie to this, but a proportion of the TVEI budget continued to be allocated to evaluation, including commissioned studies by the NFER, Leeds University and Trent Polytechnic, and the funding of an in-house evaluation division. At the local level, participating projects had to allocate a minimum of one per cent of their annual budgets towards evaluation, part of which was invariably used to buy in consultancy from local university education departments, often as part of a consortium of projects. Other projects used the money to fund their own evaluators, often at relatively senior positions.

Monitoring and evaluation were clearly high profile elements of TVEI, but the fact that many projects made little progress towards the targets which were set for them begs the question of the primary purpose of evaluation. A controversial 1991 document on TVEI performance indicators argued that they were 'intended to function primarily as a management tool within a wider framework of planning, monitoring, evaluating and reviewing' (Employment Department, 1991, p.3), yet Dale et al argue that there is no evidence to suggest that earlier evaluation and monitoring had in any way fed into planning for TVEI Extension and that TVEI's huge programme of evaluation was 'little more than a symbolic and legitimating exercise' (Dale et al, 1990, p.179).

Against this backdrop, the Information Systems Strategy was promoted as a model for monitoring equal opportunities which went beyond a ritualistic collection of data, towards encouraging a constructive debate on the gender differences which existed in student outcomes and then moving towards change in those areas. However, as highlighted in chapter 5, many schools had difficulty in moving beyond the data collection stage. The expectation of the ISS was that the 'hard facts' would convince people of the rightness of the equal opportunities argument, yet this was often an ill-founded hope. Thus, one of the main problems with the ISS was its over-reliance on rational argument to win the day, and it seemed unable to move beyond this to take account of the power struggles which would inevitably follow in schools which followed the ISS approach. More recent concerns over school 'league tables' only serve to underline the inherent problems of a performance indicator-led approach to evaluation and the management of change.

As TVEI moved into its extension phase, data on subject choices and examination results by gender, aggregated to a project-wide level, were collected annually by the national TVEI Unit as part of the requirements of the extension database. Consequently, by the early 1990s every secondary school within an LEA involved in TVEI extension was obliged to provide data on gendered outcomes on an annual basis - and by then, TVEI had been established in all LEAs in England and Wales. Thus, the Training Agency succeeded in establishing a monitoring system which ensured that this information was routinely collected from all secondary schools in England and Wales. The impact of this exercise should not be underestimated, and the greater awareness of gender inequalities which this exercise would have promoted may well be an important factor in understanding current trends with respect to gendered educational attainment. This is a point underlined by Arnot et al's recent evaluation of gender equality in England and Wales:

> The positive identification of *strong central direction* with increased gender awareness - eg OFSTED equal opportunities criteria or TVEI equal opportunities requirements - suggests that equality initiatives that demand targets and accountability are likely to be more effective than those mainly dependent on individual commitment or voluntary effort (Arnot et al, 1996, p.161 - emphasis in original).

However, such evidence did not always have the desired effect of spurring teachers on to change their practice, and the next section considers how TVEI sought to influence teacher's attitudes with respect to gender inequalities in education.

Changing teachers' minds

The successful implementation of TVEI was highly dependent on the receptivity to change of individual teachers. However, this was never going to be a straightforward task:

> Those delivering TVEI were teachers who were trained and experienced in particular approaches. They worked in institutions and with colleagues who, like themselves, had certain aims and values predating, and different from, those of the initiative. In some respects, TVEI could be seen to carry an implicit criticism of these approaches, aims and values and of what had gone on before. This obviously coloured teachers' attitudes towards the change (Dale et al, 1990, p.82).

Teachers involved in TVEI were thus expected to change their practice in a number of areas, but none provoked such a strong personal reaction as equal opportunities (Ruddock, 1994). In the early days of TVEI, there was a strong reliance on awareness-raising as a strategy for change. The national equal opportunities workshops (discussed in chapter 3) were based very much on this approach. The workshops were based on the premise that:

> If you explained things with sufficient clarity, developed a necessary level of awareness and consciousness about the importance and value to be gained educationally and socially from adopting new styles, approaches and attitudes then action and implementation would follow (Chambers and Raffe, undated, p.8).

However, 'after some two years in pursuit of these beliefs... it became clear that this approach wasn't working nor would it work' (ibid). One of the obstacles to wider success identified by Jones and Gray was that all too often the workshop delegates were not the key decision makers in their schools or LEAs. Many of those who attended already had a high awareness of the issues involved, but tended to lack the institutional power necessary to bring about change. Others were in relatively powerful positions but lacked an effective strategy for delivering equal opportunities. It was from these concerns that the ISS was born, promising a way forward and a means of making equal opportunities a mainstream concern. Nonetheless, many individual projects continued to use awareness raising workshops as a key strategy for change. However, whilst some projects reported a measure of success in changing the attitudes of teachers or opening their eyes to the existence of gender inequalities, the most antagonistic teachers tended not to attend these workshops (Bridgwood and Betteridge, 1989).

In shifting their focus from awareness raising towards the promotion of the ISS, the new approach promoted by Jones and Gray moved away from trying to persuade people of the rightness of equal opportunities on moral grounds, only to replace it with a belief in the persuasive power of hard data. The ISS Handbook argued, for example, that a Head of Department would be more open to persuasion when faced with 'irrefutable evidence' of inequality in achievement, because they would feel it was 'their professional responsibility to deal with the problem'. This, the Handbook went on to argue,

> is quite a different aspect from arguing the 'Philosophy' or 'Policy' of Equal Opportunities as a moral issue... In so doing one is reducing the coercive nature of such a management of change strategy to the extent that the motivation for change does not come from some authoritarian source, outside the individual, but comes as a result of their own convictions. Changes, as a result of this approach, are much more likely to be successful and ongoing since they depend on self-motivation. Such an approach consciously avoids anti-sexist, anti-racist

approaches and is unifying rather than divisive (Jones and Gray, undated, p.13).

However, what was interpreted as irrefutable evidence of girls' underachievement by one teacher was liable to be interpreted by another as irrefutable evidence of girls' lesser abilities. GIST constantly faced this attitude with regard to the achievement of girls in the physical sciences and CDT (Whyte, 1986), and TVEI was equally unable to persuade the most resistant teachers of the need for an equal opportunities approach, whether on moral *or* educational grounds. This problem was commented on by a representative from the EOC:

> I think that what perhaps people didn't take account of was the raw material that you were actually dealing with, though. I mean, we know that a lot of teachers were very resistant to equal opportunities at that time and some still are, although I think it has improved greatly, but that was never taken into account when TVEI was introduced (August 1992).

However, Jones and Gray expressed the view that one of the main potential obstacles to turning equal opportunities into a mainstream educational concern arose not from difficulties of raising awareness amongst resistant teachers, but from the negative attitudes expressed by certain feminist teachers:

> JG: A number of people were quite hostile to it, because quite deliberately what we were doing was getting it out of the preserve of the feminists in the staffroom and actually making it a mainstream curriculum issue, and arguing that you should have senior and significant members of staff (on the working parties).
>
> LJ: And they didn't want that, feminists, did they? Because they said, oh well, that's depowering us, I mean what you're doing is you're giving it to the male power people on the staff, and our response to that was if they (senior management) are not accepting responsibility for equal opportunities, how do you think you are going to change things? And that was the problem.
>
> JG: But I mean its a political position that the two of us take up... its a view we have in relation to the ultra-left and also to the rarefied feminists in a sense, that our feeling was that they would keep moving the goalposts, because in a sense they wanted to be part of an out-group, their rationale was because they weren't getting anywhere, they were exploited or whatever, and that was always the danger with equal opportunities.

These comments are very significant in understanding TVEI's underlying equal opportunities philosophy. Not only do they play down the role of feminist teachers over many years in promoting grassroots anti-sexist practices within education, and trivialise the opposition with which their efforts have often been met, but they also highlight the ideological vacuum which lay at the heart of TVEI's equal opportunities policy. It is unlikely that a desire to make equal opportunities a mainstream issue would have been widely opposed by feminist teachers, although many undoubtedly had concerns about the model of equal opportunities that was emerging from the ISS approach. Power and self-interest are also rendered of little consequence in this account, and the arguments for caution expressed by feminist teachers are dismissed as unreasonable. There is no recognition that in a male-dominated educational system it is a matter of considerable importance if women teachers feel that they are being further disempowered. The fact that this disempowerment occurred in the name of equal opportunities would have been particularly hard to stomach, and it is not surprising within this context if the ISS was criticised by some feminist teachers.

Jones and Gray's comments also reveal an implicit view that the arguments of feminist teachers were irrational and subjective, and that feminist teachers were liable to do more harm than good by voicing their opinions. This was by no means an isolated view. For example, Bridgwood and Betteridge's review of equal opportunities strategies notes that 'a few interviewees felt that the tone of some INSET sessions had been 'too feminist'. Many people have deeply-held views about gender and respond better to gradual persuasion than to abrupt challenges' (Bridgwood and Betteridge, 1989, p.34). A similar attitude was expressed in a newsletter produced by TVEI evaluators at the University of East Anglia. A (male) TVEI Coordinator wrote that,

> The role of feminists in the staff group is one which needs particularly sensitive handling, not least by the feminists themselves. I firmly believe that equal opportunities must always be portrayed as an 'educational' issue in the widest sense, and therefore *sexual politics must not be allowed to cloud it* if we are to engage the hearts and minds of all staff (CARE, 1986, p.6 - emphasis added).

Again, there was no argument with the need for equal opportunities to be made a mainstream educational issue. However, attempting to divorce sexual politics from gender issues in education, portraying them instead as primarily pedagogic issues, essentially undermined a key issue which lay at the heart of the issue. Thus, there was always an inherent danger that TVEI would attempt to make equal opportunities a mainstream issue by means of 'sanitising' the debate, essentially transforming and containing the more radical concerns of many feminist teachers (Yates, 1993).

TVEI and organisational change

To a very large extent, then, the direction and success of TVEI's equal opportunities emphasis was shaped by key aspects of TVEI's model of implementation. Firstly, contract compliance proved to be a crucial tool for the management of change, arguably resulting in TVEI achieving a far greater impact on educational organisation and policy making over the five year pilot phase than the EOC had managed to achieve by legislative means in the previous ten year period. Secondly, TVEI's monitoring procedures placed an emphasis on the collection of data disaggregated by gender, culminating in the establishment of a database which contained information on the subject choices and post-16 destinations of boys and girls from every secondary school in England and Wales. Thirdly, TVEI's equal opportunities policy relied very much on 'carrying' teachers along with it, and much effort was put into devising ways of persuading teachers of the wisdom of equal opportunities, firstly by means of moral persuasion, and latterly by means of appealing to the professionalism of teachers. By such means, an awareness of gender inequalities in education undeniably became much more widespread amongst the teaching profession.

These features also had inherent limitations. Given that the threat of the withdrawal of funding was never followed through, it was possible for some pilot projects and schools merely to pay lip service to TVEI's equal opportunities criterion. The emphasis on measurable outcomes resulted in a concentration on aspects of equal opportunities which were most amenable to quantifiable measurement which, whilst fitting in with TVEI's most immediate concerns, marginalised more 'qualitative' issues. Finally, TVEI had a troubled relationship with more radical approaches to gender inequalities, manifest in a widespread unease vis-a-vis feminist approaches which emphasised the centrality of sexual politics. This had serious implications for TVEI's impact on the experiences of pupils and teachers, particularly female pupils and teachers, and pinpoints a general ambivalence on the part of the educational establishment towards more radical approaches. TVEI's limited impact on pupil outcomes forms the focus of the next section.

TVEI's impact on pupils

TVEI's stated *raison d'être* was the preparation of young people for adult life. As we have seen, in most projects this led to a focus on career planning and the prior step of option choice. Accordingly, TVEI resources were concentrated on efforts to promote non-traditional option choices and career plans. In tackling these issues, TVEI developed an emphasis upon the importance of individual decision making and highlighted the centrality of awareness raising to the removal of discrimination, a liberal approach which tended to perpetuate a deficit model of girls and their aspirations. Despite the concentration of effort in this area, however, TVEI proved to have little success in encouraging young people to opt for the non-traditional, both pre- and post-16.

There is some evidence to suggest that the young people who were involved in TVEI were well aware of its equal opportunities emphasis and that their preconceptions had been challenged by the message that non-traditional choices were acceptable. Despite their awareness of the policy, however, TVEI's equal opportunities emphasis proved to be largely irrelevant to them. The vast majority of school leavers had not even the faintest desire to pursue non-traditional options and careers, although many insisted that they would not have hesitated to choose such routes if they had so wished. They argued that they were perfectly happy for others to choose the non-traditional, but that such routes were not for them. Consequently, because resources were concentrated on encouraging young people into non-traditional pathways, TVEI's equal opportunities policy had little to offer the vast majority of students, even though once in the labour market they were acutely aware of the nature of gender inequalities. Whilst issues such as sexual harassment were occasionally discussed in the context of the promotion of non-traditional occupations, TVEI had relatively little to say about similar problems associated with gender relations within traditional areas of employment, and left pupils unprepared to cope with problems such as a lack of access to promotion and training, or the effects of discrimination on their day to day working lives.

TVEI's obvious limitations in this respect brings us right back to the issues raised in the opening chapters of this book, and the dilemma that vocational education has *always* presented to policy makers. Can schools ever hope to make a significant impact in changing existing gender relations in the labour market when schools themselves are key agents in promoting and reinforcing those very divisions? To put it another way: was TVEI setting itself a theoretically impossible task? Or would it be possible to achieve a measure of success (that is, within TVEI's own restricted terms of reference), yet still maintain the role of the school as a key site for the reproduction of sexual divisions within the labour market? Walby (1990), for example, has argued that the mass movement of women into the labour market represents a transition from private to public forms of patriarchy. Thus, women are no longer subordinated primarily within the household by individual men but, in order to meet the changing needs of capitalism, have been allowed access to the waged economy - where they find themselves subordinated to men in general within the public sphere, overwhelmingly located within low paid, often temporary and part-time, positions. From this perspective, it could be argued that post-war educational policies which provided greater opportunities to women facilitated this move to a public form of patriarchy, simultaneously meeting the needs of both capitalism and patriarchy. Thus, the needs of capital may change over time, but the relations between those whom capitalism privileges and those whom it disadvantages will arguably remain broadly the same.

A version of this argument could be applied to educational initiatives, TVEI included, which have overtly promoted the movement of young people into non-traditional curricular and occupational areas. Kelly (1985), writing in the context of GIST, has argued that it is possible that 'highly gendered' subjects and associated occupations may well become acceptable routes for young women, but that this need not affect the fundamental nature of a sexually divided labour market. Young women may gain qualifications which equip them for careers in male-dominated occupational areas, but this will not necessarily guarantee them subsequent employment or positions of power and influence if they do succeed in gaining employment in traditionally male areas, a point reinforced by Kenway (1993) in the context of similar policies to promote 'non-traditional pathways' in Australia. Similarly, it could be argued that routes more commonly associated with young women could become attractive to young men without substantially changing the nature of gender relations. Riddell (1992a), for example, argues that boys may be encouraged by teachers and careers advisers to pursue non-traditional occupations largely because of the opportunities such routes provide for young men to outstrip their female competitors. Thus, a move to break down horizontal gender segregation may ultimately serve to reinforce vertical segregation. Both these examples suggest that the net result of initiatives to promote equal opportunities within a vocational context, even when successful, will inevitably be to strengthen the labour market position of men vis-a-vis women, lending support to Walby's thesis. Recent examination successes by young women in traditionally male subject areas (Elwood and Comber, 1995; Elwood, 1996) similarly reinforce this argument, as there does not appear to be a marked corollary within the youth labour market.

However, even if it was theoretically possible for these shifts to occur without substantially fracturing patriarchal relations between men and women, the fact remains that TVEI had very little impact, even within the narrow parameters of the areas it identified as priorities for change. Despite the concerted efforts of many educators, boys and girls did not move into non-traditional subject areas, let alone non-traditional occupations, in vast numbers. The tiny minority who did, though, served an important ideological function, providing 'proof' that it was possible for a woman to break into a man's world, and vice versa. By such means, broader gender inequalities within TVEI (not least those affecting female teachers) were made legitimate by the existence of an equal opportunities policy which encouraged young people to 'choose' the non-traditional if they so wished. Any resulting inequality could thus be constructed as an artifact of individual choice and a lack of motivation and/or ability. There is of course a strong parallel here with Bowles and Gintis' critique of the meritocratic ideal within liberal education. They argued that class-based inequalities in educational outcomes were similarly represented as the inevitable result of different levels of ability and motivation, thereby giving legitimacy to the social reproductive functions of schooling (Bowles and Gintis, 1976). Thus, 'the ideology of free choice has been used as a means of persuading individual pupils to accept responsibility for educational outcomes which are in reality due to structural forces beyond their control' (Riddell, 1992a, p.72).

It is undoubtedly the case that many young women *will* benefit from an emphasis on equal opportunities (Weiner, 1990), adding further weight to the legitimation argument. But who are these women? The careers which tend to be promoted by equal opportunities policies within vocational contexts are predominantly professional-level careers such as engineering, medicine and science, and the pupils most likely to benefit will be young women from middle class backgrounds. In particular, Devine (1993 and 1994) has pointed out that a high proportion of young women who pursue non-traditional careers are strongly influenced by fathers working in similar areas. Thus, to choose a career in a similar field was to reproduce the class advantage of the family of origin. The likely futures of the majority of working class pupils, both male and female, remain largely unaffected by a policy commitment which offers a middle class notion of 'career'. Attempts to promote equal opportunities for women which ignore the interaction between gender and race will, therefore, result in a widening of the class gap between women (Arnot, 1992), as well as a perpetuation of inequalities between men and women: selective access is offered to individuals, at the expense of the empowerment of subordinated groups (Kessler et al, 1985, p46).

The logical conclusion of these arguments is, however, rather pessimistic, suggesting that however hard schools might try to overcome gender inequalities their actions will inevitably reinforce the status quo. This is a key difficulty associated with deterministic social reproduction theories and, for those who are genuinely committed to progressive change through education, this is a deeply depressing picture. It seems to suggest that they are wasting their time - or, as Kelly (1985) puts it, are perhaps 'suffering from a bad case of false consciousness.' As a counter to the over-determinism of much social reproduction theory, Arnot (1984) has argued that whilst schools undoubtedly *do* act as forces of social control, *simultaneously* they have the potential to act as a progressive force vis-a-vis the predominant values within society. She concludes that individual schools or classrooms may actually succeed in becoming sites of resistance, enjoying 'relative autonomy' from the wider aims of the education system. However, one of the chief difficulties of TVEI was that it often *failed* to challenge those predominant values, and instead brought them straight into the classroom, by virtue of its necessary and central link to the 'world of work'. TVEI was by definition explicitly allied with the needs of the labour market (even though national objectives were often out of step with the needs of *local* labour markets). In seeking to forge links with the 'world of work' pupils of necessity were brought face to face with the dominant values of capitalism and patriarchy, the injustices of which were obvious to many teachers. However, by integrating the world of work into the curriculum and exposing young people directly and often uncritically to the discriminatory practices and assumptions of the labour market, TVEI further reinforced those practices and assumptions by association, one of the most crucial being the general subordination of women to men within paid labour. As Turner et al (1995) argue in their evaluation of TVEI in Scotland,

> it is possible that, despite its ostensible commitment to widening access to employment, TVEI might, because of its vocational orientation, have contributed to the process of pupil socialisation into a gender differentiated labour market (ibid, p.56).

Thus, even though TVEI made efforts to counterbalance the influences of the 'real world', ultimately these forces proved too strong: TVEI's impact on gender relations within the labour market proved to be negligible and, if anything, retrogressive.

The real issue for TVEI practitioners was not *whether* schools should have engaged with the world of work (a non-starter in the context of TVEI), but the *nature* of that engagement. Pilot schools would have been accused of failing their pupils if they had refused point-blank to engage with the labour market. Even anti-vocationalists would presumably support the provision of basic careers education, for example, but that is quite different from gearing the curriculum specifically to the needs of employers, whatever those needs may be. There was, and still is, therefore, a need for a framework which allows schools to tackle these issues in a way which does not simply reflect the dominant values of the labour market, but which rather engages critically with the world of work. Of course, many of the issues which such an approach might seek to tackle arise not just within the labour market, but within the school itself: issues such as discrimination, the 'policing' of sexuality, sexual violence and harassment, and the lack of training and promotion opportunities for women are as relevant to the school experiences of young women - and their female teachers - as they are to the wider world of work. However, for schools to effectively tackle issues such as these would necessitate an acknowledgement that 'the social scaffolding of modern state secondary schooling is informed by differentiated masculinities and femininities and the power relations that are contained within them' (Mac an Ghaill, 1994, p.4). In contrast, TVEI quite deliberately attempted to bring about change within a depoliticised agenda, underpinned by a belief that this was the only way to transform gender issues from being a fringe interest into a mainstream educational concern. Whilst done with laudable intent, the consequence was that the issue was sanitised by excising any 'unhelpful' references to sexual politics, which were considered the preserve of extremists.

Redefining gender inequalities

The radical, anti-sexist work which had been developing prior to TVEI, particularly within New Left authorities, had been focused almost exclusively on girls and women, the argument being that to concentrate resources on girls was not to give them something extra, but to give them the same treatment that boys had effectively enjoyed throughout their schooling (Mahony, 1985). The rationale of these earlier initiatives was to boost women's self-confidence and esteem in order to fight back against patriarchal relations within the school, within the home and within wider society, rather than to encourage them to pursue non-traditional occupations in order to meet the specific short-term needs of the labour market. If boys were discussed in this more radical framework, it tended to be in the context of providing support for gay men alongside lesbian women (both pupils and teachers), although some schools tried to initiate anti-sexist work with boys. However, by developing a high profile equal opportunities policy of its own, TVEI claimed the right to redefine the nature of the problem. As we have seen, this meant redefining the issue in purely vocational terms and as an educational problem demanding an educational solution. Most significantly, gender inequality was redefined as a problem for boys as much as it was for girls, and any measures that were to be taken under the auspices of TVEI had to be seen to be scrupulously fair to the interests of both sexes. Thus, TVEI acknowledged the existence of gender inequalities, but it failed to acknowledge the relations of power on which those inequalities were based and, as Weiler (1993) has argued, the meanings of 'race' and 'gender' which were adopted within this framework tended to perpetuate white male control and their positions of power. More radical interpretations of the problem of gender inequality clearly posed an unwelcome threat to those in positions of power and were therefore 'transformed and contained' into a less threatening policy (Yates, 1993).

The more radical initiatives for change which had begun to emerge in the early 1980s had increasingly sought to address not only gender inequalities in education, but racial inequalities also (Jones, 1989; Lupton and Russell, 1990). 'Race' was largely neglected by TVEI during the pilot years, which meant that TVEI's equal opportunities policy tended to universalise the experiences of girls and young women, ignoring differences between girls from different ethnic and cultural backgrounds, as well as girls from different class backgrounds. Towards the end of pilot, consideration began to be paid to 'race' as a dimension of equal opportunities work (and the TVEI Extension criteria included a commitment to equal opportunities for young people from 'all ethnic origins' as well as on grounds of gender), but in practice it tended to be seen as a separate issue, rather than an issue interlinked with gender inequality. Within Masonfield, for example, the view was expressed by some of the pilot school coordinators that gender had been the focus of equal opportunities work for too long, and that it was now time to look at 'race': it was a question of either/or, rather than both. Thus, whilst the need to address race and racism within education was eventually recognised by TVEI, debates concerning the interrelationship between race and gender tended to be marginalised, in the same way that radical voices on gender were marginalised; again, the more radical discourses regarded schools as part of the problem for black pupils.

Weiner (1990) has argued that TVEI's success in transforming equal opportunities into a mainstream concern has meant that there is now little future for the more radical edge of feminist activity in schools, although the institutional base for equal opportunities work is now stronger than ever. This begs the question of whether TVEI's success was at too high a price for feminism, whether the point at which it went mainstream was actually the 'kiss of death' for more radical strategies. Cockburn's comments with regards to equal opportunities policies in employment are pertinent:

> It could be that positive action for sex equality in organisations is a passing fad. The 1980s may be remembered as the period in which the new wave feminism of the seventies drained away into the sands of institutionalism. If this is so it will be because the movement was sanitised, immobilised and defeated in its

encounter with men in places of power (Cockburn, 1991, p.227).

It *may* be the case that radical policies are now unlikely to become incorporated into the mainstream, and it is *certainly* the case that policies such as TVEI have marginalised more radical voices, but this does not necessarily imply that radical voices will disappear altogether. Radical feminist strategies have traditionally blossomed in 'unofficial' spaces within schools, where much of the politics of gender is worked out (Arnot, 1993). TVEI did not prevent feminist teachers from continuing to develop subversive strategies on these sites nor from subverting male-dominated educational practices within their own classrooms. Indeed, rather than seeing TVEI's success as a monolithic threat to more radical approaches, it should be recognised that within the classroom TVEI positively encouraged the development of new teaching strategies, giving official sanction to feminist teachers to develop 'girl-friendly' and 'girl-centred' approaches to teaching and learning. It also increased the potential for the 'subversion' of subjects beyond those which had most commonly been taught by feminists (English and history), whilst TVEI's emphasis on other developments - Records of Achievement, for example, or residential experience - provided the opportunity to extend an equal opportunities influence beyond the confines of the traditional curriculum. These are precisely the areas of TVEI which were less amenable to quantification, yet where the greatest influence on girls may have been felt.

TVEI in perspective

TVEI pilot funding came to an end in the late 1980s for the majority of LEAs, with extension funding expiring in the early 1990s. Masonfield's extension funding ceased in summer 1995, and the few remaining projects were finally wound up in summer 1997. In spite of the huge financial investment of TVEI, its overall legacy has been challenged by the demands of the National Curriculum and other educational changes. Davies et al (1992), for example, point out that TVEI only merited two brief comments in the National Curriculum consultation document, whilst Saunders (1990) argues that the influence TVEI had on developing progressive teaching styles will have been undermined by the reinstatement of a traditional curriculum. Perhaps this is the ultimate revenge of the DES; its authority and influence having been usurped in the early 1980s by an outsider in the shape of the MSC, it has now reasserted its authority in the form of the National Curriculum. It is, of course, a fairly weak form of revenge, given that the education and employment functions of government have now been merged with the creation in 1996 of the Department For Education and Employment.

This reassertion has, however, had important ramifications for the future of equal opportunities initiatives within education. As a former chief executive of the EOC has noted, 'in relation to gender issues the DES can hardly be regarded as a trail blazer and usually follows well behind enlightened educational opinion when it comes to promoting equal opportunities in schools' (Amos, 1990, p.8). Indeed, there is plenty of evidence to suggest that more recent educational developments have undermined many of the gains made under TVEI and have 'placed reintrenchment above change on the agenda' (Gleeson and McLean, 1994, p.242). The longer-term impact of the 1988 Education Reform Act continues to be a source of concern, firstly with regard to certain integral features of the National Curriculum (Carr, 1989; Davies et al, 1990; Shah, 1990; Miles and Middleton, 1990), and secondly with regard to the devolution of powers away from Local Education Authorities and the associated granting of increased powers to school governing bodies (Deem, 1989; Reynolds, 1992). Moreover, the 1994 White Paper on education and training (DTI, 1994), singled out one of TVEI's most problematic features, its work experience programme, for particular praise. The White Paper went on to pledge to provide *all* pupils with a work experience placement, organised via Training and Enterprise Councils. The White Paper also called for a major investment in careers education, to be provided by the now privatised network of local careers services.

The policies and pledges noted above were, of course, made under a Conservative administration. However, the change of government in May 1997 has not resulted in any indication of a substantial change of direction. A few weeks after taking office, David Blunkett, Secretary of State for Education and Employment, announced the formation of a new body - the Qualifications and Curriculum Authority (QCA) - which will combine the functions of the School Curriculum Assessment Authority and the National Council for Vocational Qualifications, thus signalling a desire for a stronger partnership between the academic and the vocational. Indeed, the Deputy Chairman (sic) of the QCA has been named as Dominic Cadbury, Chairman of Cadbury's Schweppes plc and of the CBI's Education and Training Committee, an appointment which, as David Blunkett noted, 'brings a powerful voice from business to the world of education and emphasises the new Government's strong support for links between schools, colleges and industries' (DFEE, 1997, p.1). Indeed, we seem to be heading for a 1990s version of the Great Debate, embroiled in a more general debate about educational standards, but tied to concerns about the problems that are thus caused *for industry*. Not untypically, Prince Charles has also added to this debate (Carvel, 1997a), whilst the *Times Educational Supplement's* 32 page 'Business Links' pull-out included headlines such as 'We need business to help us raise standards', 'Our customers, our pupils' and 'You're never too young to work: Even nursery children can be given a feel for factory life' (TES, 1997).

Much of the current debate around the apparent skills-gap is also being conducted within a broader discussion about the weaknesses of existing vocational qualifications, not just the inadequacies of an overwhelmingly academic curriculum. Regardless of their academic merits, recent evidence has highlighted the perpetuation of a gender gap with respect to participation and attainment in vocational qualifications (such as NVQ, GNVQ, RSA, BTEC and City and Guilds courses).

Felstead et al (1995) have shown that young women are less likely than young men to receive vocational qualifications, for example, and that young men are more likely than their female counterparts to be taking higher level courses. Other research has highlighted strong horizontal segregation within BTEC courses, although young women are more likely to complete their course than young men, including female students in male-dominated subject areas such as agriculture, computing and construction (Bailey, 1992).

On the few occasions when official concerns have been expressed around gender issues in recent years, it has arisen overwhelmingly from a concern for *boys*. Thus, Chris Woodhead, Her Majesty's Chief Inspector of Schools, recently stated that 'the failure of boys, and in particular white working class boys' is one of the most disturbing problems we face within the whole education system' (Woodhead, 1996). This is despite research which has highlighted that white working class boys actually tend to do better than afro-caribbean working class boys (Gilborn and Gipps, 1996). Woodhead's statement played into the hands of a frenzied media debate on gender and educational attainment (Raphael Reid, 1997), and was followed shortly afterwards by an OFSTED report which, in rather more measured terms, reiterated a concern for boys' examination performance (OFSTED, 1996). Not to be outdone, Estelle Morris, at the time Labour spokesperson on education and now a key member of David Blunkett's team at the DFEE, made a speech in the House of Commons which *also* repeated this theme (Morris, 1996). Now in office, one of the solutions to educational underachievement which is being mooted is the introduction of schemes allowing 'disaffected youths' to spend part of their school week learning vocational skills with local firms (Carvel, 1997b).

All of these developments have very serious implications for the future of equal opportunities policies within education. During the TVEI years, categorical funding from the MSC kept the issue on the policy agenda, yet in the post-TVEI era, equal opportunities have effectively been sidelined from the major policy debates. The DFEE may possibly have felt that TVEI had largely succeeded in making equal opportunities a mainstream concern, or at least had done as much as was realistically possible, and that a further concentration of resources was therefore considered unnecessary, especially given that all pupils now follow the same curriculum. Regardless of the motivation behind the failure to systematically address equal opportunities in recent policy, however, the gains that were made under TVEI, for all their weaknesses, could potentially be lost as a result of these various policy developments.

Lessons for the future

Vocationalism is clearly not just a passing fad within the British education system. TVEI, as part of the New Vocationalism of the 1980s, emerged in response to very specific concerns about the supposed inadequacies of school leavers and was very much a *political* response to those concerns. Current discussions of declining standards, skills gaps and underachieving boys are equally politicised, and situated very much in contemporary concerns. It seems highly possible that a vocationalist scheme along the lines of TVEI will be proposed as the solution, showing once again the tendency for history to repeat itself within the British education system. Whatever happens, though, it is extremely unlikely that the same generous levels of funding will be made available: vocationalism on a shoe string is not likely to place a very high priority on 'extras' such as equal opportunities appointments. What, then, are the lessons of TVEI in attempting to shape a feminist response to the ongoing emphasis on vocationalism within the pre-16 curriculum, particularly given the downgrading of girls' equal opportunities concerns relative to those of boys? Given that vocationalism is here to stay, what might a feminist response look like?

Firstly, it is important that the continuing success of high-achieving girls is celebrated, rather than problematised. However, it should not be allowed to cloud the issue of continuing post-16 inequalities, both in terms of academic and vocational credentialism and in relation to the youth labour market. Discrimination against women exists as much within traditionally female spheres as it does within male-dominated spheres, albeit in slightly different forms, and in numerical terms affects a far greater number of women. Thus, whilst acknowledging the extreme difficulties faced by a growing number of young men as they attempt a smooth transition into the labour market (Haywood and Mac an Ghaill, 1996), the difficulties experienced by young women should also be flagged up in any programmes of careers education and guidance. Moreover, the existence of discrimination on the basis of other factors needs to be overtly addressed, not least because one of the most serious weaknesses of vocational education is a failure to acknowledge the unlevel playing field upon which school leavers are situated not just due to gender differences, but also by virtue of socially ascribed characteristics such as 'race' and class. Schemes such as TVEI may constantly emphasise equal opportunity and equal access, yet many leavers still find themselves excluded from the opportunities they most desire. By ignoring the structural basis of these inequalities, a heavy burden is placed upon school leavers and many will undoubtedly individualise their inability to achieve their career goal, rather than attribute it to structural factors.

Secondly, the aims of work experience programmes need to be carefully evaluated. To say that work experience is an essential element in preparing young people for adult life is an overstatement, not least because of the importance of other forms of exposure to the world of work. If this point is conceded, then imaginative responses can be developed, in which issues of gender inequality in the labour market can be specifically addressed. The wider use of work shadowing, for example, would allow pupils to spend time with people in unconventional careers or with those who are challenging stereotypical expectations in unusual or high-ranking positions. This would act to widen pupils' horizons and to counteract a common problem of many pupils being assigned to workplaces where they end up merely making the tea and standing in front of the photocopier all day. To justify such activities by arguing that this is what many young people will be doing once they leave school is to miss the point wildly. It may also be possible, as some schools have attempted to do, to allow pupils to choose two placements, on the condition that one placement is an area which they would not normally consider (and not necessarily non-traditional in gender terms). At the very least, pupils should be actively encouraged to reflect upon the gender dynamics of their workplace in any debriefing exercises. It is worth noting in passing the recent popularity of the annual 'Take our daughters to work' day, an idea imported from the USA. There is a danger that this programme merely reinforces gender divisions, alongside divisions based on race and class. A better approach might be a programme which, where possible, encourages fathers to take their daughters to work, and mothers to take their sons to work; the latter may do more to raise awareness amongst young men of the poor conditions under which women often work than any amount of classroom-based awareness-raising.

Thirdly, it is imperative that the idiosyncratic responses of young men and women to vocational equal opportunities initiatives are taken seriously. This will involve a movement away from an assumption which underpins much equal opportunities work that the message which is transmitted is identical to the message that is received. The evidence of ethnographic research confirms the complex responses of young people to calls to consider non-traditional curriculum areas or subsequent careers (see chapter 8), whilst Kenway et al have highlighted the danger of much girl-centred work inadvertently presenting a rather drab, anti-pleasure and consequently unappealing version of femininity. Moreover,

> whilst they didn't seem to mind being critical of patriarchy - seen as 'out there' - their hackles often rose if critique got too close to family and friends. Strong fluctuations of opinion often occurred in the transition from single-sex to co-educational classes, when female solidarity with feminist teachers often gave way to peer solidarity against femininity and feminist teachers (Kenway et al, 1994, p.195).

Foster (1996) has similarly noted the discomfort experienced by girls *on behalf of their male peers* when gender issues are raised in the classroom. Thus, feminist teachers and researchers need to be acutely aware of these interpretations, and should seek not to condemn them but to try to understand them and work both with and through them, an approach which Kenway et al (1994) refer to as 'deconstructionist'. Further, Foster's argument points to the need for opportunities to conduct single sex awareness-raising work with girls, away from the pressures which many of them may feel whilst in the same classroom as boys. This is a call which would also be welcomed by many men seeking to conduct gender work with boys (Jackson and Salisbury, 1996).

Finally, there needs to be greater awareness of the extent to which questions of masculine and feminine identity are tied up in the vocational choices made by young people. Thus, certain subjects and careers are extremely appealing because of the unambiguous version of masculinity or femininity which they represent; conversely, some subjects pose a threat to one's sense of identity and perhaps give other pupils reason to call into question one's sexual identity. These concerns are invariably played down, or ignored, within many initiatives designed to encourage pupils to 'experiment' with non-traditional subjects or occupational areas. If the promotion of the non-traditional is seen to be an important goal in itself, then this would again imply the need for single sex provision in subjects which have a strong prior gender association. Although post-structuralists would argue that this strategy reinforces an unhelpful binary divide, this would seem to be an occasion when treating boys and girls as homogenous categories may actually be to their advantage. Moreover, the single sex classroom will arguably allow girls *more* freedom, not less, to experiment with notions of femininity; away from the 'male gaze', it may be much easier to take on supposedly 'male' traits. Given sensitive classroom teaching, the same could apply in reverse for boys in single sex environments.

To conclude, TVEI's equal opportunities policy marked an important, albeit unintended, moment of transition in the politics of gender inequalities in education. From being a peripheral if not neglected issue in most schools, the issue of gender inequality moved centre stage under TVEI funding and had a major impact on the place of equal opportunities in official policy making. Ultimately, though, the policy was fatally flawed. The apparent lack of initial thought behind the policy was reflected in a false assumption that boys and girls formed homogenous categories undifferentiated by social characteristics such as class and 'race'. The policy was further weakened by its deficit model of young women and by the subsequent failure of TVEI's architects to address the theoretical issues which lay at the heart of the practical challenge that had been set. Consequently, it developed a restricted focus for its work, and offered little to the vast majority of young men and women who chose to be involved in TVEI pilot. Although it always had the potential to develop a far more radical edge, TVEI was constrained by the perceived need not only to be 'fair' to both boys and girls, but to be 'reasonable' in the approach it adopted. Ironically, despite these limitations, TVEI's attempts to tackle gender inequalities in education may ultimately come to be regarded as something of a 'golden age' for equal opportunities. However, whilst TVEI represented, without question, an unprecedented opportunity to make an impact on gender relations both within school and more widely, it failed to address some of the most pressing equal opportunities concerns of young people, particularly women, as they moved into the labour market. As such, TVEI can perhaps be said to have offered as many *lost* opportunities as it did *equal* opportunities.

Appendix 1:
A note on method

1. Researching the policy makers' perspectives

Two major sources of data have been drawn upon to explore the policymakers' perspectives on TVEI: (i) documentary evidence relating to the introduction of TVEI and its pilot phase in Masonfield; and (ii) interviews with key LEA personnel, as well as two interviews with national figures. Each will be examined in turn.

(i) Documentary analysis

It was imperative that I turned to documentary evidence for two main reasons: firstly, to put developments within an 'historical' context, but secondly in order to examine and attempt to understand the underlying philosophy of equal opportunities which emerged over time, and the implications that philosophy then had for the strategies which were considered to be feasible. The Central Coordinator granted me access to a wide range of materials, which are described below (a full list of documentation is provided in the bibliography):

TVEI Coordinators Meeting Minutes, September 1986-1992

These are a formal record of the regular meetings of school-based coordinators, convened by the Central Coordinator. These documents proved to be extemely disappointing: they are very formal minutes, rarely capturing the 'flavour' of a meeting.

Minutes and papers of the Pilot Equal Opportunities Working Group, 1989

These are very detailed minutes of a group set up as a forum for the sharing of experience and progress on the Information Systems Strategy which was launched in Masonfield in late 1988. Four of the pilot schools officially attended these meetings, although the coordinator of the school which was not involved in ISS used to attend informally. I also managed to trace a number of papers which were presented at these meetings. It should be noted that these minutes give only a partial picture: the meetings were regarded as a confidential forum and the minutes only captured the 'public face'; more sensitive concerns would not, apparently, have been minuted.

Minutes and papers of the TVEI Consultative Committee, 1988

This committee was set up to monitor TVEI developments in Masonfield (see chapter 4). The group ceased to exist after 1988 and minutes of meetings held in earlier years proved impossible to track down. Equal opportunities was a frequent topic of discussion.

Annual reports of the pilot schools, 1986-1991

These proved to be the most valuable source of information, particularly for giving a sense of development over time. Equal opportunities were discussed in each report, and the growing importance of the issue is evident from the space given to it in successive reports. These reports, usually written by the schools' TVEI coordinators, also contain a wealth of contextual detail relating to the project as a whole, including data on subject take-up, staffing, exam results and post-16 destinations.

Minutes and papers of the LEA Equal Opportunities (Curriculum) Working Group, 1989

These are the minutes of a group operating at the LEA level to produce a policy statement on equal opportunities. The Central TVEI Coordinator was a member of this group. The group carried out a comprehensive survey of the priority given to equal opportunities in each of the LEA's schools.

Minutes and papers of the Regional Equal Opportunities Steering Group, 1989-1990

As well as giving a broad picture of regional developments, these papers include specific references to developments within Masonfield, including Masonfield's entry in the regional 'good practice' directory.

Miscellaneous

A number of other documents have been drawn upon: an HMI report on one of the pilot schools (Seddon Park); notes from visits to the pilot schools made by the Senior Adviser prior to the start of TVEI; the original submission document sent to the MSC; minutes of a national equal opportunities meeting attended by the Central Coordinator; Training Agency review document on equal opportunities; documentation of the 'Women In Industry' event.

In addition to the sources released to me by the Central Coordinator, I drew extensively upon the minutes of the City Council Education Committee (housed in the local history library), from 1982 through to 1988, to capture the sequence of events in the genesis of TVEI in Masonfield LEA. These minutes were fairly detailed and proved to be invaluable for building up the broader picture of developments in the run-up to the launch of TVEI in Masonfield.

(ii) In-depth interviews

Interviews were held with the following 'policy makers', in chronological order:

Equal Opportunities Coordinator, Greenwood High School	20th October 1989
TVEI Coordinator, St Catherine's High School	12th July 1991
Principal Careers Officer, Masonfield LEA	2nd August 1991
Former national TVEI Equal Opportunities Advisers (Len Jones & Joan Gray)	20th August 1991
Central TVEI Coordinator, Masonfield LEA ('David James')	6th January 1992
Equal Opportunities Coordinator, Mosslands High School	31st January 1992
TVEI Coordinator, Seddon Park High School	6th February 1992
Chair of the Education Committee, Masonfield City Council	3rd June 1992
TVEI Coordinator, The Croft High School	17th June 1992
Two education specialists from the EOC	13th August 1992

The interviews with school-based coordinators (with the exception of the interview with the Greenwood High School equal opportunities coordinator) were all held on the school premises. The exception was held in the home of the person in question, as she had retired the previous summer. Interviews with LEA officers were held in their offices, and the interview with the Chair of the Education Committee was held in a committee room at the Town Hall. The interview with the two national advisers was held in the garden of Len Jones' home, and the interview with the EOC officials was held at the EOC. All but two of the interviews were tape-recorded and fully transcribed.

2. Researching the young people's perspectives

The data used in piecing together the perspectives of young people who had been involved in TVEI pilot were gathered in a three-stage process: (i) secondary analysis of Careers Service destinations data for pupils from pilot schools six months and eighteen months after they had left in summer 1989; (ii) a postal survey conducted a year after they had left school (summer 1990); and (iii) a series of interviews with young people two to two and a half years after they had left school (summer-autumn 1991). Each is described in turn.

(i) Secondary analysis of Masonfield Careers Service destinations data

All school leavers in Masonfield are routinely tracked by the LEA's Careers Service for up to three years, and this data is added to an already rich database of information gathered whilst the young people are still at school. In September 1989, I approached Masonfield Careers Service to ask permission to carry out secondary analysis on the December data relating to school leavers (both TVEI and non-TVEI) from the five pilot schools. Every year, the Careers Service produced a set of statistics relating to young people's post-school destinations in November/December of the autumn after leaving school. In most cases, the December destination is the first recorded destination, whilst for those who have already had jobs or started courses in the intervening six months, the December destination is deemed to be the most accurate picture of long-term destinations, as many young people move into short-term jobs immediately on leaving school before settling into a more permenant job or course.

I was sent a print-out containing individual records for 866 young people - all the summer 1989 leavers from the pilot High Schools, including the 244 young people who had been involved in Cohort II. I had information on the following variables for each leaver: individual client record number (no names), gender, name of high school, TVEI status (cohort/non-cohort), predicted GCSE performance, job of interest whilst at school (expressed as an OTF code), actual destination, job title code, details of employer, and details of college (if applicable)

In December 1990, the Careers Service sent me an update for all the Cohort II leavers. This included greater detail than before, with an entry for every position held by the young people since leaving school and the relevant dates. I was aware of certain limitations of both sets of data. The picture is firstly dependent for its accuracy on the reliability of the data held by the Careers Service, and they are the first to admit that the data is held primarily for administrative purposes rather than broader research purposes. Destinations six months after leaving school are deemed to be the most accurate and complete picture that the Careers Service can gather and, although in principle young people are tracked for three years, it becomes inceasingly difficult to keep tabs on them after the first six months. Sixth form and FE college students are relatively easily monitored, but the accuracy of data on the majority of young people becomes increasingly inaccurate as time goes on, although the Careers Service make a concerted effort to update their records.

(ii) The Masonfield School Leavers' Survey

The second phase of the 'leavers' research was focussed on a postal questionnaire which was sent to a representative sample of leavers in summer 1990, a year after they had first left school. The questionnaire was designed with two broad purposes in mind: firstly, to gain a broad picture of the experiences of leavers from the pilot schools and their views of TVEI to inform the work of individual pilot coordinators, Careers Service personnel and Central Team members, and secondly to generate data relating to equal opportunities outcomes for the purposes of my own research.

The initial questionnaire was piloted in March 1990 amongst 40 leavers, with the Careers Service acting as an intermediary to overcome the restraints placed on me by the Data Protection Act, and the final version was sent out in June 1990. Both the pilot and the final version included a covering letter from the Principle Careers Officer and the Central Coordinator which stressed the importance of the survey to future provision for young people in the city and offered to put the young people in touch with a careers officer if they so wished (and several young people did indeed avail themselves of the offer).

The final version was sent to 300 leavers from the pilot schools: 200 ex-TVEI pupils (82 per cent of all TVEI pupils in Cohort II) and 100 non-TVEI pupils (16 per cent of all non-TVEI pupils). The sample was weighted towards young people in the labour market, as a disproportionate number of full-time students had responded to the pilot exercise. By the end of July, 92 questionnaires had been returned: a 31 per cent response rate. Although I was slightly disappointed by the response rate, I was assured that the Careers Service had never achieved a higher response rate for their own periodic surveys. However, I was unable to send out a reminder because I did not have direct access to the full mailing list of the Careers Service, so could not check who had not responded.

The number of respondents who had been TVEI pupils in high school was equivalent to 23 per cent of all Cohort II pupils, and the sample as a whole represented 11 per cent of all the pilot school leavers. The characteristics of the respondents were broadly representative of the wider school-leaving population in terms of their academic ability and their post-school destinations, although there was a slightly higher proportion of young people in the labour market amongst the questionnaire respondents (reflecting the weighting noted above). They were of course very much a self-selected group; presumably, only the more motivated young people would have taken the time to complete the survey, and the non-respondents may well have shared a completely different set of characteristics, with possibly a very different view of TVEI. It is, however, impossible for me to draw any firm conclusions on this.

(iii) In-depth interviews with school leavers

The final phase of the fieldwork consisted of a series of interviews conducted over the summer and autumn of 1991 with 12 young people who had been TVEI pupils in high school. All twelve had responded to the Leavers Survey the summer before and at the time of the interview were either 18 or 19 years old. The interviews lasted from fifty minutes to an hour and a half, and explored a number of key themes within an open-ended framework. Topics covered included career histories, career aspirations whilst still at school, work experience, part-time and domestic work, subject choice at school, careers education and guidance, experiences of TVEI (including reflections on TVEI's various core elements), post-16 training/further education, promotion hopes, and equality issues in school and the workplace.

Profiles of the young people

David
David agreed to see me during a week's holiday and, even though the weather was foul, he arrived on time, rather bedraggled! He was dressed casually in jeans, trainers and a baggy sweatshirt, with short, spiky hair. He was very confident which, given his occupation as a salesperson, is hardly surprising. David had been part of Cohort II at Mosslands High School, which is where the interview was held. His TVEI subjects had been Business Studies and IT, and he had also studied physics, history and CDT: Control Technology. He had not been on work experience, but he had had a number of part-time jobs whilst still at school, including a paper round, farm work and occasional baby-sitting. He had been thinking about a career in sales since he was 14; before that, he had thought about athletics, motor racing and demolition work! At the time of the interview he was coming to the end of his period as a YTS trainee with a 'High Street' electrical retailer, and he fully expected to be kept on as a permanent employee. Previous jobs included farm work and telephone sales. He had eventually got his YTS placement through the Careers Service. He also had a weekend job at a cash and carry ware-house to earn extra money. His long-term ambition was to become a sales executive with his own team of sales reps.

Amanda
Amanda agreed to be interviewed at her old school on an evening when the school was open for a parents' evening. A very confident young woman was waiting for me - who turned out to be Amanda's friend Jane! Amanda turned up five minutes later, dressed very stylishly in 501s and a baggy blue T-shirt. Amanda struck me as less confident than Jane, and seemed to take longer to relax into the interview. However, the presence of her friend ensured a lively flow of interjections, as well as a lot of laughter! It was a very hot evening that night, and we spent the interview drinking cans of Pepsi. Amanda had attended The Croft High School, and her TVEI options were Business Studies and IT, alongside modular science, geography and home economics. Amanda had originally wanted to join the Police Force and had been given a work experience placement at the Police Training College (where she had worked in the laundry). She had also thought about being a social worker or an air hostess. Whilst at school, she had a Saturday job selling cards on the local market, as well as occasional baby sitting. Since leaving school, Amanda had

worked as a trainee on British Rail's own clerical training scheme. At the time of the interview she was now a permanent employee in the staff travel section, and hoped to make a sideways move into the Transport Police.

Jane

Jane was equally as fashion-conscious as her friend; she was dressed in jeans and an orange zip-up top. Her blonde hair was cut into a bob, and she wore a gold chain and gold rings. Jane had also been a TVEI student, and had also taken Business Studies and IT. She had always wanted to be a nurse or a midwife and had been given a work experience placement in a dental surgery. (Amanda claimed that Jane had wanted to be a model, a claim which Jane denied vigorously!) She had had a couple of part-time jobs, too: washing up at a local pub, working in a shoe shop and, whilst at college, bar work. Jane had initially remained in full-time education. Her long-term plan had been - and still was - to become a nurse, and she had studied for further GCSEs and a City and Guilds in Health Studies. She had left after a year, even though she still needed an additional GCSE, partly because she felt that she should be bringing money into her family. Believing that it would only be a temporary stop-gap, she had found work with a mail order company, and had been promoted to the position of merchandiser (a supervisory position). She didn't enjoy her work, though, not least because of the discrimination she faced as a woman, but had doubts now about her commitment to nursing, particularly because of the loss of earnings it would incur.

Keith

I interviewed Keith in the afternoon at my workplace, Masonfield Education Centre. He had just returned from a week in Morocco and consequently was sporting an extraordinary tan. He was dressed in a football-style shirt (complete with a pair of shades stuck in to the 'V' of the shirt collar), cycling shorts and trainers, and had short, thin blond hair and three earrings. Despite his rather imposing appearance - he was easily 18 inches taller than me! - he was quite shy and quietly-spoken and had to be prompted a lot during interview. He came over, however, as very shrewd and canny, and evidently very bright and mature. Keith had attended Mosslands High School. His TVEI option had been Business Studies and IT, and he had also studied history, chemistry and English literature. Whilst at school he had been uncertain about his future, although he was sure that he did not want to stay on into the sixth form At school, he had done a paper round and had had a Saturday job in a cash and carry warehouse. He had had a work experience placement in a bank which he had enjoyed. When much younger, he had considered a career in medicine or accountancy, but realised he would have to stay on after 16 to pursue both options. On leaving school, therefore, he had applied for banking jobs, and had been working for a major bank for two years. He had also continued working for the warehouse on Saturdays. When he was old enough, he hoped to join the Police, in the traffic division.

John

I interviewed John at his old school, St Catherine's, on an evening when it was open for night school. John had come straight from work and was clutching a rather large and impressive-looking briefcase. He was smartly dressed in black 'work' trousers, a pin-striped shirt and a stripy tie. His hair was quite long, but neat and parted to the side, and he wore a ring on his right hand which he played with throughout the interview. He came across as a confident and mature young man, sure of himself and the correctness of his outlook on life. He needed very little prompting and talked at great length, particularly about his work. John's TVEI subjects had been Business Studies and Food Studies. He had also taken Technology, Design and Realisation and physics. He had always wanted to work as a draughtsman and accordingly he had been given a work experience placement in a drawing office. He had had a Saturday job in a DIY shop whilst at school, as well as a paper round. On first leaving school, John had been recruited as a YTS trainee by a fire safety equipment company, but it had been a sales job and not the promised drawing job. He had then found work with his current employer, a large insurance company, initially as a YTS trainee, and latterly as a full-time trainee building surveyor. Looking to the long term, John hoped that he would one day become head of a surveying department.

Mike

Mike agreed to meet me early one evening at Masonfield Education Centre. When I arrived, he was already there, dressed in blue jeans, a white cotton shirt and a leather flying jacket, complete with Biggles-style furry collar. He had a dark complexion, and a very thin, straight moustache. The interview was extremely short, less than 45 minutes, and Mike was short and to the point in his responses to my questions. Mike had been a TVEI student at St Catherine's High School, where he had taken IT and Media Studies. He had had a paper round whilst at school, and had worked briefly on a market stall. He had also babysat on a number of occasions. His work experience placement had been in a bank. On leaving school, Mike had been unclear quite what he wanted to do, but hoped it might involve computers. The careers service had eventually found him a YTS placement with a travel agency, which he had enjoyed very much. He was there for 18 months before being made redundant. After a short stint as a YTS trainee in an advertising company, he had found his present job, and for the last three months had been working for a 'flights only' travel agency. In the longer term, Mike hoped that one day he would own his own travel agency.

Karen

I interviewed Karen at her old school, St Catherines. She was dressed in a black and white patterned blouse, a black miniskirt and thick black tights. She was quite short, with shoulder length permed hair. She was extremely 'chatty', and surprised herself by this, commenting later that she couldn't believe how quickly the time had gone and that she had not talked about herself for so long before! Karen told me that she had been extremely shy at school, but that she had changed a lot since starting work. Karen's TVEI subjects had been Business Studies and IT, alongside biology, media studies and community studies. She had had a number of career ideas whilst still in school: vet work, shop work, and latterly personnel work. She had been given a work experience placement in the bakery at the local Tescos superstore. On leaving school, she accepted a place on a BTEC course in Business and Finance, but then took a YTS post as a purchase ledge clerk as she was promised BTEC by day release. After a year, Karen had been made redundant, which had left her shocked and upset, but she had been able to find a second post. After three months, she had moved to her current post, a full-time post as a purchase ledger clerk. In the long-term, she hoped to be doing something quite different; she was uncertain quite what she would be doing, but was just about to start studying for 'A' levels in her spare time as a first step.

Paul

I met Paul at his old school, St Catherines, on a cold, wet night. I wondered if he would turn up, but he had got a lift with two of his friends, who sat in the car and waited for him! Paul was tall and thick-set; he was dressed in shell suit bottoms, a black raincoat-cum-track suit top, and red trainers/bumper boots. He had short brown hair, and wore a gold chain. He seemed quite shy on arrival, but he relaxed quite quickly and chatted away quite happily, thinking long and hard about his responses. Paul's TVEI subjects had been Food Studies and Business Studies. He had had a work experience placement in a car parts distribution warehouse, and had even been offered paid work at the end of it. Whilst at school, he had considered joining the Army Air Corps, but decided against this as they wanted him to start before he had taken his exams. Paul worked as an assistant manager in a high street sports shop, and he had been working for them since his last month or so at school, when he had managed to get a Saturday job in another shop in the chain. He regarded his job very much as a stop-gap. however, as his real ambition was to join the Fire Service: he was hoping to apply in about six months time.

Tina

I interviewed Tina at her old school, Seddon Park, on one of the evenings it was open for night school. Tina was wearing baggy trousers in 'sweatshirt' material, with a matching top worn over her trousers, and trainers. Her hair was swept up into a ponytail cascading over her head, and she wore large earrings, several gold chains and at least four chunky gold rings. She was immediately at ease and seemed very interested in the research. Tina's TVEI subjects had been Business Studies and IT. Whilst at school, she had baby sat on a number of occasions and had also worked in a bakery on a Saturday for a short time. She had originally hoped to join the Police Force, but had eventually favoured a career in graphic design. She had had a work experience placement in an office at the City Council, and the experience had put her off clerical work! On first leaving school, she had started a BTEC in art and design, but fell out with her tutor and left the course. She had then applied for a number of jobs and eventually secured a secretarial post at the local university which, to her surprise, she had enjoyed and was still in. Longer-term, she hoped to have moved higher up in the university administrative structure, either as a personal secretary, or in a job where she would be able to utilise her design skills.

Nick

Nick was a full-time student in a local sixth form college, and I arranged to interview him at his college. Nick was wearing black jeans, a sweatshirt-material top, and a baseball jacket. He was at ease from the start and was very interested in the research, asking quite a few questions himself. Nick had been a TVEI student at St Catherine's High School. His TVEI subjects had been Business Studies and Business French. Whilst at school, he had considered a career in the Police Force and had been given a work experience placement at the Police Headquarters where he had worked in an office. Nick was in his third year at sixth form college, and had started a number of courses over his three years: he had originally opted for 'A' levels in German, English and Business Studies, with GCSE Law, but had dropped German at the end of the first year. He had passed Business Studies and was now taking 'A' levels in Geography and Law. His original choice had been influenced by the hope of a career with the Foreign Office using his languages, but he now hoped to study law, and was in the process of applying for a Law degree at a number of universities.

Jennifer

I interviewed Jennifer at Masonfield Education Centre during the Christmas vacation, as she was in her first year of a degree at a Northern university. She wore a black blazer over a big baggy sweater and T-shirt, a short black skirt and thick black tights. She had long blond hair and wore dangly gold and pearl earrings. Jennifer was very friendly and bright and seemed to be very relaxed throughout the interview. Jennifer had attended St Catherine's High School, with Business French and Social Studies as her TVEI options. Whilst at school she had had vague ideas about a career in one of the caring professions and had been given a work experience placement at a geriatric hospital in Masonfield. With these ideas in mind, she had considered taking Sociology or Social Biology 'A levels, but in the end had opted for 'A' levels in history, English and French as a TVEI student at sixth form college. She had had a number of part-time jobs during this period: work in a newsagent and work in a chemist's shop. At the time of the interview she was in her first year of a degree in English and Philosophy, and was now considering a future career in television research. She had even arranged a placement at a TV studio on her own initiative.

Andrew

Andrew was also interviewed during the Christmas vacation, as he was a student at a university in the Midlands. He was tall and stocky, with spiky ginger hair, and was wearing jeans, a T-shirt and an anorak. He was extremely friendly - indeed, I found him chatting away to the receptionist like a long-lost friend! He was clearly very bright, and considered his responses carefully before replying. Andrew had been a student at St Catherine's, where he had studied Business Studies and IT as his TVEI subjects. Whilst still at school he had wanted to be a Police Officer, but had begun to think about a career in banking and accordingly had had a work experience placement in a bank. He had not had any part-time jobs whilst at high school, but as an 'A' level student had taken on casual labouring jobs over the summer holidays. His career plans had influenced his choice of 'A' levels - maths with statistics, computer studies and economics, plus GCSE Law. At the time of the interview Andrew was in his first year of a degree in Banking and Finance, and remained very keen on pursuing a career in banking when he had finished his course.

Bibliography

This bibliography is presented in two sections. The first section lists all the local documentary sources used in researching the case study, including all the Masonfield documentation referenced in the main body of the book. Some, but by no means all, of these documents are in the public domain, but none have been formally published. The second section contains the main bibliography, including all TVEI documentation published outside of Masonfield.

Local sources

Minutes of regular meetings

Minutes and papers of the TVEI cross-LEA Equal Opportunities Working Party, 1989-1990.
Minutes and papers of the LEA Equal Opportunities Working Party, 1988-1989.
Minutes and papers of Regional TVEI Equal Opportunities Steering Group, 1989-1990.
Minutes of Masonfield City Council Education Committee, 1982-1988.
Minutes and papers of the TVEI Consultative Committee, 1986-1988.
Minutes and papers of TVEI Pilot Coordinators Meetings, 1986-1989.

Annual reports

First Annual Report of TVEI Pilot in Masonfield, 1987.
Second Annual Report of TVEI Pilot in Masonfield, 1988.
Third Annual Report of TVEI Pilot in Masonfield, 1989.
Fourth Annual Report of TVEI Pilot in Masonfield, 1990.

Final Annual Report of TVEI Pilot in Masonfield, 1991.
Annual reports for individual pilot schools 1987-1991.
Annual Reports for TVEI Extension, 1990-1992.
Final Report of TVEI in Masonfield, 1995.

Miscellaneous

Interim report of LEA Equal Opportunities Working Party, 11/89.
Minutes of TVEI Pilot Wind-Up Meeting, 10/7/91.
Masonfield Careers Service (1991), *Destinations of 1991 School Leavers*.
Masonfield Research and Information Planning Unit (1990), *Briefing on Unemployment*.
Masonfield Training and Enterprise Council (1990), *Masonfield: The demand for labour*.
TVEI Submission Document to the Manpower Services Commission, 1985.
Unattributed (undated), *Labour Market Intelligence*.

Research reports by the author

City of Masonfield (1990a), *Girls and Option Choice: A study of fourth year girls in four Masonfield High Schools*, City of Masonfield Education Department.
City of Masonfield (1990b), *Boys and Option Choice: A follow-up to the 'Girls and Option Choice' Study*, City of Masonfield Education Department.
City of Masonfield (1990c), *The Masonfield School Leavers Survey: A report based on the experiences of 1989 leavers from the five TVEI Pilot schools*, City of Masonfield Education Department.
City of Masonfield (1991a), *On the Way Out: Young people's views of option and career choice on the eve of leaving high school*, City of Masonfield Education Department.
City of Masonfield (1991b), *A report on the introduction of balanced science in TVEI Extension High Schools*, City of Masonfield Education Department.

Main bibliography

Abraham, J (1995), *Divide and School: Class and Gender Dynamics in Comprehensive Education*, London: Falmer Press.
Acker, Sandra (1984), 'Women in higher education: what is the problem?', in Acker, S and Warren Piper, D (eds), *Is Higher Education Fair to Women?*, Guildford: SRHE/NFER-Nelson.
Acker, S (1988), 'Teachers, gender and resistance', *British Journal of Sociology of Education*, Vol. 9, No. 3, pp.307-322.
Acker, S (1994), *Gendered Education*, Buckingham: Open University Press.

Ainley, P and Corney, M (1990), *Training for the Future: The Rise and Fall of the Manpower Services Commission*, London: Cassell.

Althusser, L (1971), 'Ideology and Ideological State Apparatuses', in Cosin, R (ed), *Education, Structure and Society*, Harmondsworth: Penguin.

Amos, V (1990), 'Policy and Practice', *Paper presented at EOC Education Network Conference, 'Equal Opportunities in the 1990s: The Changing Era'*, Manchester, 17.5.90.

Anyon, J (1983), 'Intersections of gender and class: Accommodation and resistance by working class and affluent females to contradictory sex-role ideologies', in Walker, S and Barton, L (eds), *Gender, Class and Education*, Lewes: Falmer Press.

Apple, M (1982), *Education and Power*, Boston: Routledge and Kegan Paul.

Arnot, M (1982), 'Male hegemony, social class and women's education', *Journal of Education (Boston University)*, Vol. 164, No. 1, pp.64-89.

Arnot, M (1983), 'A cloud over co-education: An analysis of the forms of transmission of class and gender relations', in Walker, S and Barton, L (eds), *Gender, Class and Education*, Lewes: Falmer Press.

Arnot, M (1984), 'A feminist perspective on the relationship between family life and school life', *Journal of Education (Boston University)*, Vol. 166, No. 1, pp.5-24.

Arnot, M (1986), 'State education policy and girls' educational experiences', in Beechey, V and Whitelegg, V (eds), *Women in Britain Today*, Milton Keynes: OUP.

Arnot, A (1987), 'Political lip-service or radical reform? Central government responses to sex equality as a policy issue', in Arnot, M and Weiner, G (eds), *Gender and the Politics of Schooling*, London: Hutchinson.

Arnot, M (1989), 'Crisis or challenge: Equal opportunities and the National Curriculum', *National Union of Teachers Review*, Vol. 3, No. 2, pp.7-13.

Arnot, M (1991), 'Equality and democracy: A decade of struggle over education', *British Journal of Sociology of Education*, Vol. 12, No. 4, pp.447-466.

Arnot, M (1992), 'Feminism, education and the New Right', in Arnot, M. and Barton, L., *Voicing Concerns: Sociological perspectives on contemporary education reforms*, Wallingford: Triangle Books.

Arnot, M (1993), 'A crisis in patriarchy? British feminist educational politics and state regulation of gender', in Arnot, M and Weiler, K (eds), *Feminism and Social Justice in Education: International Perspectives*, London: Falmer Press.

Arnot, M., David, M and Weiner, G (1996), *Educational Reforms and Gender Equality in Schools*, Manchester: Equal Opportunities Commission.

Arnot, M and Whitty, G (1982), 'From reproduction to transformation: Recent radical perspectives on the curriculum from the USA', *British Journal of Sociology of Education*, Vol. 3, No. 1, pp.93-103.

Ashton, D (1988), 'Educational institutions, youth and the labour market', in Gallie, D (ed), *Employment in Britain*, Oxford: Basil Blackwell.

Ashton, D and Field, D (1976), *Young Workers*, London: Hutchinson.

Ashton, D, Maguire, M and Spilsbury, M (1987), 'Labour market segmentation and the structure of the youth labour market', in Brown, P and Ashton, D (eds), *Education, Unemployment and Labour Markets*, Lewes: Falmer Press.

Attar, D (1990), *Wasting Girls' Time: The History and Politics of Home Economics*, London: Virago.

Bailey, C (1988), 'What hopes for liberal education?', *Cambridge Journal of Education*, Vol. 18, No. 1, pp.27-37.

Bailey, V (1992), *Student Non-Completion of BTEC Programmes and Awards*, London: BTEC.

Ball, S (1990a), *Politics and Policy Making in Education: Explorations in Policy Sociology*, London: Routledge.

Ball, S (1994), *Education Reform: A critical and Poststructural Approach*, Buckingham: Open University Press.

Banks, M, Bates, I, Breakwell, G, Bynner, J, Emler, N, Jamieson, L, and Roberts, K (1992), *Careers and Identities*, Milton Keynes:OUP.

Barnes, D, Johnson, G, and Jordan, S (1989a), *Work Experience in TVEI: 14-16*, Sheffield: Training Agency/ School of Education, University of Leeds.

Barnes, D, Johnson, G, and Jordan, S (1989b), *Work Experience in TVEI: 16-18*, Sheffield: Training Agency/ School of Education, University of Leeds.

Barnes, J A (1979), *Who Should Know What? Social Science, Privacy and Ethics*, Harmondsworth: Penguin.

Bates, I, Clarke, J, Cohen, P., Finn, D, Moore, R, and Willis, P (1984), *Schooling for the Dole: The New Vocationalism*, Basingstoke: Macmillan.

Bates, I (1993a), 'A job which is 'Right for me'? Social class, gender and individualisation', in Bates, I and Riseborough, G (eds), *Youth and Inequality*, Buckingham: OUP.

Bates, I (1993b), '"When I have my own studio..." The making and shaping of 'designer' careers', in Bates, I and Riseborough, G (eds), *Youth and Inequality*, Buckingham: OUP.

Bates, I and Riseborough, G (1993), *Youth and Inequality*, Buckingham: OUP.

Beavis, S (1988), 'Ticking 'demographic timebomb' as women await the back-to-work call', *The Guardian*, 4.11.88.

Bell, C and Raffe, D (1991), 'Working together? Research, policy and practice: The experience of the Scottish evaluation of TVEI', in Walford, G (ed), *Doing Educational Research*, London: Routledge.

Benn, C and Fairley, J (1986), *Challenging the MSC on Jobs, Training and Education*, London: Pluto Press.

Bernstein, B (1971), *Class, Codes and Control Volume I*, London: Routledge and Kegan Paul.

Bernstein, B (1977), *Class, Codes and Control Volume III*, London: Routledge and Kegan Paul.

Bernstein, B (1990), *Class, Codes and Control Volume IV: The Structuring of Pedagogic Discourse*, London: Routledge.

Bernstein, B (1996), *Pedagogy, Symbolic Control and Identity: Theory, Research, Critique*, London: Taylor and Francis.

Blackman, S J (1987), 'The labour market in schools: New Vocationalism and issues of socially ascribed discrimination', in Brown, P and Ashton, D N, *Education, Unemployment and Labour Markets*, Lewes: Falmer Press.

Blackmore, J (1992), 'The gendering of skill and vocationalism in twentieth century Australian education', *Journal of Education Policy*, Vol. 7, No. 4, pp.351-377.

Boseley, S (1988), 'Our beautiful launderette', *The Guardian*, 7.11.88.

Boseley, S (1995), 'Need to be liked still blocks girls' hopes of better jobs', *The Guardian*, 27.4.95.

Bourdieu, P (1973), 'Cultural reproduction and social reproduction', in Brown, R (ed), *Knowledge, Education and Cultural Change*, London: Tavistock.

Bourdieu, P (1976a), 'The school as a conservative force: scholastic and cultural inequalities', in Dale, R., Esland, G., and MacDonald, M (eds), *Schooling and Capitalism: A Sociological Reader*, London: Routledge and Kegan Paul.

Bourdieu, P (1976b), 'Systems of education and systems of thought', in Dale, R, Esland, G, and MacDonald, M (eds), *Schooling and Capitalism: A Sociological Reader*, London: Routledge and Kegan Paul.

Bourdieu, P and Passeron, C (1977), *Reproduction in Education, Society and Culture*, London: Sage.

Bowles, S and Gintis, H (1976), *Schooling in Capitalist America*, London: Routledge and Kegan Paul.

Brelsford, P, Smith, G and Rix, A (1982), *Give us a Break: Widening Opportunities for Young Women within YOP/YTS*, Sheffield: Manpower Services Commission.

Bridgwood, A (1988), 'Moving on: Views of TVEI from final year students', in Bridgwood, A, Hinckley, S, Sims, D, and Stoney, S, *Perspectives on TVEI*, Sheffield: Training Commission/ NFER.

Bridgwood, A (1990), Equal Opportunities in TVEI: Issues and Strategies, *Paper presented to EOC Education Network Conference 'Equal Opportunities in the 1990s: The Changing Era'*, Manchester, 17.5.90.

Bridgwood, A and Betteridge, J (1989), *Equal Opportunities for Girls and Boys within TVEI: Issues and Strategies*, Training Agency/NFER.

Brown, P (1988), 'The New Vocationalism: A policy for inequality?', in Coles, B (ed), *Young Careers: The search For Jobs and the New Vocationalism*, Milton Keynes: OUP.

Brown, R (1997), 'Unemployment, youth and the employment relationship', *Youth and Policy*, No. 55, pp.28-39.

Bryman, A (1988), *Quality and Quantity in Social Research*, London: Unwin Hyman Ltd.

Buckley, M (1992), *Perestroika and Soviet Women*, Cambridge: Cambridge University Press.

Burnhill, P & McPherson, A (1984), 'Careers and gender: The expectations of able

Scottish school leavers in 1971 and 1981', in Acker, S and Warren Piper, D (eds), *Is Higher Education Fair to Women?*, Guildford: SRHE/NFER-Nelson.

Byrne, E M (1975), Inequality in Education, *Education Review*, 27, 3, 179-191.

Byrne, E M (1978), *Women and Education*, London: Tavistock.

Byrne, E M (1985), 'Equality or equity? A European overview', in Arnot, M (ed), *Race and Gender: Equal Opportunities Policies in Education*, Oxford: Pergamon Press.

Byrne, E M (1989), 'Grounded theory and the snark syndrome: The role of the international organisations in research in gender and education', *Evaluation and Research in Education: The Durham and Newcastle Research Review*, Vol. 3, No. 3, pp.111-123.

CARE (1986), *TVEI Working Papers 1*, Spring 1986, Norwich: CARE, University of East Anglia.

Carnoy, M (1982), 'Education, economy and the state', in Apple, M (ed), *Cultural and Economic Reproduction in Education: Essays on Class Ideology and the State*, London: Routledge and Kegan Paul.

Carr, L (1989), *Equal opportunities and the Education Reform Act*, Paper presented at the EOC Education Network Seminar, 15/3/89.

Carvel, J (1997a), 'Prince to meet Blunkett on schools', *The Guardian*, 16.6.97.

Carvel, J (1997b), 'Job learning proposed for schools', *The Guardian*, 3.6.97.

Central Advisory Council for Education (1959), *15 to 18* (Crowther Report), London: HMSO.

Central Advisory Council for Education (1963), *Half Our Future* (Newsom Report), London: HMSO.

Centre for Contemporary Cultural Studies [CCCS] (1981), *Unpopular Education: Schooling and Social Democracy in England since 1944*, London: Hutchinson.

Chambers, J (1988), Equal opportunities in TVEI - Theory and practice, in *TVEI Developments 2: Equal Opportunities*, Sheffield: MSC.

Chamber, J and Raffe, M (undated), *Users Handbook on the Information System Strategy*, North West Region Equal Opportunities Steering Group.

Chiosso, R and Tizard, J (1990), 'Women and girls in engineering and construction courses in further education', *The Vocational Aspect of Education*, Vol. 42, No. 1, pp.101-107.

Chitty, C (1989), *Towards A New Education System: The Victory of the New Right*, Lewes: Falmer Press.

Cockburn, C (1987), *Two-Track Training: Sex Inequalities and the YTS*, Basingstoke: Macmillan.

Cockburn, C (1988), 'The gendering of jobs: workplace relations and reproduction of sex segregation', in Walby, S, *Gender Segregation at Work*, Milton Keynes: OUP.

Cockburn, C (1991), *In The Way of Women: Men's Resistance to Sex Equality in Organisations*, London: Macmillan.

Cohen, L and Manion, L (1985), *Research Methods in Educational Research* (2nd edition), London: Routledge.

Coles, B and Maynard, M (1990), 'Moving towards a fair start: equal gender opportunities and the careers service', *Gender and Education*, Vol. 2, No. 3, pp.297-308.

Connell, R (1985), *Teachers' Work*, Sydney: George Allen and Unwin.

Connell, R (1987), *Gender and Power: Society, The Person and Sexual Politics*, Cambridge: Polity Press.

Connell, R (1995), *Masculinities*, Cambridge: Polity Press.

Cooper, D (1989), 'Positive images in Haringey: A struggle for identity', in Jones, C and Mahony, P (eds), *Learning Our Lines: Sexuality and Social Control in Education*, London: Women's Press.

Courtenay, G (1989a), *England and Wales Youth Cohort Study: Report on Cohort 2, Sweep 1*, Research and Development No.48 - Youth Cohort Series No.5, Sheffield: MSC.

Courtenay, G (1989b), *England and Wales Youth Cohort Study: Report on Cohort 3, Sweep 1*, Research and Development No.53 - Youth Cohort Series No.3, Sheffield: MSC.

Cox, C and Dyson, A (1969), *Fight for Education: A Black Paper*, Critical Quarterly Society.

Cox, B and Dyson, A (1970a), *Black Paper 2: The Crisis in Education*, Critical Quarterly Society.

Cox, B and Dyson, A (1970b) *Goodbye Mr Short*, Critical Quarterly Society.

Cox, B and Boyson, R (1975), *Black Paper 4: The Fight for Education*, London: Dent.

Crompton, R and Sanderson, K (1990), 'Credentials and careers', in Payne, G and Abbott, P (eds), *The Social Mobility of Women: Beyond Male Mobility Models*, Lewes: Falmer Press.

Cross, J (1987), *Work Experience: A Report by the TVEI Careers Officer*, Great Yarmouth: Norfolk TVEI.

Cross, J (1988), Foreword, *Developments in TVEI 2: Equal Opportunities*, Sheffield: MSC.

Dale, R (1985), 'The background and inception of the TVEI', in Dale, R, (ed) *Education, Training and Employment: Towards a New Vocationalism*, Milton Keynes: OUP/Pergamon Press.

Dale, R (1992), 'Recovering from a pyrrhic victory? Quality, relevance and impact in the sociology of education', in Arnot, M and Barton, L (eds), *Voicing Concerns: Sociological perspectives on contemporary education reforms*, Wallingford: Triangle Books.

Dale, R., Bowe, R., Harris, D., Loveys, M., Moore, R., Shilling, C., Sikes, P.Trevitt, J. and Velsecchi, V. (1990), *The TVEI Story: Policy, Practice and Preparation for the Workforce*, Milton Keynes: OUP.

Dant, T (1991), *Knowledge, Ideology and Discourse: A Sociological Perspective*, London: Routledge.

David, M (1980), *The State, The Family and Education*, London: Routledge and Kegan Paul.
David, M (1993), *Parents, Gender and Education Reform*, Cambridge: Polity Press.
David, M, West, A and Ribbens, J (1994), *Mothers Intuition? Choosing Secondary Schools*, London: Falmer Press.
Davies, A M, Holland, J and Minhas, R (1992), *Equal Opportunities in the New Era*, Hillcole Group Paper 2, London: Tufnell Press.
Deem, R (1978), *Women and Schooling*, London: Routledge and Kegan Paul.
Deem, R (1980), *Schooling for Women's Work*, London: Routledge and Kegan Paul.
Deem, R (1981), 'State policy and ideology in the education of women, 1944-1980', *British Journal of Sociology of Education*, Vol. 2, No. 2, pp.131-144.
Deem, R (1987), 'Bringing gender equality into schools', in Walker, S and Barton, L (eds), *Changing Policies, Changing Teachers*, Milton Keynes: OUP.
Deem, R (1989), 'The new school governing bodies: are gender and race on the agenda?', *Gender and Education*, Vol. 1, No. 3, pp.247-260.
Deem, R, Brehony, K, and Heath, S (1995), *Active Citizenship and the Governing of Schools*, Buckingham: Open University Press.
Denzin, N K (1970), *The Research Act in Sociology: A Theoretical Introduction to Sociological Methods*, London: Butterworth.
Department for Education and Employment (1997), 'David Blunkett unveils new Qualifications and Curriculum Authority appointments', *DFEE Press Release*, London: DFEE.
Department of Education and Science (1975), *Curricular Differences for Boys and Girls*, Education Survey 21, London: HMSO.
Department of Education and Science (1977), *Education in Schools: A Consultative Document*, Cmnd 6869, London: HMSO.
Department of Education and Science (1978), *Girls and Science*, HMI Series: Matters for Discussion 13, London: HMSO.
Department of Education and Science (1979a) *Local Authority Arrangements for the School Curriculum*, London: HMSO.
Department of Education and Science (1979b), *Aspects of Secondary Education in England*, London: HMSO.
Department of Education and Science (1984), *Becoming an Engineer*, London: DES.
Department of Education and Science (1988), *Education At Work: A Guide for Schools*, London: HMSO.
Department of Education and Science (1991a), *Technical and Vocational Education Initiative (TVEI): England and Wales 1983-1990*, London: HMSO.
Department of Education and Science (1991b), Educational and economic activity of young people aged 16 to 18 years in England from 1974/5 to 1989/90, *Statistical Bulletin*, 3/91, London: DES.
Department of Trade and Industry (1994), *Competitiveness: Helping Business To Win*, Cmnd 2563, London: HMSO.

Devine, F (1993), 'Gender segregation and labour supply on 'choosing' gender-atypical jobs', *British Journal of Education and Work*, Vol. 6, No. 3, pp.61-74.

Devine, F (1994), 'Segregation and supply: Preferences and plans among 'self-made' women', *Gender, Work and Organisation*, Vol. 1, No. 2, pp.94-109.

Dex, S (1988), 'Gender and the labour market', in Gallie, D (ed), *Employment in Britain*, Oxford: Basil Blackwell.

Dixon, C (1996), '"Having a laugh, having a fight": Masculinity and the conflicting needs of the self in Design and Technology', *International Studies in Sociology of Education*, Vol. 6, No. 2, pp.147-166.

Dixon, C (1997), 'Pete's tool: Identity and sex play in the design and technology classroom', *Gender and Education*, Vol. 9, No. 1, pp.89-104.

Eden, C and Aubrey, K (1988), 'YTS and Gender: Continuity or Challenge?', in Coles, B (ed), *Young Careers: The Search for Jobs and the New Vocationalism*, Milton Keynes: OUP.

Elwood, J and Comber, C (1995) 'Gender differences in 'A' level examinations: The reinforcement of stereotypes?' *Paper presented at British Educational Research Association annual conference*, University of Bath.

Elwood, J (1996), 'Differential performance in public examinations - are boys in terminal decline?' *Paper presented at British Educational Research Association annual conference*, Lancaster University.

Employment Department (1991), *Guidance on TVEI Performance Indicators*, Moorfoot: Employment Department.

Engineering Council (1988), *Women In Science and Engineering*, London: The Engineering Council.

Epstein, D (1994), *Challenging Lesbian and Gay Inequalities in Education*, Buckingham: Open University Press.

Epstein, D (1997), 'Boyz' own stories: Masculinities and sexualities in schools', *Gender and Education*, Vol. 9, No. 1, pp.105-115.

Equal Opportunities Commission (1979), *Do You Provide Equal Opportunities?*, Manchester: EOC.

Equal Opportunities Commission (1985), *Equal Opportunities in TVEI*, Manchester: EOC.

Equal Opportunities Commission (1991), *Equal Opportunities in Schools: A Guide for Governors*, Manchester: EOC.

Evans, B (1992), *The Politics of the Training Market: From Manpower Services Commission to the Training and Enterprise Councils*, London: Routledge.

Evans, W G (1990), *Education and Female Emancipation: The Welsh Experience, 1847-1914*, Cardiff: University of Wales Press.

Faludi, S (1992), *Backlash: The Undeclared War Against Women*, London: Chatto and Windus.

Felstead, A, Goodwin, J and Green, F (1995), *Measuring up to the National Training Targets: Women's Attainment of Vocational Qualifications*, Centre for Labour Market Studies, University of Leicester.

Fielding, N and Fielding, J (1986), *Linking Data*, London: Sage.

Finch, J (1986), *Research and Policy: The Uses of Qualitative Methods in Social and Educational Research*, Lewes: Falmer Press.

Finn, D (1982), 'Whose needs? Schooling and the 'needs' of industry', in Rees, T L and Atkinson, P (eds), *Youth Unemployment and State Intervention*, London: Routledge and Kegan Paul.

Foster, V (1996), 'Space invaders: Desire and threat in the schooling of girls', *Discourse*, Vol. 17, No. 1, pp.43-63.

Friedan, B (1965), *The Feminine Mystique*, London: Penguin Books.

Fuller, A (1987), *Post-16 Work-Experience in TVEI: A Report to the MSC*, Institute for Research in Post Compulsory Education, Lancaster University.

Fulton, O, Leach, M, and Saunders, M (1986), *Beyond TVEI: A Study of 16+ Leavers from the Six First Round TVEI Projects*, University of Lancaster: IPCE.

Furlong, A (1986), 'Schools and the structure of female occupational aspirations', *British Journal of Sociology of Education*, Vol. 7, No. 4, pp.367-377.

Furlong, A (1987), 'Coming to terms with the declining demand for youth labour', in Brown, P and Ashton, D (eds), *Education, Unemployment and Labour Markets*, Lewes: Falmer Press.

Furlong, A and Cartmel, F (1997), *Young People and Social Change: Individualisation and Risk in Late Modernity*, Buckingham: Open University Press.

Game, A and Pringle, R (1983), *Gender at Work*, London: Pluto Press.

Gaskell, J (1984), 'Gender and option choice: The orientation of male and female students', *Journal of Education (Boston University)*, Vol. 166, No. 1, pp.89-102.

Gaskell, J (1992), *Gender Matters From School to Work*, Buckingham: OUP.

GATE (undated), *The What, Why and How of Girls and Technology Education*, London: Chelsea College.

Gewirtz, D (1991), 'Analyses of racism and sexism in education: strategies for change', *British Journal of Sociology of Education*, Vol. 12, No. 2, pp.183-201.

Gintis, H and Bowles, S (1988), 'Contradictions and reproduction in educational theory', in Coles, M (ed), *Bowles and Gintis Revisited: Correspondence and reproduction in educational theory*, Lewes: Falmer Press.

Gleeson, D (1988), *TVEI and Secondary Education*, Milton Keynes: OUP.

Gleeson, D and McLean M (1994), 'Whatever happened to TVEI? TVEI, Curriculum and Schooling', *Journal of Education Policy*, Vol. 9, No. 3, pp.233-244.

Goffman, I (1961), *Encounters*, New York: Bobbs Merrill Co. Inc.

Gomersall, M (1997), *Working Class Girls in Nineteenth Century England: Life, Work and Schooling*, Basingstoke: Macmillan.

Grant, M and Harding J (1987), 'Changing the polarity', *International Journal of Science Education*, Vol. 9, No. 33, pp.335-342.

Greed, C (1990), '"You're just imagining it, everything's all right really, don't worry about it": The position of women in surveying education and practice', *Gender and Education*, Vol. 2, No. 1, pp.49-61.

Gregory, J (1987), *Sex, Race and the Law: Legislating for Equality*, London: Sage.

Griffin, C (1985), *Typical Girls? Young Women from School to the Job Market*, London: Routledge.

Hakim, C (1993), 'The myth of rising female employment', *Work, Employment and Society*, Vol. 7, No. 1, pp.97-120.

Hansard (1984), vol. 60, col. 11, 15/5/84.

Hansard (1985), vol. 73, col. 138, 12/2/85.

Hansard (1986), vol. 98, col. 217, 21/5/86.

Harland, J (1987), 'The TVEI experience: issues of control, response and the professional role of teachers', in Gleeson, D (ed), *TVEI and Secondary Education*, Milton Keynes: OUP.

Haw, K F (1991), 'Intersections of gender and race: A problem for teachers? A review of the emerging literature', *Educational Research*, Vol. 33, No. 1, pp.12-21.

Haywood, C and Mac an Ghaill, M (1996), '"What about the boys?" Regendered local labour markets and the recomposition of working class masculinities', *British Journal of Education and Work*, Vol. 9, No. 1, pp.19-30.

Heath, S (1994), *Preparation for Life? The Technical and Vocational Education Initiative and Equal Opportunities (Gender)*, Unpublished PhD thesis, Lancaster University.

Henwood, F (1996), 'WISE choices? Understanding occupational decision-making in a climate of equal opportunities for women in science and technology', *Gender and Education*, Vol. 8, No. 2, pp.199-214.

Hitchcock, G (1988), *Education and Training 14-18: A Survey of New Initiatives*, Harlow: Longman.

HMI (1985), *The Technical and Vocational Education Initiative: Early Developments*, London: DES.

Hollands, R G (1990), *The Long Transition: Class, Culture and Youth Training*, Basingstoke: Macmillan.

Hopkins, D (1986), 'Sex role stereotyping and self-fulfilling prophecies in a local TVEI evaluation', *TVEI Working Papers 2: Autumn*, Norwich: CARE, University of East Anglia.

Howieson, C (1990, 'Beyond the gate: Work experience and part-time work among secondary school pupils in Scotland', *British Journal of Education and Work*, Vol. 3, No. 3, pp.49-62.

Hughes, P (1989), 'Evaluating an Equal Opportunities Initiative', *Gender and Education*, Vol. 1, No. 1, pp.5-15.

Hunt, F (1987), 'Divided aims: The educational implications of opposing ideologies in girls' secondary schooling, 1850-1940', in Hunt, F (ed), *Lessons for Life: The Schooling of Girls and Women 1850-1950*, Oxford: Basil Blackwell.

Hunt, F (1991), *Gender and Policy in English Education: Schooling for Girls 1902-1944*, Hemel Hempstead: Harvester Wheatsheaf.

Hurman, A (1978) *A Charter For Choice: A Study of Option Schemes*, Windsor: NFER-Nelson.

Jackson, D and Salisbury, J (1996), 'Why should secondary schools take working with boys seriously?' *Gender and Education*, Vol. 8, No. 1, pp.103-115.

Jones, C (1985), 'Sexual tyranny: Male violence in a mixed secondary school', in Weiner, G (ed), *Just a Bunch of Girls: Feminist Approaches to Schooling*, Milton Keynes:OUP.

Jones, C and Mahony, P (1989), *Learning Our Lines: Sexuality and Social Control in Education*, London: Women's Press.

Jones, K (1989), *Right Turn: The Conservative Revolution in Education*, London: Hutchinson Radius.

Jones, P (1988), 'Policy and praxis: local government, a case for treatment', in Coyle, A and Skinner, J (eds), *Women and Work: Positive Action for Change*, London: Macmillan.

Kelly, A (1985), 'Changing schools and changing society: Some reflections on the Girls Into Science and Technology project', in Arnot, M (ed), *Race and Gender: Equal Opportunities Policies in Education*, Oxford: Pergamon Press.

Kelly, G P and Nihlen, A S (1982), 'Schooling and the reproduction of patriarchy: Unequal workloads, unequal rewards', in Apple, M (ed), *Cultural and Economic Reproduction in Education: Essays on Class Ideology and the State*, London: Routledge and Kegan Paul.

Kenway, J (1993), 'Non-traditional pathways: Are they the way to the future?', in Blackmore, J and Kenway, J (eds), *Gender Matters in Educational Administration and Policy*, London: Falmer Press.

Kenway, J (1995), 'Masculinities in schools: Under siege, on the defensive and under reconstruction', *Discourse*, Vol. 16, No. 1, pp.59-79.

Kenway, J., Willis, S., Blackmore, J., and Rennie, L (1994), 'Making 'hope practical' rather than 'despair convincing': Feminist post-structuralism, gender reform and educational change', *British Journal of Sociology of Education*, Vol. 15, No. 2, pp.187-210.

Kessler, S., Ashenden. D J., Connell, R W and Dowsett, G W (1985), 'Gender relations in secondary schooling', *Sociology of Education*, No. 58, pp.34-48.

Lane, C (1988), 'New technology and clerical work', in Gallie, D (ed), *Employment in Britain*, Oxford: Basil Blackwell.

Lees, S (1986), *Losing Out: Sexuality and Adolescent Girls*, London: Hutchinson.

Lines, A and Stoney, S (1989), *Managing TVEI in Schools: Four Years On*, Moorfoot: Training Agency/NFER.

Lupton, C and Russell, D (1990), 'Equal opportunities in a cold climate', in Savage, S P and Robins, L (eds), *Public Policy Under Thatcher*, Basingstoke: Macmillan.

Mac an Ghaill, M (1994), *The Making of Men: Masculinities, Sexualities and Schooling*, Buckingham: OUP.

MacDonald, M (1980), 'Socio-cultural reproduction and women's education', in Deem, R (ed), *Schooling for Women's Work*, London: Routledge and Kegan Paul.

Mackinnon, D., Statham, J and Hales, M (1995), *Education in the UK: Facts and Figures*, Buckingham: Open University Press.

Mackinnon, M and Ahola-Sidaway, J (1995), '"Workin' with the boys": A North American perspective on non-traditional work initiatives for adolescent females in secondary schools', *Gender and Education*, Vol. 17, No. 1, pp.327-339.

Maguire, T (1992), 'The role of employers in the labour market', in McLaughlin, E (ed), *Understanding Unemployment: New Perspectives on Active Labour Market Policies*, London: Routledge.

Mahony, P (1985), *Schools for the Boys? Coeducation Reassessed*, London: Hutchinson.

Mahony, P (1989), 'Sexual violence in mixed schools', in Jones, C and Mahony, P (eds), *Learning Our Lines: Sexuality and Social Control in Education*, London: Women's Press.

Manpower Services Commission (1976), *Training Opportunities for Women*, Training Services Agency, London: MSC.

Manpower Services Commission (1977), *Young People and Work* (The Holland Report), Sheffield: MSC.

Manpower Services Commission (1979), *Opportunities for Girls and Women in the MSC Special Programmes for the Unemployed*, London: MSC.

Manpower Services Commission (1981a), *Skills For Working Life*, Sheffield: MSC.

Manpower Services Commission (1981b), *A New Training Initiative*, London: MSC.

Manpower Services Commission (1984), *TVEI Review*, Sheffield: MSC.

Marsh, C (1988) 'Unemployment in Britain', in Gallie, D (ed), *Employment in Britain*, Oxford: Basil Blackwell.

Marsh, S (1986), 'Women and the MSC', in Benn, C and Fairley, J (eds), *Challenging the MSC on Jobs, Education and Training: Enquiry into a National Disaster*, London: Pluto Press.

Martin, B (1988), 'Feminism, criticism and Foucault', in Diamond, I and Quinby, L (eds), *Feminism and Foucault: Reflections and Resistance*, Boston: North Eastern University Press.

Mason, J (1994), 'Linking qualitative and quantitative data analysis', in Bryman, A and Burgess, R (eds), *Analysing Qualitative Data*, London: Routledge.

Mason, J (1996), *Qualitative Researching*, London: Sage.

McIntyre, T (1987), *Equal Opportunities for Boys and Girls*, Evaluation Working Paper No. 1, London: TVEI Unit.

McIntyre, T (1988), *TVEI Work Experience: An Overview of Evaluation Findings*, Evaluation Working Paper No. 2, London: TVEI Unit.

McRobbie, A (1978), 'Working class girls and the culture of femininity', in Women's Study Group (eds), *Women Take Issue*, London: Hutchinson.

McRobbie, A and Garber, J (1975), 'Girls and sub-cultures', in Hall, S and Jefferson, T (eds), *Resistance Through Rituals: Youth Sub-Cultures in Post-War Britain*, London: Hutchinson.

Meehan, E M (1985), *Women's Rights at Work: Campaigns and Policy in Britain and the United States*, Basingstoke: Macmillan.

Middleton, S (1993), 'A post-modern pedagogy for the sociology of women's education', in Arnot, M and Weiler, K (eds) *Feminism and Social Justice in Education: International Perspectives*, London: Falmer Press.

Middleton, S (1995), 'Doing feminist educational theory: A post-modern perspective', *Gender and Education*, Vol. 17, No. 1, pp.87-99.

Miles, S and Middleton, C (1990), 'Girls' education in the balance: the Education Reform Act and Inequality', in Flude, M and Hammer, M (eds), *The Education Reform Act 1988*, Lewes: Falmer Press.

Miller, J (1996), *Schooling for Women*, London: Virago.

Millman, V (1985), 'The New Vocationalism in secondary schools: its influence on girls', in Whyte, J, Deem, R, Kant, L, and Cruickshank, M (eds), *Girl-Friendly Schooling*, London: Methuen.

Millman, V and Weiner, G (1987), 'Engendering equal opportunities: The case of TVEI', in Gleeson, D, *TVEI and Secondary Education: A Critical Appraisal*, Milton Keynes: OUP.

Ministry of Labour (1958), *Training for Skills: Recruitment and Training of Young Workers in Industry* (Carr Report), London: HMSO.

Mirza, H S (1992), *Young, Female and Black*, London: Routledge.

Mitchell, J (1974), *Psychoanalysis and Feminism*, London: Allen Lane.

Mizen, P (1992), 'Learning the hard way: The extent and significance of child working in Britain', *British Journal of Education and Work*, Vol. 5, No. 1, pp.5-18.

Moore, R (1988), 'The correspondence principle and the Marxist sociology of education', in Coles, M (ed), *Bowles and Gintis Revisited: Correspondence and reproduction in educational theory*, Lewes: Falmer Press.

Morris, E (1996), 'Labour's plans to give boys new hope', *The Guardian*, 1.11.96.

NEON (1987), *The Newsletter of the National Equal Opportunities Network*, 1, London: Training Agency.

NEON (1989), *The Newsletter of the National Equal Opportunities Network*, 6, London: Training Agency.

New, S (1993), '"This is the teacher here": Governing bodies and the teacher voice', *Journal of Teacher Development*, Vol. 2, No. 2, pp.70-80.

Office of Population Censuses and Surveys (1993), *1991 Census County Report: Sandfordshire (Part 1)*, London: HMSO.

OFSTED (1996), *The Gender Divide: Performance Differences Between Boys and Girls at School*, London: HMSO.

Oram, A (1987), 'Inequalities in the teaching profession: The effect on teachers and pupils, 1910-39', in Hunt, F (ed), *Lessons For Life: The Schooling of Girls and Women 1850-1950*, Oxford: Basil Blackwell.

Ord, F and Quigley, J (1985), 'Anti-sexism as good educational practice: What can feminists realistically achieve?' in Weiner, G (ed), *Just a Bunch of Girls: Feminist Approaches to Schooling*, Milton Keynes:OUP.

Orr, P (1985), 'Sex bias in schools: a national perspective', in Whyte, J., Deem, R., Kant, L., and Cruickshank, M, (eds) *Girl-Friendly Schooling*, London: Methuen.

Panorama (1995), *Men Aren't Working*, BBC Television, 16.10.95.

Payne, G., Hustler, D., and Cuff, T (1984), *GIST or PIST: Teachers' Perceptions of the Project Girls Into Science and Technology*, Didsbury: Manchester Polytechnic.

Platt, J (1988), 'What can case studies do?', *Studies in Qualitative Methodology*, No. 1, pp.1-23.

Pratt, J., Bloomfield., and Seale, C. (1984), *Option Choice: A Question of Equal Opportunity*, Windsor: NFER/ Nelson.

Purcell, K (1988), 'Gender and the experience of employment', in Gallie, D (ed), *Employment in Britain*, Oxford: Basil Blackwell.

Purvis, J (1991), *A History of Women's Education in England*, Buckingham: Open University Press.

Pye, D, Haywood, C and Mac an Ghaill, M (1996), 'The training state, deindustrialisation and the production of white working class trainee identities', *International Studies in Sociology of Education*, Vol. 6, No. 2, pp.133-146.

Quicke, J (1996), 'Work, education and democratic identity', *International Studies in Sociology of Education*, Vol. 6, No. 1, pp.49-66.

Raffe, D (1987), 'Youth unemployment in the United Kingdom 1979-1984', in Brown, P and Ashton, D (eds), *Education, Unemployment and Labour Markets*, Lewes: Falmer Press.

Raphael Reed, L (1997), 'Troubling boys and disturbing discourses on masculinity and schooling: A feminist exploration of current debates and interventions around boys in school, *Paper presented at 'Gender and Education' conference*, University of Warwick.

Rauta, I and Hunt, A (1975), *Fifth Form Girls: Their Hopes for the Future*, London: HMSO.

Rees, T (1992), *Women and the Labour Market*, London: Routledge.

Rees, T and Atkinson, P (1982), *Youth Unemployment and State Intervention*, London: Routledge and Kegan Paul.

Reid, M I., Barnett, B R., and Rosenberg, H A (1974), *A Matter of Choice: A Study of Guidance and Subject Options*, Windsor: NFER.

Rendel, M (1985), 'The winning of the Sex Discrimination Act', in Arnot, M (ed), *Race and Gender: Equal Opportunities Policies in Education*, Oxford: Pergamon Press.

Reskin, B and Roos, P (1990), *Job Queues, Gender Queues*, Philadelphia: Temple University Press.

Reynolds, K (1992), "Equal opportunities' and Local Management of Schools - what happens now?', *Gender and Education*, Vol. 4, No. 3, pp.289-300.

Riboswki, G (1992), 'Work experience schemes and part-time jobs in a recruitment context', *British Journal of Education and Work*, Vol. 5, No. 1, pp.19-46.

Rich, A (1980), 'Compulsory heterosexuality and lesbian existence', *Signs*, Vol. 5, No. 4, pp.631-660.

Riddell, S (1989), 'Pupils, resistance and gender codes: A study of classroom encounters', *Gender and Education*, Vol. 1, No. 2, pp.183-197.

Riddell, S (1992a), *Gender and the Politics of the Curriculum*, London: Routledge.

Riddell, S (1992b), 'Gender and education: Progressive and conservative forces in the balance', in Brown, S and Riddell, S (eds), *Class, Race and Gender in Schools: A New Agenda for Policy and Practice in Scottish education*, Edinburgh: SCRE.

Roberts, K (1984), *School Leavers and their Prospects: Youth and the Labour Market in the 1980s*, Milton Keynes: Open University Press.

Roberts, K, Richardson, D, and Dench, S. (1988), 'Sex discrimination in youth labour markets and employers' interests', in Walby, S (ed) *Gender Segregation at Work*, Milton Keynes: OUP.

Rubery, J and Fagan, C (1995), 'Gender segregation in societal context', *Work, Employment and Society*, Vol. 9, No. 2, pp.213-240.

Ruddock, J (1994) *Developing a Gender Policy in Secondary Schools*, Buckingham: OUP.

Ryrie, A C (1981), *Routes and Results: A Study of the Later Years of Schooling*, Edinburgh: SCRE/ Hodder and Stoughton

Ryrie, A C, Furst, A, and Lauder, M (1979), *Choices and Chances: A Study of Pupils' Subject Choices and Future Career Intentions*, London: Hodder and Stoughton/ SCER.

Sadovnik, A (1991), 'Basil Bernstein's theory of pedagogic practice: A structuralist approach', *Sociology of Education*, Vol. 64, No. 1, pp.48-63.

Salisbury, J (1996), *Educational Reform and Gender Equality in Welsh Schools*, Cardiff: Equal Opportunities Commission.

Sanders, S and Sprigg, G (1989), 'Section 28 and Education', in Jones, C and Mahony, P (eds), *Learning Our Lines: Sexuality and Social Control in Education*, London: Women's Press.

Saunders, M (1990), 'Control and influence: Recent government policy on technical and vocational education in British schools', in Summerfield, P and Evans, E (1990), *Technical Education and the State Since 1850: Historical and Contemporary Perspectives*, Manchester: Manchester University Press.

Savage, S P and Robins, L (1990), *Public Policy Under Thatcher*, Basingstoke: Macmillan.

Scott, H (1976), *Women and Socialism: Experiences from Eastern Europe*, London: Allison and Busby.

Secondary Schools Examination Council (1943), *Curriculum and Examinations in Secondary Schools* (Norwood Report), London: HMSO.

Shah, S (1990), 'Equal opportunities issues in the context of the National Curriculum: a black perspective', *Gender and Education*, Vol. 2, No. 3, pp.309-318.

Sharpe, S (1976), *Just Like a Girl: How Girls Learn to be Women*, London: Penguin.

Sheratt, N (1983), 'Girls, jobs and glamour', *Feminist Review*, No. 15, 47-60.

Shilling, C (1991), 'Labouring at school: Work experience in the TVEI', *Work,*

Employment and Society, Vol. 5, No. 1, pp.59-80.

Sims, D (1987), 'Work experience in TVEI: Student views and reactions - A preliminary study', in Hinckley, S M., Pole, C J., Sims, D and Stoney, S (eds) *The TVEI Experience: Views from Teachers and Students*, Sheffield: MSC/ NFER.

Sims, D (1989), *Project Management in TVEI: Continuity and Change*, Moorfoot: Training Agency/NFER.

Skeggs, B (1991), 'Challenging masculinity and using sexuality', *British Journal of Sociology of Education*, Vol, 12, No. 1, pp.127-140.

Skinner, J and Jones, P (1988), *Promoting Equal Opportunities for Girls and Boys within TVEI: A Strategy Guide*, London: TVEI Unit.

Smart, C (1989), *Feminism and the Power of the Law*, London: Routledge.

Spence, J (1996), 'Feminism in work with girls and women', *Youth and Policy*, No. 52, pp.38-53.

Stafford, A (1991), *Trying Work: Gender, Youth and Work Experience*, Edinburgh: Edinburgh University Press.

Stone, L (1994), *The Education Feminism Reader*, London: Routledge.

Stoney, S and Froud, K (1988), 'The parental dimension in TVEI', in Bridgwood, A., Hinckley, S M., Sims, D and Stoney, S (eds), *Perspectives on TVEI*, Sheffield: Training Commission/ NFER.

Stromquist, N P (1990), 'Gender inequality in education: accounting for women's subordination', *British Journal of the Sociology of Education*, Vol. 11, No. 2, pp.137-153.

Stronach, I (1984), 'Work experience: The sacred anvil', in Varlaam, C (ed), *Rethinking Transition: Educational Innovation and the Transition to Adult Life*, Lewes: Falmer Press.

Summerfield, P (1989), *Women Workers in the Second World War: Production and Patriarchy in Conflict*, London: Routledge.

Tapp, R (1990), *Preliminary report on the data collected by the Post-Work Experience Survey (Survey 2)*, Stockport TVEI Unit: Stockport.

Tenne, R (1987), *TVEI Students and Studies - Three Years On: Second Report of the Student/ Teacher Database*, London: TVEI Unit.

Tett, L (1997), 'Single-sex work with working class boys and young men', *Paper presented to 'Gender and Education' conference'*, University of Warwick.

Thane, P (1982), *The Foundations of the Welfare State*, Harlow: Longman.

Times Educational Supplement (1997), Business Links pull-out, *Times Educational Supplement*, 13.6.97.

Trent Polytechnic (1988), *Curricular Changes 1982-1987*, London: Training Agency.

Turnbull, A (1987), 'Learning her womanly work: The Elementary School curriculum, 1870-1914', in Hunt, F (ed), *Lessons for Life: The Schooling of Girls and Women 1850-1950*.

Turner, E., Riddell, S., and Brown, S (1995), *Gender Equality in Scottish Schools: The Impact of Recent Educational Reforms*, Manchester: Equal Opportunities Commission.

TVEI Unit (Undated), *TVEI National Handbook*, London: TVEI Unit.
TVEI Unit (1985), *Supporting TVEI*, Sheffield: MSC.
TVEI Unit (1986), *TVEI Evaluation*, London: TVEI Unit.
Varlaam, C (1984), *Rethinking Transition: Educational Innovation and the Transition to Adult Life*, Lewes: Falmer Press.
Vincent, C (1996), *Parents and Teachers: Power and Participation*, London: Falmer Press.
Walby, S (1990), *Theorizing Patriarchy*, Oxford: Basil Blackwell.
Walker, J (1988), *Louts and Legends: Male Youth Cultures in an Inner City School*, Sydney: Allen and Unwin.
Wallace, C (1986), *For Richer, For Poorer: Growing Up In and Out of Work*, London: Tavistock.
Watson, S (1990), *Playing the State: Australian Feminist Interventions*, London: Verso.
Watts, A G (1985), 'Education and employment: The traditional bonds', in Dale, R (ed), *Education, Training and Employment: Towards a New Vocationalism?*, Oxford: Pergamon Press.
Weedon, C (1987), *Feminist Practice and Post-Structuralist Theory*, Oxford: Basil Blackwell.
Weiler, K (1988), *Women Teaching for Change: Gender, Class and Power*, South Hadley. Bergin and Garvey.
Weiler, K (1993), 'Feminism and the struggle for a democratic education: A view from the United States', in Arnot, M and Weiler, K (eds) *Feminism and Social Justice in Education: International Perspectives*, London: Falmer Press.
Weiner, G (1985a), 'The Schools Council and gender: A case study in the legitimation of curriculum policy', in Arnot, M (ed), *Race and Gender: Equal Opportunities Policies in Education*, Oxford: Pergamon Press.
Weiner, G (1985b), *What the Customers Have to Say: Interviews with Pupils who made Non-Traditional Option Choices*, Bedfordshire TVEI.
Weiner, G (1986), 'Feminist education and equal opportunities: Unity or discord?', *British Journal of Sociology of Education*, Vol. 7, No. 3, pp.265-274.
Weiner, G (1989), Feminism, equal opportunities and vocationalism: The changing context, in Burchell, H and Millman, V., *Changing Perspectives on Gender: New initiatives in secondary education*, Milton Keynes: OUP.
Weiner, G (1990a), 'Ethical practice in an unjust world: educational evaluation and social justice', *Gender and Education*, Vol. 2, No. 2, pp.231-238.
Weiner, G (1990b), 'What price vocationalism - the feminist dilemma! Equal opportunities in the new government initiatives', *British Journal of Education and Work*, Vol. 4, No. 1, pp.23-30.
Weiner, G (1993), 'Shell-shock or sisterhood: English school history and feminist practice', in Arnot, M and Weiler, K (eds) *Feminism and Social Justice in Education: International Perspectives*, London: Falmer Press.
Weiner, G (1994), *Feminisms in Education: An introduction*, Buckingham: Open

University Press.

Weiner, G and Arnot, M (1987), 'Teachers and gender politics', in Arnot, M and Weiner, G (eds), *Gender and the Politics of Schooling*, London: Hutchinson.

Weiner, G, Arnot, M and David, M (1997) 'Is the future female? Female success, male disadvantage and changing gender patterns in education', in Halsey, A, Lauder, H, Brown, P, and Wells, A (eds), *Education: Culture, Economy, Society*, Oxford: Oxford University Press.

Weiner, M (1981), *English Culture and the Decline of the Industrial Spirit 1950-1980*, Cambridge: Cambridge University Press.

Weis, L (1990), *Working Class Without Work: High School Students in a Deindustrialising Economy*, New York: Routledge.

West, M and Newton, P (1983), *The Transition from School to Work*, Croom Helm/ Nichols Publishing Company.

Whyte, J (1986), *Girls into Science and Technology*, London: Routledge and Kegan Paul.

Wickham, A (1985), 'Gender divisions, training and the State', in Dale, R (ed), *Education, Training and Employment: Towards a New Vocationalism?*, Oxford: Pergamon Press.

Wickham, A (1986), Women and Training, Milton Keynes: OUP.

Willis, P (1977), *Learning to Labour: How Working Class Kids Get Working Class Jobs*, Farnborough: Saxon House.

Wolpe, A (1978), 'Education and the sexual division of labour', in Kuhn, A and Wolpe, A (eds), *Feminism and Materialism*, London: Routledge and Kegan Paul.

Wolpe, A (1981), 'The official ideology of education for girls', in Dale, T., Esland, G., Fergusson, R and MacDonald, M. (eds), *Politics, Patriarchy and Practice*, Basingstoke: Falmer Press/OUP.

Wolpe, A (1988), "Experience' as analytical framework: does it account for girls' education?', in Cole, M (ed), *Bowles and Gintis Revisited: Correspondence and Contradiction in Educational Theory*, Lewes: Falmer Press.

Woodhead, C (1996), 'Boys who learn to be losers', The Times, 6.3.96.

Woods, P (1976), 'The myth of subject choice', *British Journal of Sociology of Education*, Vol. 27, No. 2, pp.130-149.

Wright, M (1988), 'We must change the norm', *TVEI Developments 2: Equal Opportunities*, Sheffield: MSC.

Yates, L (1985), 'Is 'girl-friendly schooling' really what girls need?', in Whyte, J, Deem, R, Kant, L, and Cruickshank, M (eds), *Girl-Friendly Schooling*, London: Methuen.

Yates, L (1993), 'Feminism and Australian state policy: Some questions for the 1990s', in Arnot, M and Weiler, K (eds) *Feminism and Social Justice in Education: International Perspectives*, London: Falmer Press.

Yeatman, A (1993), 'Contemporary issues for feminism: The politics of the state', in Blackmore, J and Kenway, J (eds), *Gender Matters in Educational Administration and Policy*, London: Falmer Press.

Yin, R (1984), *Case Study Research: Design and Methods*, London: Sage Publications.

Index

Blunkett, David 180-181
Board of Education 8-9, 13
boys and achievement 3, 25, 29, 181, 182

careers education and guidance 114-118
Carr Report 10, 12
case studies 76-78
comprehensive schools 13
cultural reproduction theory 23, 26-29
Crowther Report 10, 11

Department for Education and Employment 179-181
Department of Education and Science 16-18, 19, 46-47, 48-49, 50, 118, 167, 179

Education Reform Act (1988) 180
Equal Opportunities Commission 4, 15-16, 18, 19, 59, 61, 62, 99, 162, 167
Europe 59-60

family 25, 26, 27-28, 29, 35, 55, 91
femininities 32, 38, 41, 42, 129-135, 177, 184
feminism 22-44, 85, 87, 129, 171-172, 173, 182-184
   liberal feminism 23, 30-33, 37, 40, 87, 99
   post-structural feminism 3, 23, 39, 40-43, 145, 184
   radical feminism 23, 36-39, 40, 41-42, 177-179
   socialist feminism 23, 33-36

Girls and Technology Education (GATE) 37
Girls into Science and Technology (GIST) 31-32, 171, 174
Great Debate, The 45, 46-47

Holland Report 47-48, 51

industry 46-47, 118, 176-177, 180

labour market (see also youth labour market) 10, 19, 20, 33, 34, 56, 174
   segregation 56, 141-142, 155-156

Manpower Services Commission 45, 47-49, 50, 59, 60, 69, 118-119,

167, 179
equal opportunities record 51-52
masculinities 32, 38, 39, 41, 42, 100, 177, 184
Masonfield LEA 65-79
    central team 70, 81, 83-84, 185-186
    cohort membership 101-102
    equal opportunities coordinators 84-88, 163
    Information Systems Strategy 88-90, 94
    local councillors 66-70, 86, 162-164, 186
    local labour market 66, 73, 135-137
    pilot schools 70-72, 90-94, 186
    post-16 destinations 135-143, 149-159, 188-190
    single sex provision 109-111
    subject choice 103-108
    TVEI bid 67-70
    work experience 121-126

National Curriculum 31, 37, 50, 59, 162, 167, 179, 180
New Left 39, 58-59, 66, 72, 73, 86
Newsom Report 10, 11-12
New Vocationalism 1, 29, 35, 45, 181
non-traditional occupations 53, 56, 57, 97-100, 116, 132-135, 158-159, 173-175, 184
Norwood Report 9, 10-11

OFSTED 167, 181
option choice (see subject choice)

'race' 3, 36, 39, 43, 130-132, 134, 178, 181, 182

science 17-18, 19, 31-32, 37, 59
Sex Discrimination Act 14-16, 22, 51, 52, 86, 111, 167
sexuality 36, 38, 39, 40, 42, 43, 86, 130, 132-133, 177, 184
single sex provision 13, 38-39, 109-111, 133, 183, 184
social class 23-29, 13, 32, 33-36, 39, 43, 130-131, 175-176, 182-183
social reproduction theory 23, 24-26, 34, 35, 94, 175, 176
subject choice 19, 26, 31, 33, 37, 38, 40, 55, 59, 89, 91-93, 97-100, 145-148, 173-175, 184

technology 31-32, 37, 56-57, 59, 81, 92, 93, 97-100, 103, 110-111
Thatcher, Margaret 1, 14, 53
training 51-52, 59-60, 151-152, 180-181
triangulation 77-78
TVEI
    awareness raising 62-63, 169-172
    cohort membership 100-103
    contract compliance 165-168
    entitlement curriculum 49-50
    equal opportunities national advisers 60-61, 62-64, 87, 88, 90, 170-172
    equal opportunities coordination 83-88
    equal opportunities policy 50-51, 52-64, 76, 99-100, 145-148, 161, 166, 173-174, 184
    evaluation and monitoring 49, 81, 99, 113, 168-169
    extension 50, 76, 16
    funding 49-50, 58, 67, 165-168, 179
    Information Systems Strategy 64, 77, 84, 88-90, 94, 168-169, 170-171
    National Equal Opportunities Network (NEON) 63-64, 128
    origins 1, 45-49

staffing 80-88, 166
subject choice 103, 105-108, 169

UNESCO 59-60

vocational training (see training)

Women into Science and Engineering (WISE) 31-32, 37
Women's National Commission 59, 62

work experience 118-127, 182-183

youth unemployment 47-49, 53, 57
youth labour market 4, 20, 33, 38, 42, 46, 47-49, 51, 53, 128-135, 149-159, 182
Youth Opportunities Programme 20, 52, 59, 132
Youth Training Scheme 38, 52, 119, 132, 137-143